Christopher Lasch is an American historian, teacher and writer. He has been on the faculty of the University of Rochester since 1970 and his books include *The New Radicalism in America*, *The Agony of the American Left*, and *Haven in a Heartless World*.

'Christopher Lasch has gone to the heart of our culture. The insights into personality and its social context are stunning. This is a courageous, important book.'

> Michael Rogin, professor of political
> science, University of California, Berkeley

'Cultural history at its best – but something more: a challenging critique of both modern American capitalism and the New Left criticism of it . . . Whether one agrees or disagrees, one must recognize that Lasch has written a book of fundamental importance.'

> Bruce Mazlish, professor of history and head
> of the humanities department, Massachusetts
> Institute of Technology

THE CULTURE OF
NARCISSISM

American Life in an Age of
Diminishing Expectations

Christopher Lasch

First published in Great Britain in ABACUS 1980 by
Sphere Books Ltd, 30 /32 Gray's Inn Road, London, WC1X 8JL
Reprinted 1982

Reproduced, printed and bound in Great Britain by
Hazell Watson & Viney Ltd, Aylesbury, Bucks

To Kate

For she is wise, if I can judge of her,
And fair she is, if that mine eyes be true,
And true she is, as she hath prov'd herself;
And therefore, like herself, wise, fair, and true,
Shall she be placed in my constant soul.

THE MERCHANT OF VENICE, II. vi

Contents

III

Changing Modes of Making It:
From Horatio Alger to the Happy Hooker

IV

The Banality of Pseudo-Self-Awareness:
Theatrics of Politics and Everyday Existence

V

The Degradation of Sport

VI

Schooling and the New Illiteracy

VII

The Socialization of Reproduction and the Collapse of Authority

VIII

The Flight from Feeling: Sociopsychology of the Sex War

IX

The Shattered Faith in the Regeneration of Life

X

Paternalism Without Father

Preface

Hardly more than a quarter-century after Henry Luce proclaimed "the American century," American confidence has fallen to a low ebb. Those who recently dreamed of world power now despair of governing the city of New York. Defeat in Vietnam, economic stagnation, and the impending exhaustion of natural resources have produced a mood of pessimism in higher circles, which spreads through the rest of society as people lose faith in their leaders. The same crisis of confidence grips other capitalist countries as well. In Europe, the growing strength of communist parties, the revival of fascist movements, and a wave of terrorism all testify, in different ways, to the weakness of established régimes and to the exhaustion of established tradition. Even Canada, long a bastion of stolid bourgeois dependability, now faces in the separatist movement in Quebec a threat to its very existence as a nation.

The international dimensions of the current malaise indicate that it cannot be attributed to an American failure of nerve. Bourgeois society seems everywhere to have used up its store of constructive ideas. It has lost both the capacity and the will to confront the difficulties that threaten to overwhelm it. The political crisis of capitalism reflects a general crisis of western culture, which reveals itself in a pervasive despair of understanding the course of modern history or of subjecting it to rational direction. Liberalism, the political theory of the ascendant bourgeoisie, long ago lost the capacity to explain events in the world of the welfare state and the multinational corporation; nothing has taken its place. Politically bankrupt, liberalism is intellectually bankrupt as well. The sciences it has fostered, once confident of their ability to dispel the darkness of the ages, no longer provide satisfactory explanations of the phenomena they profess to elucidate.

Neoclassical economic theory cannot explain the coexistence of unemployment and inflation; sociology retreats from the attempt to outline a general theory of modern society; academic psychology retreats from the challenge of Freud into the measurement of trivia. The natural sciences, having made exaggerated claims for themselves, now hasten to announce that science offers no miracle cures for social problems.

In the humanities, demoralization has reached the point of a general admission that humanistic study has nothing to contribute to an understanding of the modern world. Philosophers no longer explain the nature of things or pretend to tell us how to live. Students of literature treat the text not as a representation of the real world but as a reflection of the artist's inner state of mind. Historians admit to a "sense of the irrelevance of history," in David Donald's words, "and of the bleakness of the new era we are entering." Because liberal culture has always depended so heavily on the study of history, the collapse of that culture finds an especially poignant illustration in the collapse of the historical faith, which formerly surrounded the record of public events with an aura of moral dignity, patriotism, and political optimism. Historians in the past assumed that men learned from their previous mistakes. Now that the future appears troubled and uncertain, the past appears "irrelevant" even to those who devote their lives to investigating it. "The age of abundance has ended," Donald writes. "The 'lessons' taught by the American past are today not merely irrelevant but dangerous. . . . Perhaps my most useful function would be to disenthrall [students] from the spell of history, to help them see the irrelevance of the past, . . . [to] remind them to what a limited extent humans control their own destiny."

Such is the view from the top—the despairing view of the future now widely shared by those who govern society, shape public opinion, and supervise the scientific knowledge on which society depends. If on the other hand we ask what the common man thinks about his prospects, we find plenty of evidence to confirm the impression that the modern world faces the future without hope, but we also find another side of the picture, which qualifies that impression and suggests that western civilization may yet generate the moral resources to transcend its present crisis. A pervasive distrust of those in power has made society increasingly difficult to govern, as the governing class repeatedly complains without understanding its own contribution to the difficulty; but this same distrust may furnish the basis of a new capacity for self-government, which would end by doing away with the need that gives rise to a governing class in the first place. What looks to political scientists like voter apathy may represent a healthy skepticism about a political system in which public lying has become endemic and routine. A distrust of experts may help to diminish the dependence on experts that has crippled the capacity for self-help.

Modern bureaucracy has undermined earlier traditions of local action, the revival and extension of which holds out the only hope that a decent society will emerge from the wreckage of capitalism. The inadequacy of solutions dictated from above now forces people to invent solutions from below. Disenchantment with governmental bureaucracies has begun to extend to corporate bureaucracies as well—the real centers of power in contemporary society. In small towns and crowded urban neighborhoods, even in suburbs, men and women have initiated modest experiments in cooperation, designed to defend their rights against the corporations and the state. The "flight from politics," as it appears to the managerial and political elite, may signify the citizen's growing unwillingness to take part in the political system as a consumer of prefabricated spectacles. It may signify, in other words, not a retreat from politics at all but the beginnings of a general political revolt.

Much could be written about the signs of new life in the United States. This book, however, describes a way of life that is dying—the culture of competitive individualism, which in its decadence has carried the logic of individualism to the extreme of a war of all against all, the pursuit of happiness to the dead end of a narcissistic preoccupation with the self. Strategies of narcissistic survival now present themselves as emancipation from the repressive conditions of the past, thus giving rise to a "cultural revolution" that reproduces the worst features of the collapsing civilization it claims to criticize. Cultural radicalism has become so fashionable, and so pernicious in the support it unwittingly provides for the status quo, that any criticism of contemporary society that hopes to get beneath the surface has to criticize, at the same time, much of what currently goes under the name of radicalism.

Events have rendered liberationist critiques of modern society hopelessly out of date—and much of an earlier Marxist critique as well. Many radicals still direct their indignation against the authoritarian family, repressive sexual morality, literary censorship, the work ethic, and other foundations of bourgeois order that have been weakened or destroyed by advanced capitalism itself. These radicals do not see that the "authoritarian personality" no longer represents the prototype of the economic man. Economic man himself has given way to the psychological man of our times—the final product of bourgeois individualism. The new narcissist is haunted not by guilt but by anxiety. He seeks not to inflict his own certainties on others but to find a meaning in life. Liberated from the superstitions of the past, he doubts even the reality of his own existence. Superficially relaxed and tolerant, he finds little use for dogmas of racial and ethnic purity but at the same time forfeits the security of group loyalties and regards everyone as a rival for the favors conferred by a paternalistic state. His sexual attitudes are permissive rather than puritanical, even though his emancipation from ancient taboos brings him no sexual peace. Fiercely competitive in his demand for approval and acclaim, he distrusts competition because he associates it unconsciously with an unbridled urge to destroy. Hence he repudiates the competitive ideologies that flourished at an earlier stage of capitalist development and distrusts even their limited expression in sports and games. He extols cooperation and teamwork while harboring deeply antisocial impulses. He praises respect for rules and regulations in the secret belief that they do not apply to himself. Acquisitive in the sense that his cravings have no limits, he does not accumulate goods and provisions against the future, in the manner of the acquisitive individualist of nineteenth-century political economy, but demands immediate gratification and lives in a state of restless, perpetually unsatisfied desire.

The narcissist has no interest in the future because, in part, he has so little interest in the past. He finds it difficult to internalize happy associations or to create a store of loving memories with which to face the latter part of his life, which under the best of conditions always brings sadness and pain. In a narcissistic society—a society that gives increasing prominence and encouragement to narcissistic traits—the cultural devaluation of the past reflects not only the poverty of the prevailing ideologies, which have lost their grip on reality and abandoned the attempt to master it, but the poverty of the narcissist's inner life. A society that has made "nostalgia" a marketable commodity on the cultural exchange quickly repudiates the suggestion that life in the past was in any important way better than life today. Having trivialized the past by equating it with outmoded styles of consumption, discarded fashions and attitudes, people today resent anyone who draws on the past in serious discussions of contemporary conditions or attempts to use the past as a standard by which to judge the present. Current critical dogma equates every such reference to the past as itself an expression of nostalgia. As Albert Parr has observed, this kind of reasoning "rules out entirely any insights gained, and any values arrived at by personal experience, since such experiences are always located in the past, and therefore in the precincts of nostalgia."

To discuss the complexities of our relation to the past under the heading of "nostalgia" substitutes sloganeering for the objective social criticism with which this attitude tries to associate itself. The fashionable sneer that now automatically greets every loving recollection of the past attempts to exploit the prejudices of a pseudoprogressive society on behalf of the status quo. But we now know—thanks to the work of Christopher Hill, E. P. Thompson, and other historians—that many radical movements in the past have drawn strength and sustenance from the myth or memory of a golden age in the still more distant past. This historical discovery reinforces the psychoanalytic insight that loving memories constitute an indispensable psychological resource in maturity, and that those who cannot fall back on the memory of loving relations in the past suffer terrible torments as a result. The belief that in some ways the past was a happier time by no means rests on a sentimental illusion; nor does it lead to a backward-looking, reactionary paralysis of the political will.

My own view of the past is just the opposite of David Donald's. Far from regarding it as a useless encumbrance, I see the past as a political and psychological treasury from which we draw the reserves (not necessarily in the form of "lessons") that we need to cope with the future. Our culture's indifference to the past—which easily shades over into active hostility and rejection—furnishes the most telling proof of that culture's bankruptcy. The prevailing attitude, so cheerful and forward-looking on the surface, derives from a narcissistic impoverishment of the psyche and also from an inability to ground our needs in the experience of satisfaction and contentment. Instead of drawing on our own experience, we allow experts to define our needs for us and then wonder why those needs never seem to be satisfied. "As people become apt pupils in learning how to need," Ivan Illich writes, "the ability to shape wants from experienced satisfaction becomes a rare competence of the very rich or the seriously undersupplied."

For all these reasons, the devaluation of the past has become one of the most important symptoms of the cultural crisis to which this book addresses itself, often drawing on historical experience to explain what is wrong with our present arrangements. A denial of the past, superficially progressive and optimistic, proves on closer analysis to embody the despair of a society that cannot face the future.

Acknowledgments

Some of the ideas in this book were sharpened in correspondence and conversation with Michael Rogin and Howard Shevrin, whom I wish to thank for their interest in my work and for their valuable suggestions. I should also like to underscore my indebtedness to the writings of Philip Rieff and Russell Jacoby, which have done so much to clarify the cultural and psychological issues this book addresses. None of these scholars should be held responsible for my conclusions, some of which they may find it impossible to agree with.

The manuscript has benefited from a critical reading by my wife and by Jeannette Hopkins, who has saved me more than once from careless or unnecessarily abstract formulations. I want to thank Jean DeGroat, once again, for her skill and patience as a typist.

Preliminary versions of some of this material—now reworked beyond much resemblance to these earlier essays—appeared in the *New York Review* ("The Narcissist Society," 30 September 1976; "Planned Obsolescence," 28 October 1976; "The Corruption of Sports," 28 April 1977; "The Siege of the Family," 24 November 1977); *Partisan Review* ("The Narcissistic Personality of Our Time," 1977, no. 1); *Hastings Center Report* ("Aging in a Culture without a Future," August 1977); *Marxist Perspectives* ("The Flight from Feelings," spring 1978); and *Psychology Today* ("To Be Young, Rich, and Entitled," March 1978).

THE CULTURE OF NARCISSISM

I

The Awareness Movement and
the Social Invasion of the Self

> *The Marivaudian being is, according to Poulet, a pastless futureless man, born anew at every instant. The instants are points which organize themselves into a line, but what is important is the instant, not the line. The Marivaudian being has in a sense no history. Nothing follows from what has gone before. He is constantly surprised. He cannot predict his own reaction to events. He is constantly being overtaken by events. A condition of breathlessness and dazzlement surrounds him.*
>
> DONALD BARTHELME

> *It is only irritating to think one would like to be somewhere else. Here we are now.*
>
> JOHN CAGE

The Waning of the Sense of Historical Time   As the twentieth century approaches its end, the conviction grows that many other things are ending too. Storm warnings, portents, hints of catastrophe haunt our times. The "sense of an ending," which has given shape to so much of twentieth-century literature, now pervades the popular imagination as well. The Nazi holocaust, the threat of nuclear annihilation, the depletion of natural resources, well-founded predictions of ecological disaster have fulfilled poetic prophecy, giving concrete historical substance to the nightmare, or death wish, that avant-garde artists were the first to express. The question of whether the world will end in fire or in ice, with a bang or a whimper, no longer interests artists alone.

Impending disaster has become an everyday concern, so commonplace and familiar that nobody any longer gives much thought to how disaster might be averted. People busy themselves instead with survival strategies, measures designed to prolong their own lives, or programs guaranteed to ensure good health and peace of mind.*

Those who dig bomb shelters hope to survive by surrounding themselves with the latest products of modern technology. Communards in the country adhere to an opposite plan: to free themselves from dependence on technology and thus to outlive its destruction or collapse. A visitor to a commune in North Carolina writes: "Everyone seems to share this sense of imminent doomsday." Stewart Brand, editor of the *Whole Earth Catalogue*, reports that "sales of the *Survival Book* are booming; it's one of our fastest moving items." Both strategies reflect the growing despair of changing society, even of understanding it, which also underlies the cult of expanded consciousness, health, and personal "growth" so prevalent today.

After the political turmoil of the sixties, Americans have retreated to purely personal preoccupations. Having no hope of improving their lives in any of the ways that matter, people have convinced themselves that what matters is psychic self-improvement: getting in touch with their feelings, eating health food, taking lessons in ballet or belly-dancing, immersing themselves in the wisdom of the East, jogging, learning how to "relate," overcoming the "fear of pleasure." Harmless in themselves, these pursuits, elevated to a program and wrapped in the rhetoric

---

* "The sense of an ending . . . is . . . endemic to what we call modernism," writes Frank Kermode. ". . . In general, we seem to combine a sense of decadence in society—as evidenced by the concept of alienation, which, supported by a new interest in the early Marx, has never enjoyed more esteem—with a technological utopianism. In our ways of thinking about the future there are contradictions which, if we were willing to consider them openly, might call for some effort toward complementarity. But they lie, as a rule, too deep." Susan Sontag, noting that "people take the news of their doom in diverse ways," contrasts the apocalyptic imagination of earlier ages with that of today. In the past, expectations of the apocalypse often furnished "the occasion for a radical disaffiliation from society," whereas in our time they provoke "an inadequate response," being received "without great agitation."

of authenticity and awareness, signify a retreat from politics and a repudiation of the recent past. Indeed Americans seem to wish to forget not only the sixties, the riots, the new left, the disruptions on college campuses, Vietnam, Watergate, and the Nixon presidency, but their entire collective past, even in the antiseptic form in which it was celebrated during the Bicentennial. Woody Allen's movie *Sleeper*, issued in 1973, accurately caught the mood of the seventies. Appropriately cast in the form of a parody of futuristic science fiction, the film finds a great many ways to convey the message that "political solutions don't work," as Allen flatly announces at one point. When asked what he believes in, Allen, having ruled out politics, religion, and science, declares: "I believe in sex and death—two experiences that come once in a lifetime."

To live for the moment is the prevailing passion—to live for yourself, not for your predecessors or posterity. We are fast losing the sense of historical continuity, the sense of belonging to a succession of generations originating in the past and stretching into the future. It is the waning of the sense of historical time—in particular, the erosion of any strong concern for posterity—that distinguishes the spiritual crisis of the seventies from earlier outbreaks of millenarian religion, to which it bears a superficial resemblance. Many commentators have seized on this resemblance as a means of understanding the contemporary "cultural revolution," ignoring the features that distinguish it from the religions of the past. A few years ago, Leslie Fiedler proclaimed a "New Age of Faith." More recently, Tom Wolfe has interpreted the new narcissism as a "third great awakening," an outbreak of orgiastic, ecstatic religiosity. Jim Hougan, in a book that seems to present itself simultaneously as a critique and a celebration of contemporary decadence, compares the current mood to the millennialism of the waning Middle Ages. "The anxieties of the Middle Ages are not much different from those of the present," he writes. Then as now, social upheaval gave rise to "millenarian sects."*

* Hougan's book reflects the current belief in the futility of "mere political solutions" ("revolution would accomplish nothing more than a change in the management of the disease") and exemplifies the inadequate response in the face of disas-

Both Hougan and Wolfe inadvertently provide evidence, however, that undermines a religious interpretation of the "consciousness movement." Hougan notes that survival has become the "catchword of the seventies" and "collective narcissism" the dominant disposition. Since "the society" has no future, it makes sense to live only for the moment, to fix our eyes on our own "private performance," to become connoisseurs of our own decadence, to cultivate a "transcendental self-attention." These are not the attitudes historically associated with millenarian outbreaks. Sixteenth-century Anabaptists awaited the apocalypse not with transcendental self-attention but with ill-concealed impatience for the golden age it was expected to inaugurate. Nor were they indifferent to the past. Ancient popular traditions of the "sleeping king"—the leader who will return to his people and restore a lost golden age—informed the millenarian movements of this period. The Revolutionary of the Upper Rhine, anonymous author of the *Book of a Hundred Chapters*, declared, "The Germans once held the whole world in their hands and they will do so again, and with more power than ever." He predicted that the resurrected Frederick II, "Emperor of the Last Days," would reinstate the primitive German religion, move the capital of Christendom from Rome to Trier, abolish private property, and level distinctions between rich and poor.

Such traditions, often associated with national resistance to foreign conquest, have flourished at many times and in many forms, including the Christian vision of the Last Judgment. Their egalitarian and pseudohistorical content suggests that even the most radically otherworldly religions of the past expressed a hope of social justice and a sense of continuity with earlier generations. The absence of these values characterizes the survivalist mentality of the seventies. The "world view emerging among us," writes Peter Marin, centers "solely on the self" and has "individual survival as its sole good." In an attempt to identify the peculiar features of contemporary religiosity, Tom Wolfe himself notes that

---

ter that Sontag finds so characteristic of our age. "It's amazingly simple," Hougan announces at the outset. "Things fall apart. There's nothing you can do. Let a smile be your umbrella."

"most people, historically, have *not* lived their lives as if thinking, 'I have only one life to live.' Instead they have lived as if they are living their ancestors' lives and their offspring's lives. . . ." These observations go very close to the heart of the matter, but they call into question his characterization of the new narcissism as a third great awakening.*

The Therapeutic Sensibility   The contemporary climate is therapeutic, not religious. People today hunger not for personal salvation, let alone for the restoration of an earlier golden age, but for the feeling, the momentary illusion, of personal well-being, health, and psychic security. Even the radicalism of the sixties served, for many of those who embraced it for personal rather than political reasons, not as a substitute religion but as a form of therapy. Radical politics filled empty lives, provided a sense of meaning and purpose. In her memoir of the Weathermen, Susan Stern described their attraction in language that owes more to psychiatry and medicine than to religion. When she tried to evoke her state of mind during the 1968 demonstrations at the Democratic National Convention in Chicago, she wrote instead about the state of her health. "I felt good. I could feel my body supple and strong and slim, and ready to run miles, and my legs moving sure and swift under me." A few pages later, she says: "I felt real." Repeatedly she explains that association with important people made her feel important. "I felt I was part of a vast network of intense, exciting and brilliant people." When the leaders she idealized disappointed her, as they always did, she looked for new heroes to take their place, hoping to warm herself in their "brilliance" and to overcome her feeling of insignificance. In their presence, she occasionally felt "strong and solid"—only to

---

* As an example of the new disposition, which repudiates the view of the self "as part of a great biological stream," Wolfe cites an advertisement for hair dye: "If I've only one life, let me live it as a blonde!" Other examples could be cited *ad infinitum:* the slogan for Schlitz ("You only go around once in life, so you have to grab all the gusto you can"); the title of a popular soap opera, *One Life to Live,* and so on.

find herself repelled, when disenchantment set in again, by the "arrogance" of those whom she had previously admired, by "their contempt for everyone around them."

Many of the details in Stern's account of the Weathermen would be familiar to students of the revolutionary mentality in earlier epochs: the fervor of her revolutionary commitment, the group's endless disputes about fine points of political dogma, the relentless "self-criticism" to which members of the sect were constantly exhorted, the attempt to remodel every facet of one's life in conformity with the revolutionary faith. But every revolutionary movement partakes of the culture of its time, and this one contained elements that immediately identified it as a product of American society in an age of diminishing expectations. The atmosphere in which the Weathermen lived—an atmosphere of violence, danger, drugs, sexual promiscuity, moral and psychic chaos—derived not so much from an older revolutionary tradition as from the turmoil and narcissistic anguish of contemporary America. Her preoccupation with the state of her psychic health, together with her dependence on others for a sense of selfhood, distinguish Susan Stern from the kind of religious seeker who turns to politics to find a secularized salvation. She needed to establish an identity, not to submerge her identity in a larger cause. The narcissist differs also, in the tenuous quality of his selfhood, from an earlier type of American individualist, the "American Adam" analyzed by R. W. B. Lewis, Quentin Anderson, Michael Rogin, and by nineteenth-century observers like Tocqueville. The contemporary narcissist bears a superficial resemblance, in his self-absorption and delusions of grandeur, to the "imperial self" so often celebrated in nineteenth-century American literature. The American Adam, like his descendants today, sought to free himself from the past and to establish what Emerson called "an original relation to the universe." Nineteenth-century writers and orators restated again and again, in a great variety of forms, Jefferson's doctrine that the earth belongs to the living. The break with Europe, the abolition of primogeniture, and the looseness of family ties gave substance to their belief (even if it was finally an illusion) that Americans, alone among the people of the world, could escape the entangling influence of the past. They imagined, according to Tocqueville, that "their whole destiny is in their own hands." Social conditions in the United States, Tocqueville wrote, severed the tie that formerly united one generation to another. "The woof of time is every instant broken and the track of generations effaced. Those who went before are soon forgotten; of those who will come after, no one has any idea: the interest of man is confined to those in close propinquity to himself."

Some critics have described the narcissism of the 1970s in similar language. The new therapies spawned by the human potential movement, according to Peter Marin, teach that "the individual will is all powerful and totally determines one's fate"; thus they intensify the "isolation of the self." This line of argument belongs to a well-established American tradition of social thought. Marin's plea for recognition of "the immense middle ground of human community" recalls Van Wyck Brooks, who criticized the New England transcendentalists for ignoring "the genial middle ground of human tradition." Brooks himself, when he formulated his own indictment of American culture, drew on such earlier critics as Santayana, Henry James, Orestes Brownson, and Tocqueville.* The critical tradition they established still has much to tell us about the evils of untrammeled individualism, but it needs to be restated to take account of the differences between nineteenth-century Adamism and the narcissism of our own time. The critique of "privatism," though it helps to keep alive the need for community, has become more and more misleading as the possibility of genuine privacy recedes. The contemporary American may have failed, like his predecessors, to establish any sort of common life, but the integrating tendencies of modern industrial society have at the same time undermined his "isolation." Having surrendered most of his technical skills to the

---

* In 1857, Brownson criticized the atomizing individualism of modern life in words that anticipate similar complaints in the twentieth century. "The work of destruction, commenced by the Reformation, which had introduced an era of criticism and revolution, had, I thought, been carried far enough. All that was dissoluble had been dissolved. All that was destructible had been destroyed, and it was time to begin the work of reconstruction—a work of reconciliation and love. . . . The first thing to be done is to cease our hostility to the past."

corporation, he can no longer provide for his material needs. As the family loses not only its productive functions but many of its reproductive functions as well, men and women no longer manage even to raise their children without the help of certified experts. The atrophy of older traditions of self-help has eroded everyday competence, in one area after another, and has made the individual dependent on the state, the corporation, and other bureaucracies.

Narcissism represents the psychological dimension of this dependence. Notwithstanding his occasional illusions of omnipotence, the narcissist depends on others to validate his self-esteem. He cannot live without an admiring audience. His apparent freedom from family ties and institutional constraints does not free him to stand alone or to glory in his individuality. On the contrary, it contributes to his insecurity, which he can overcome only by seeing his "grandiose self" reflected in the attentions of others, or by attaching himself to those who radiate celebrity, power, and charisma. For the narcissist, the world is a mirror, whereas the rugged individualist saw it as an empty wilderness to be shaped to his own design.

In the nineteenth-century American imagination, the vast continent stretching westward symbolized both the promise and the menace of an escape from the past. The West represented an opportunity to build a new society unencumbered by feudal inhibitions, but it also tempted men to throw off civilization and to revert to savagery. Through compulsive industry and relentless sexual repression, nineteenth-century Americans achieved a fragile triumph over the id. The violence they turned against the Indians and against nature originated not in unrestrained impulse but in the white Anglo-Saxon superego, which feared the wildness of the West because it objectified the wildness within each individual. While celebrating the romance of the frontier in their popular literature, in practice Americans imposed on the wilderness a new order designed to keep impulse in check while giving free rein to acquisitiveness. Capital accumulation in its own right sublimated appetite and subordinated the pursuit of self-interest to the service of future generations. In the heat of the struggle to win the West, the American pioneer gave full vent to his rapacity and murderous cruelty, but he always envisioned the result—not without misgivings, expressed in a nostalgic cult of lost innocence—as a peaceful, respectable, churchgoing community safe for his women and children. He imagined that his offspring, raised under the morally refining influence of feminine "culture," would grow up to be sober, law-abiding, domesticated American citizens, and the thought of the advantages they would inherit justified his toil and excused, he thought, his frequent lapses into brutality, sadism, and rape.

Today Americans are overcome not by the sense of endless possibility but by the banality of the social order they have erected against it. Having internalized the social restraints by means of which they formerly sought to keep possibility within civilized limits, they feel themselves overwhelmed by an annihilating boredom, like animals whose instincts have withered in captivity. A reversion to savagery threatens them so little that they long precisely for a more vigorous instinctual existence. People nowadays complain of an inability to feel. They cultivate more vivid experiences, seek to beat sluggish flesh to life, attempt to revive jaded appetites. They condemn the superego and exalt the lost life of the senses. Twentieth-century peoples have erected so many psychological barriers against strong emotion, and have invested those defenses with so much of the energy derived from forbidden impulse, that they can no longer remember what it feels like to be inundated by desire. They tend, rather, to be consumed with rage, which derives from defenses against desire and gives rise in turn to new defenses against rage itself. Outwardly bland, submissive, and sociable, they seethe with an inner anger for which a dense, overpopulated, bureaucratic society can devise few legitimate outlets.

The growth of bureaucracy creates an intricate network of personal relations, puts a premium on social skills, and makes the unbridled egotism of the American Adam untenable. Yet at the same time it erodes all forms of patriarchal authority and thus weakens the social superego, formerly represented by fathers, teachers, and preachers. The decline of institutionalized authority in an ostensibly permissive society does not, however, lead to a "decline of the superego" in individuals. It encourages instead the development of a harsh, punitive superego that derives most of its psychic energy, in the absence of authoritative social prohibitions, from the destructive, aggressive impulses within the id. Unconscious, irrational elements in the superego come to dominate its operation. As authority figures in modern society lose their "credibility," the superego in individuals increasingly derives from the child's primitive fantasies about his parents— fantasies charged with sadistic rage—rather than from internalized ego ideals formed by later experience with loved and respected models of social conduct.*

The struggle to maintain psychic equilibrium in a society that demands submission to the rules of social intercourse but refuses to ground those rules in a code of moral conduct encourages a form of self-absorption that has little in common with the primary narcissism of the imperial self. Archaic elements increasingly dominate personality structure, and "the self shrinks back," in the words of Morris Dickstein, "toward a passive and primeval state in which the world remains uncreated, unformed." The egomaniacal, experience-devouring imperial self regresses into a grandiose, narcissistic, infantile, empty self: a "dark wet hole," as Rudolph Wurlitzer writes in *Nog*, "where everything finds its way sooner or later. I remain near the entrance, handling goods as they are shoved in, listening and nodding. I have been slowly dissolving into this cavity."

---

* The superego, society's agent in the mind, always consists of internalized representations of parents and other symbols of authority, but it is important to distinguish between those representations which derive from archaic, pre-Oedipal impressions and those resting on later impressions and therefore reflecting a more realistic assessment of parental powers. Strictly speaking, these latter contribute to the formation of the "ego ideal"—the internalization of others' expectations and of the traits we love and admire in them; whereas the superego, in distinction to the ego ideal, derives from early fantasies that contain a large admixture of aggression and rage, originating in the parents' inevitable failure to satisfy all the child's instinctual demands. But the aggressive, punishing, and even self-destructive part of the superego is usually modified by later experience, which softens early fantasies of parents as devouring monsters. If that experience is lacking—as it so often is in a society that has radically devalued all forms of authority—the sadistic superego can be expected to develop at the expense of the ego ideal, the destructive superego at the expense of the severe but solicitous inner voice we call conscience.

Plagued by anxiety, depression, vague discontents, a sense of inner emptiness, the "psychological man" of the twentieth century seeks neither individual self-aggrandizement nor spiritual transcendence but peace of mind, under conditions that increasingly militate against it. Therapists, not priests or popular preachers of self-help or models of success like the captains of industry, become his principal allies in the struggle for composure; he turns to them in the hope of achieving the modern equivalent of salvation, "mental health." Therapy has established itself as the successor both to rugged individualism and to religion; but this does not mean that the "triumph of the therapeutic" has become a new religion in its own right. Therapy constitutes an antireligion, not always to be sure because it adhreres to rational explanation or scientific methods of healing, as its practitioners would have us believe, but because modern society "has no future" and therefore gives no thought to anything beyond its immediate needs. Even when therapists speak of the need for "meaning" and "love," they define love and meaning simply as the fulfillment of the patient's emotional requirements. It hardly occurs to them—nor is there any reason why it should, given the nature of the therapeutic enterprise—to encourage the subject to subordinate his needs and interests to those of others, to someone or some cause or tradition outside himself. "Love" as self-sacrifice or self-abasement, "meaning" as submission to a higher loyalty— these sublimations strike the therapeutic sensibility as intolerably oppressive, offensive to common sense and injurious to personal health and well-being. To liberate humanity from such outmoded ideas of love and duty has become the mission of the post-Freudian therapies and particularly of their converts and popularizers, for whom mental health means the overthrow of inhibitions and the immediate gratification of every impulse.

From Politics to Self-Examination   Having displaced religion as the organizing framework of American culture, the therapeutic outlook threatens to displace politics as well, the last refuge of ideology. Bureaucracy transforms collective grievances into personal problems amenable to therapeutic intervention; in clarifying this process, this trivialization of political conflict, the new left of the sixties made one of its most important contributions to political understanding. In the seventies, however, many former radicals have themselves embraced the therapeutic sensibility. Rennie Davis leaves radical politics to follow the teenage guru, Maharaj Ji. Abbie Hoffman, former leader of the Yippies, decides that it is more important to get his own head together than to move multitudes. His onetime associate, Jerry Rubin, having reached the dreaded age of thirty and having found himself face to face with his private fears and anxieties, moves from New York to San Francisco, where he shops voraciously—on an apparently inexhaustible income—in the spiritual supermarkets of the West Coast. "In five years," Rubin says, "from 1971 to 1975, I directly experienced est, gestalt therapy, bioenergetics, rolfing, massage, jogging, health foods, tai chi, Esalen, hypnotism, modern dance, meditation, Silva Mind Control, Arica, acupuncture, sex therapy, Reichian therapy, and More House—a smorgasbord course in New Consciousness."

In his coyly titled memoir, *Growing (Up) at Thirty-seven*, Rubin testifies to the salutary effects of his therapeutic regimen. After years of neglecting his body, he gave himself "permission to be healthy" and quickly lost thirty pounds. Health foods, jogging, yoga, sauna baths, chiropractors, and acupuncturists have made him feel, at thirty-seven, "like twenty-five." Spiritual progress proved equally gratifying and painless. He shed his protective armor, his sexism, his "addiction to love," and learned "to love myself enough so that I do not need another to make me happy." He came to understand that his revolutionary politics concealed a "puritan conditioning," which occasionally made him uneasy about his celebrity and its material rewards. No strenuous psychic exertions seem to have been required to convince Rubin that "it's O.K. to enjoy the rewards of life that money brings."

He learned to put sex "in its proper place" and to enjoy it without investing it with "symbolic" meaning. Under the influence of a succession of psychic healers, he raged against his parents and the righteous, punitive "judge" within himself, eventually learning to "forgive" his parents and his superego. He cut his hair, shaved his beard, and "liked what I saw." Now "I entered rooms and no one knew who I was, because I didn't fit their image of me. I was thirty-five but I looked twenty-three."

Rubin sees his "journey into myself" as part of the "consciousness movement" of the seventies. Yet this "massive self-examination" has produced few indications of self-understanding, personal or collective. Self-awareness remains mired in liberationist clichés. Rubin discusses the "female in me," the need for a more tolerant view of homosexuality, and the need to "make peace" with his parents, as if these commonplaces represented hard-won insights into the human condition. As a skillful manipulator of the common coin, a self-confessed "media freak" and propagandist, he assumes that all ideas, character traits, and cultural patterns derive from propaganda and "conditioning." Apologizing for his hetereosexuality, he writes, "Men do not turn me on, because I was propagandized as a child to think that homosexuality is sick." In therapy, he attempted to reverse "the negative programming of childhood." By convincing himself that a collective deconditioning will provide the basis for social and political change, he has tried to build a rickety bridge between his political activities in the sixties and his current preoccupation with his own body and "feelings." Like many ex-radicals, he has succeeded only in exchanging current therapeutic slogans for the political slogans he used to mouth with equal disregard of their content.

Rubin claims that the "inner revolution of the seventies" grew out of an awareness that the radicalism of the sixties had failed to address itself to the quality of personal life or to cultural questions, in the mistaken belief that questions of "personal growth," in his words, could wait "until after the revolution." This accusation contains a certain amount of truth. The left has too often served as a refuge from the terrors of the inner life. Another ex-radical, Paul Zweig, has said that he became a communist in the late fifties because communism "released him . . . from the failed rooms and broken vases of a merely private life." As long as political movements exercise a fatal attraction for those who seek to drown the sense of personal failure in collective action—as if collective action somehow precluded rigorous attention to the quality of personal life—political movements will have little to say about the personal dimension of social crisis.

Yet the new left (unlike the old left) did begin to address this issue, in the brief period of its flowering in the mid-sixties. In those years, there was a growing recognition—by no means confined to those associated with the new left—that personal crisis on the scale it has now assumed represents a political issue in its own right, and that a thoroughgoing analysis of modern society and politics has to explain among other things why personal growth and development have become so hard to accomplish; why the fear of growing up and aging haunts our society; why personal relations have become so brittle and precarious; and why the "inner life" no longer offers any refuge from the danger around us. The emergence in the sixties of a new literary form, combining cultural criticism, political reportage, and reminiscence, represented an attempt to explore these issues—to illuminate the intersection of personal life and politics, history and private experience. Books like Norman Mailer's *Armies of the Night*, by disposing of the convention of journalistic objectivity, often penetrated more deeply into events than accounts written by allegedly impartial observers. The fiction of the period, in which the writer made no effort to conceal his presence or point of view, demonstrated how the act of writing could become a subject for fiction in its own right. Cultural criticism took on a personal and autobiographical character, which at its worst degenerated into self-display but at its best showed that the attempt to understand culture has to include analysis of the way it shapes the critic's own consciousness. Political upheavals injected themselves into every discussion and made it impossible to ignore the connections between culture and politics. By undermining the illusion of culture as a separate and autonomous development uninfluenced by the distribution of wealth and power, the political upheaval of the sixties also tended to undermine the distinction between high culture and popular culture and to make popular culture an object of serious discussion.

Confession and Anticonfession   The popularity of the confessional mode testifies, of course, to the new narcissism that runs all through American culture; but the best work in this vein attempts, precisely through self-disclosure, to achieve a critical distance from the self and to gain insight into the historical forces, reproduced in psychological form, that have made the very concept of selfhood increasingly problematic. The mere act of writing already presupposes a certain detachment from the self; and the objectification of one's own experience, as psychiatric studies of narcissism have shown, makes it possible for "the deep sources of grandiosity and exhibitionism—after being appropriately aim-inhibited, tamed, and neutralized— [to] find access" to reality.*

Yet the increasing interpenetration of fiction, journalism, and autobiography undeniably indicates that many writers find it more and more difficult to achieve the detachment indispensable to art. Instead of fictionalizing personal material or otherwise reordering it, they have taken to presenting it undigested, leaving the reader to arrive at his own interpretations. Instead of working through their memories, many writers now rely on mere self-disclosure to keep the reader interested, appealing not to his understanding but to his salacious curiosity about the private lives of famous people. In Mailer's works and those of his many imitators, what begins as a critical reflection on the writer's own ambition, frankly acknowledged as a bid for literary immortality, often ends in a garrulous monologue, with the writer trading on his own celebrity and filling page after page with material having no other claim to attention than its association with a famous name. Once having brought himself to public attention, the writer enjoys a ready-made market for true confessions. Thus Erica Jong, after winning an audience by writing about sex with as little feeling as a man, immediately produced another novel about a young woman who becomes a literary celebrity.

---

* Useful, creative work, which confronts the individual with "unsolved intellectual and aesthetic problems" and thereby mobilizes narcissism on behalf of activities outside the self, provides the narcissist, according to Heinz Kohut, with the best hope of transcending his predicament. "A modicum of creative potential—however narrow its scope may be—lies within the realm of the experience of many people, and the narcissistic nature of the creative act (the fact that the object of the creative interest is invested with narcissistic libido) can be approached through ordinary self-observation and empathy."

Even the best of the confessional writers walk a fine line between self-analysis and self-indulgence. Their books—Mailer's *Advertisements for Myself*, Norman Podhoretz's *Making It*, Philip Roth's *Portnoy's Complaint*, Paul Zweig's *Three Journeys*, Frederick Exley's *A Fan's Notes*—waver between hard-won personal revelation, chastened by the anguish with which it was gained, and the kind of spurious confession whose only claim to the reader's attention is that it describes events of immediate interest to the author. On the verge of an insight, these writers often draw back into self-parody, seeking to disarm criticism by anticipating it. They try to charm the reader instead of claiming significance for their narrative. They use humor not so much to detach themselves from the material as to ingratiate themselves, to get the reader's attention without asking him to take the writer or his subject seriously. Many of Donald Barthelme's stories, so brilliant and so often moving in their "Critique de la Vie Quotidienne," suffer because of Barthelme's inability to resist an easy laugh. In "Perpetua," for example, his satire of the newly divorced, with their time-killing sociability and pseudoliberate "life-styles," collapses into pointless humor.

> After the concert she . . . put on her suède jeans, her shirt made of a lot of colored scarves sewn together, her carved-wood neck bracelet, and her D'Artagnan cape with its silver lining.

> Perpetua could not remember what was this year and what was last year. Had something just happened, or had it happened a long time ago? She met many new people. "You are different," Perpetua said to Sunny Marge. "Very few of the girls I know wear a tattoo of the head of Marshal Foch on their backs."

Woody Allen, a masterful parodist of therapeutic clichés and the self-absorption from which they arise, often subverts his own ideas with the perfunctory, mandatory, self-deprecatory humor that has itself become so much a part of the American conversational style. In his parodies of pseudo-introspection in a world *Without Feathers*—without hope—Allen undermines irony with jokes that overflow all too abundantly from a limitless supply.

Good Lord, why am I so guilty? Is it because I hated my father? Probably it was the veal-parmigian incident. Well, what *was* it doing in his wallet? . . . What a sad man! When my first play, *A Cyst for Gus,* was produced at the Lyceum, he attended opening night in tails and a gas mask.

What *is* it about death that bothers me so much? Probably the hours.

Look at me, he thought. Fifty years old. Half a century. Next year, I will be fifty-one. Then fifty-two. Using this same reasoning, he could figure out his age as much as five years in the future.

The confessional form allows an honest writer like Exley or Zweig to provide a harrowing account of the spiritual desolation of our times, but it also allows a lazy writer to indulge in "the kind of immodest self-revelation which ultimately hides more than it admits." The narcissist's pseudo-insight into his own condition, usually expressed in psychiatric clichés, serves him as a means of deflecting criticism and disclaiming responsibility for his actions. "I am aware that this book is rather stunningly male chauvinistic," writes Dan Greenberg in his *Scoring: A Sexual Memoir.* "Well, what can I tell you? . . . I mean, that's what we were—so what else is new? I'm not condoning the attitude, I'm merely reporting it." At one point Greenberg describes how he made love to a woman who had collapsed into an alcoholic stupor and could not defend herself, only to inform the reader, in the next chapter, that "there wasn't a single true thing" in his entire account.

How do you feel about that now? Are you glad? Did that whole imaginary incident with Irene make you think I was too sick and disgusting to even go on reading my book? I guess not, because you obviously went on to read *this* chapter. . . .

Maybe you feel betrayed and maybe you're beginning to think that if I told you *one* untrue thing I could have told you others. I haven't though—everything else in this book . . . is absolutely true, and you can either believe that or not, as you wish.

In *Snow White*, Donald Barthelme resorts to a similar device, which again implicates the reader in the writer's invention. In the middle of the book, the reader finds a questionnaire soliciting his opinion about the progress of the story and alerting him to the ways in which the author has departed from the original fairy tale. When T. S. Eliot appended reference notes to *The Wasteland*, he became one of the first poets to call attention to his own imaginative transformation of reality, but he did so in order to expand the reader's awareness of allusions and to create a deeper imaginative resonance—not, as in these more recent instances, to demolish the reader's confidence in the author.

The unreliable, partially blinded narrator is another literary device of long standing. In the past, however, novelists often used it in order to achieve an ironic juxtaposition of the narrator's flawed perception of events with the author's own more accurate view. Today, the convention of a fictionalized narrator has been abandoned in most experimental writing. The author now speaks in his own voice but warns the reader that his version of the truth is not to be trusted. "Nothing in this book is true," Kurt Vonnegut announces on the very first page of *Cat's Cradle*. Having called attention to himself as a performer, the writer undermines the reader's ability to suspend disbelief. By fogging over the distinction between truth and illusion, he asks the reader to believe his story not because it rings true or even because he claims it is true, but simply because he claims it conceivably might be true—at least in part—if the reader chose to believe him. The writer waives the right to be taken seriously, at the same time escaping the responsibilities that go with being taken seriously. He asks the reader not for understanding but for indulgence. In accepting the writer's confession that he lied, the reader in turn waives the right to hold the writer accountable for the truth of his report. The writer thus attempts to charm the reader instead of trying to convince him, counting on the titillation provided by pseudo-revelation to hold the reader's interest.

Undertaken in this evasive mood, confessional writing degenerates into anticonfession. The record of the inner life becomes an unintentional parody of inner life. A literary genre that appears to affirm inwardness actually tells us that inner life is precisely what can no longer be taken seriously. This explains why Allen, Barthelme, and other satirists so often parody, as a deliberate literary strategy, the confessional style of an earlier time, when the artist bared his inner struggles in the belief that they represented a microcosm of the larger world. Today the artist's "confessions" are notable only for their utter banality. Woody Allen writes a parody of Van Gogh's letters to his brother, in which the artist becomes a dentist preoccupied with "oral prophylaxis," "root-canal work," and "the proper way to brush." The voyage to the interior discloses nothing but a blank. The writer no longer sees life reflected in his own mind. Just the opposite: he sees the world, even in its emptiness, as a mirror of himself. In recording his "inner" experiences, he seeks not to provide an objective account of a representative piece of reality but to seduce others into giving him their attention, acclaim, or sympathy and thus to shore up his faltering sense of self.

The Void Within   In spite of the defenses with which contemporary confessions surround themselves, these books often provide glimpses into the anguish that gives rise to the search for psychic peace. Paul Zweig speaks of his growing "conviction, amounting to a faith, that my life was organized around a core of blandness which shed anonymity upon everything I touched"; of "the emotional hibernation which lasted until I was almost thirty"; of the persisting "suspicion of personal emptiness which all my talking and my anxious attempts at charm surround and decorate, but don't penetrate or even come close to." In the same vein, Frederick Exley writes: "Whether or not I am a writer, I have . . . cultivated the instinct of one, an aversion for the herd, without, in my unhappy case, the ability to harness and articulate that aversion."

The mass media, with their cult of celebrity and their attempt to surround it with glamour and excitement, have made Americans a nation of fans, moviegoers. The media give substance to and thus intensify narcissistic dreams of fame and glory, encourage the common man to identify himself with the stars and to hate the "herd," and make it more and more difficult for him to accept the banality of everyday existence. Frank Gifford and the New York Giants, Exley writes, "sustained for me the illusion that fame was possible." Haunted and in his own view destroyed by "this awful dream of fame," this "illusion that I could escape the bleak anonymity of life," Exley depicts himself or his narrator— as usual, the distinction is unclear—as a yawning void, an insatiable hunger, an emptiness waiting to be filled with the rich experiences reserved for the chosen few. An ordinary man in most respects, "Exley" dreams of "a destiny that's grand enough for me! Like Michaelangelo's God reaching out to Adam, I want nothing less than to reach across the ages and stick my dirty fingers into posterity! . . . There's nothing I don't want! I want *this*, and I want *that*, and I want—well, everything!" The modern propaganda of commodities and the good life has sanctioned impulse gratification and made it unnecessary for the id to apologize for its wishes or disguise their grandiose proportions. But this same propaganda has made failure and loss unsupportable. When it finally occurs to the new Narcissus that he can "live not only without fame but without self, live and die without ever having had one's fellows conscious of the microscopic space one occupies upon this planet," he experiences this discovery not merely as a disappointment but as a shattering blow to his sense of selfhood. "The thought almost overcame me," Exley writes, "and I could not dwell upon it without becoming unutterably depressed."

In his emptiness and insignificance, the man of ordinary abilities tries to warm himself in the stars' reflected glow. In *Pages from a Cold Island*, Exley dwells on his fascination with Edmund Wilson and tells how he tried to get closer to his idol, after Wilson's death, by interviewing the great man's survivors. Since the record of these interviews concerns Exley himself far more than it concerns Wilson, and since Exley repeatedly praises Wilson's literary achievement in the rhetoric of conventional tribute—"one of the great men of the twentieth century"; "fifty years of relentless dedication to his craft"; "American Letters had . . . never seen his like before"—it is clear that Wilson represents for Exley a magical presence, even in death, association with whom confers vicarious importance on his literary admirers and posthumous hangers-on. Exley himself says that he acted as if "proximity to Wilson would bring me luck."

Other autobiographers describe, with none of Exley's self-consciousness, the same attempt to live vicariously through others more brilliant than oneself. Susan Stern gives the impression that she gravitated to the Weathermen because association with media stars like Mark Rudd and Bernadine Dohrn made her feel that she had finally found her "niche in life." Dohrn impressed her as a "queen," a "high priestess" whose "splendor" and "nobility" set her apart from the "secondary" and "third-ranking leadership" of SDS. "Whatever quality she possessed, I wanted it. I wanted to be cherished and respected as Bernadine was." When the trial of the Seattle 7 made Stern a media celebrity in her own right, she found herself "someone" at last, "because there were so many people hanging around me, asking me questions, looking to me for answers, or just looking at me, offering to do things for me, to get some of the glow from the limelight." Now in her "prime," she imagined herself and tried to impress others as "flashy and vulgar, hard and funny, aggressive and dramatic." "Wherever I went people loved me." Her eminence in the most violent wing of the American left enabled her to act out, before a large audience, the fantasy of destructive rage that underlay her desire for fame. She imagined herself an avenging Fury, an Amazon, a Walküre. On the wall of her house, she painted "an eight-foot-tall nude woman with flowing green-blond hair, and a burning American flag coming out of her cunt!" In her "acid frenzy," she says, she "had painted what I wanted to be somewhere deep in my mind; tall and blond, nude and armed, consuming—or discharging—a burning America."

Neither drugs nor fantasies of destruction—even when the fantasies are objectified in "revolutionary praxis"—appease the inner hunger from which they spring. Personal relations founded on reflected glory, on the need to admire and be admired, prove fleeting and insubstantial. Stern's friendships and love affairs usually ended in disillusionment, animosity, recrimination. She complains of an inability to feel anything: "I grew more frozen inside, more animated outside." Although her life revolved around politics, the political world has no reality in her memoir; it figures only as a projection of her own rage and unease, a dream of anxiety and violence. Many other books of our time, even books that are the product of political upheaval, convey the same sense of the unreality of politics. Paul Zweig, who spent ten years in Paris in the fifties and sixties and took part in the agitation against the Algerian war, says that the war "gradually became an environment pervading every aspect" of his existence; yet external events play only a shadowy part in his narrative. They have the quality of hallucination, a vague background of "terror and vulnerability." At the height of the violent protest against the Algerian war, "he recalled a phrase he had once read in a book about the inner feeling of schizophrenia. The patient, with the pungency of an oracle, had said: *'La terre bouge, elle ne m'inspire aucune confiance.'* " The same feeling, Zweig says, later overwhelmed him in the Sahara Desert, where he tried to overcome his "inner dryness" by testing himself, alone, against the rigors of nature. "The earth moves about, I can have no confidence in it."

In Zweig's account of his life, friends and lovers provide moments of what might be called happiness, but their presence fails to arrest "the vacant spin of his inner existence." He lived for a time with a girl named Michelle, who "hurled herself against his impassability without success." A carefully laid scene, intended to capture the quality of their connection, captures also the elusive quality of Zweig's narrative, the self-mockery intended to charm and to disarm criticism, and the terribly conviction of inauthenticity that lies behind it:

As if to mock the anguish in the room, the gray-lit bulk of Notre Dame floats out of the night at a distance of magic and low muttering cars. The girl is sitting on the floor next to scattered paintbrushes and a murky wooden palette. The boy, in several pieces, or so he feels, on the bed, is saying in a strangled, theatrical whisper: *"Je ne veux pas être un homme."* To make his meaning clearer, which is to say, to lift his anxiety into the intellectual realm, he repeats: *"Je ne veux pas 'être un homme,'* " hinting at a question of principle which the girl is apparently too obtuse to grasp, because she lets out a moan and begins to cry.

After six years of this, "they got married and divorced within a few bracing weeks." Zweig's exile came to an end, and with it, his attempt "to impersonate his existence with the agility of someone who has nothing more to lose."

The inner void, however, persists: "the experience of inner emptiness, the frightening feeling that at some level of existence

I'm nobody, that my identity has collapsed and deep down, no one's there." It remains for Swami Muktananda, a guru much favored by New Yorkers in search of spiritual healing, to teach Zweig how to put his "double" to sleep. "Baba"—father—teaches "the futility of mental processes." Under his instruction, Zweig has experienced "the delirium of release." Like Jerry Rubin, he attributes this "cure," this feeling of being "healed and buoyant," to the destruction of his psychic defenses. "No longer trapped in the labor of self-defense," he has anesthetized that part of himself which is "constructed of mental busyness . . . glued together by obsessive thinking and propelled by anxiety."

The Progressive Critique of Privatism   The popularization of psychiatric modes of thought, the spread of the "new conscious-ness movement," the dream of fame, and the anguished sense of failure, which all give added urgency to the quest for spiritual panaceas, share a quality of intense preoccupation with the self. This self-absorption defines the moral climate of contemporary society. The conquest of nature and the search for new frontiers have given way to the search for self-fulfillment. Narcissism has become one of the central themes of American culture, as Jim Hougan, Tom Wolfe, Peter Marin, Edwin Schur, Richard Sen-nett, and other recent writers have suggested in various ways. Unless we are content merely to moralize under the cover of psy-chiatric jargon, however, we need to use this concept more rigorously than it is used in popular social criticism, and with an awareness of its clinical implications.

Critics of contemporary narcissism and of the new therapeutic sensibility mistakenly condemn the psychiatric orientation as an opiate of the upper middle class. Self-absorption, according to Marin, insulates affluent Americans against the horrors around them—poverty, racism, injustice—and "eases their troubled con-science." Schur attacks the "awareness craze" on the grounds that it addresses problems peculiar to the well-to-do, neglects those of the poor, and converts "social discontent to personal inade-quacy." He thinks it is "criminal" for "white middle-class citizens to become complacently self-preoccupied while their less fortunate fellow Americans struggle and starve." But the self-preoccupation on which the awareness movement capitalizes arises not from complacency but from desperation; nor is this desperation confined to the middle class. Schur seems to think that the transient, provisional character of personal relations is a problem only for affluent executives always on the move. Are we to believe that things are different among the poor? that working-class marriages are happy and free of conflict? that the ghetto produces stable, loving, and nonmanipulative friendships? Studies of lower-class life have repeatedly shown that poverty undermines marriage and friendship. The collapse of personal life originates not in the spiritual torments of affluence but in the war of all against all, which is now spreading from the lower class, where it has long raged without interruption, to the rest of society.

Because the new therapies are usually expensive, Schur makes the mistake of supposing that they address problems that concern the rich alone and are inherently trivial and "unreal." He criticizes writers like George and Nena O'Neill (the apostles of "open marriage") for taking "an incredibly ethnocentric view of personal crisis, apparently based on their own middle-class values and experience." It never occurs to experts in awareness, he complains, "that economic resources might help a person confront a crisis, or avoid it to begin with." These experts write as if social classes and social conflict did not exist. For this reason, Schur finds it "hard to imagine" that the awareness movement, in spite of attempts to popularize it through inexpensive manuals and free clinics, will ever have much appeal to the poor.

Certainly, it's conceivable that even a poor person might feel somewhat better as a result of some of the new self-realization techniques. But, at best, such happiness would tend to be short-lived. Seduced into interiorizing their problems, the poor would only be diverted from the more urgent task of advancing their real collective interests.

By setting up an oversimplified opposition between "real" issues and personal issues, Schur ignores the fact that social questions inevitably present themselves also as personal ones. The real world is refracted in familial and personal experiences, which color the way we perceive it. Experiences of inner emptiness, loneliness, and inauthenticity are by no means unreal or, for that matter, devoid of social content; nor do they arise from exclusively "middle- and upper-class living conditions." They arise from the warlike conditions that pervade American society, from the dangers and uncertainty that surround us, and from a loss of confidence in the future. The poor have always had to live for the present, but now a desperate concern for personal survival, sometimes disguised as hedonism, engulfs the middle class as well.

Schur himself notes that "what seems ultimately to emerge out of this very mixed message is an ethic of self-preservation." But his condemnation of the survival ethic as a "retreat into privatism" misses the point. When personal relations are conducted with no other object than psychic survival, "privatism" no longer provides a haven from a heartless world. On the contrary, private life takes on the very qualities of the anarchic social order from which it is supposed to provide a refuge. It is the devastation of personal life, not the retreat into privatism, that needs to be criticized and condemned. The trouble with the consciousness movement is not that it addresses trivial or unreal issues but that it provides self-defeating solutions. Arising out of a pervasive dissatisfaction with the quality of personal relations, it advises people not to make too large an investment in love and friendship, to avoid excessive dependence on others, and to live for the moment—the very conditions that created the crisis of personal relations in the first place.

The Critique of Privatism: Richard Sennett on the Fall of Public Man Richard Sennett's critique of narcissism, more subtle and penetrating than Schur's in its insistence that "narcissism is the very opposite of strong self-love," nevertheless implies a similar devaluation of the personal realm. The best things in the Western cultural tradition, in Sennett's view, derive from the conventions that once regulated impersonal relations in public. These conventions, now condemned as constricting, artificial, and deadening to emotional spontaneity, formerly established civilized boundaries between people, set limits on the public display of feeling, and promoted cosmopolitanism and civility. In eighteenth-century London or Paris, sociability did not depend on intimacy. "Strangers meeting in the parks or on the streets might without embarrassment speak to each other." They shared a common fund of public signs which enabled people of unequal rank to conduct a civilized conversation and to cooperate in public projects without feeling called upon to expose their innermost secrets. In the nineteenth century, however, reticence broke down, and people came to believe that public actions revealed the inner personality of the actor. The romantic cult of sincerity and authenticity tore away the masks that people once had worn in public and eroded the boundary between public and private life. As the public world came to be seen as a mirror of the self, people lost the capacity for detachment and hence for playful encounter, which presupposes a certain distance from the self.

In our own time, according to Sennett, relations in public, conceived as a form of self-revelation, have become deadly serious. Conversation takes on the quality of confession. Class consciousness declines; people perceive their social position as a reflection of their own abilities and blame themselves for the injustices inflicted on them. Politics degenerates into a struggle not for social change but for self-realization. When the boundaries between the self and the rest of the world collapse, the pursuit of enlightened self-interest, which once informed every phase of political activity, becomes impossible. The political man of an earlier age knew how to take rather than desire (Sennett's definition of psychological maturity) and judged politics, as he judged reality in general, to see "what's in it for him, rather than if it is him." The narcissist, on the other hand, "suspends ego interests" in a delirium of desire.

Far more intricate and suggestive than a brief summary can indicate, Sennett's argument has much to teach us about the importance of self-distance in play and in dramatic reconstructions of reality, about the projection of the search for self into politics, and about the pernicious effects of the ideology of intimacy.

But Sennett's idea that politics turns on enlightened self-interest, the careful calculation of personal and class advantage, hardly does justice to the irrational elements that have always characterized the relations between dominant and subordinate classes. It pays too little heed to the ability of the rich and powerful to identify their ascendancy with lofty moral principles, which make resistance a crime not only against the state but against humanity itself. Ruling classes have always sought to instill in their subordinates the capacity to experience exploitation and material deprivation as guilt, while deceiving themselves that their own material interests coincide with those of mankind as a whole. Leaving aside the dubious validity of Sennett's equation of successful ego-functioning with the ability "to take rather than to desire," which seems to enshrine rapacity as the only alternative to narcissism, the fact is that men have never perceived their interests with perfect clarity and have therefore tended, throughout history, to project irrational aspects of themselves into the political realm. To blame the irrational features of modern politics on narcissism, the ideology of intimacy, or the "culture of personality" not only exaggerates the role of ideology in historical development but underestimates the irrationality of politics in earlier epochs.

Sennett's conception of proper politics as the politics of self-interest shares with the Tocquevillean, pluralistic tradition from which it evidently derives an ideological element of its own. The tendency of this analysis is to exalt bourgeois liberalism as the only civilized form of political life and bourgeois "civility" as the only uncorrupted form of public conversation. From the pluralist point of view, the admitted imperfections of bourgeois society remain inaccessible to political correction, since political life is regarded as inherently a realm of radical imperfection. Thus when men and women demand fundamental alterations in the political system, they are really projecting personal anxieties into politics. In this way liberalism defines itself as the outer limit of political rationality and dismisses all attempts to go beyond liberalism, including the entire revolutionary tradition, as the politics of narcissism. Sennett's adoption of a Tocquevillian perspective leaves him unable to distinguish between the corruption of radical politics in the late 1960s by the irrational elements in American culture and the validity of many radical goals. His mode of analysis makes all radicalism, all forms of politics that seek to create a society not based on exploitation, automatically suspect. In spite of its idealization of the public life of the past, Sennett's book participates in the current revulsion against politics—the revulsion, that is, against the hope of using politics as an instrument of social change.

Sennett's eagerness to restore a distinction between public and private life, moreover, ignores the ways in which they are always intertwined. The socialization of the young reproduces political domination at the level of personal experience. In our own time, this invasion of private life by the forces of organized domination has become so pervasive that personal life has almost ceased to exist. Reversing cause and effect, Sennett blames the contemporary malaise on the invasion of the public realm by the ideology of intimacy. For him as for Marin and Schur, the current preoccupation with self-discovery, psychic growth, and intimate personal encounters represents unseemly self-absorption, romanticism run rampant. In fact, the cult of intimacy originates not in the assertion of personality but in its collapse. Poets and novelists today, far from glorifying the self, chronicle its disintegration. Therapies that minister to the shattered ego convey the same message. Our society, far from fostering private life at the expense of public life, has made deep and lasting friendships, love affairs, and marriages increasingly difficult to achieve. As social life becomes more and more warlike and barbaric, personal relations, which ostensibly provide relief from these conditions, take on the character of combat. Some of the new therapies dignify this combat as "assertiveness" and "fighting fair in love and marriage." Others celebrate impermanent attachments under such formulas as "open marriage" and "open-ended commitments." Thus they intensify the disease they pretend to cure. They do this, however, not by diverting attention from social problems to personal ones, from real issues to false issues, but by obscuring the social origins of the suffering—not to be confused with complacent self-absorption—that is painfully but falsely experienced as purely personal and private.

II

The Narcissistic Personality of Our Time

Narcissism as a Metaphor of the Human Condition   Recent critics of the new narcissism not only confuse cause and effect, attributing to a cult of privatism developments that derive from the disintegration of public life; they use the term narcissism so loosely that it retains little of its psychological content. Erich Fromm, in *The Heart of Man*, drains the idea of its clinical meaning and expands it to cover all forms of "vanity," "self-admiration," "self-satisfaction," and "self-glorification" in individuals and all forms of parochialism, ethnic or racial prejudice, and "fanaticism" in groups. In other words, Fromm uses the term as a synonym for the "asocial" individualism which, in his version of progressive and "humanistic" dogma, undermines cooperation, brotherly love, and the search for wider loyalties. Narcissism thus appears simply as the antithesis of that watery love for humanity (disinterested "love for the stranger") advocated by Fromm under the name of socialism.

Fromm's discussion of "individual and social narcissism," appropriately published in a series of books devoted to "Religious Perspectives," provides an excellent example of the inclination, in our therapeutic age, to dress up moralistic platitudes in psychiatric garb. ("We live in a historical period characterized by a sharp discrepancy between the intellectual development of man . . . and his mental-emotional development, which has left him still in a state of marked narcissism with all its pathological symptoms.") Whereas Sennett reminds us that narcissism has more in common with self-hatred than with self-admiration, Fromm loses sight even of this well-known clinical fact in his eagerness to sermonize about the blessings of brotherly love.

As always in Fromm's work, the trouble originates in his

31

misguided and unnecessary attempt to rescue Freud's thought from its "mechanistic" nineteenth-century basis and to press it into the service of "humanistic realism." In practice, this means that theoretical rigor gives way to ethically uplifting slogans and sentiments. Fromm notes in passing that Freud's original concept of narcissism assumed that libido begins in the ego, as a "great reservoir" of undifferentiated self-love, whereas in 1922 he decided, on the contrary, that "we must recognize the id as the great reservoir of the libido." Fromm slides over this issue, however, by remarking, "The theoretical question whether the libido starts originally in the ego or in the id is of no substantial importance for the meaning of the concept [of narcissism] itself." In fact, the structural theory of the mind, set forth by Freud in *Group Psychology* and in *The Ego and the Id*, required modifications of his earlier ideas that have a great deal of bearing on the theory of narcissism. Structural theory made Freud abandon the simple dichotomy between instinct and consciousness and recognize the unconscious elements of the ego and superego, the importance of nonsexual impulses (aggression or the "death instinct"), and the alliance between superego and id, superego and aggression. These discoveries in turn made possible an understanding of the role of object relations in the development of narcissism, thereby revealing narcissism as essentially a defense against aggressive impulses rather than self-love.

Theoretical precision about narcissism is important not only because the idea is so readily susceptible to moralistic inflation but because the practice of equating narcissism with everything selfish and disagreeable mitigates against historical specificity. Men have always been selfish, groups have always been ethnocentric; nothing is gained by giving these qualities a psychiatric label. The emergence of character disorders as the most prominent form of psychiatric pathology, however, together with the change in personality structure this development reflects, derives from quite specific changes in our society and culture—from bureaucracy, the proliferation of images, therapeutic ideologies, the rationalization of the inner life, the cult of consumption, and in the last analysis from changes in family life and from changing patterns of socialization. All this disappears from sight if narcissism becomes simply "the metaphor of the human condition," as in another existential, humanistic interpretation, Shirley Sugerman's *Sin and Madness: Studies in Narcissism.*

The refusal of recent critics of narcissism to discuss the etiology of narcissism or to pay much attention to the growing body of clinical writing on the subject probably represents a deliberate decision, stemming from the fear that emphasis on the clinical aspects of the narcissistic syndrome would detract from the concept's usefulness in social analysis. This decision, however, has proved to be a mistake. In ignoring the psychological dimension, these authors also miss the social. They fail to explore any of the character traits associated with pathological narcissism, which in less extreme form appear in such profusion in the everyday life of our age: dependence on the vicarious warmth provided by others combined with a fear of dependence, a sense of inner emptiness, boundless repressed rage, and unsatisfied oral cravings. Nor do they discuss what might be called the secondary characteristics of narcissism: pseudo self-insight, calculating seductiveness, nervous, self-deprecatory humor. Thus they deprive themselves of any basis on which to make connections between the narcissistic personality type and certain characteristic patterns of contemporary culture, such as the intense fear of old age and death, altered sense of time, fascination with celebrity, fear of competition, decline of the play spirit, deteriorating relations between men and women. For these critics, narcissism remains at its loosest a synonym for selfishness and at its most precise a metaphor, and nothing more, that describes the state of mind in which the world appears as a mirror of the self.

Psychology and Sociology   Psychoanalysis deals with individuals, not with groups. Efforts to generalize clinical findings to collective behavior always encounter the difficulty that groups have a life of their own. The collective mind, if there is such a thing, reflects the needs of the group as a whole, not the psychic needs of the individual, which in fact have to be subordinated to the demands of collective living. Indeed it is precisely the subjection of individuals to the group that psychoanalytic theory, through a study of its psychic repercussions, promises to clarify. By conducting an intensive analysis of individual cases that rests on clinical evidence rather than common-sense impressions, psychoanalysis tells us something about the inner workings of society itself, in the very act of turning its back on society and immersing itself in the individual unconscious.

Every society reproduces its culture—its norms, it underlying assumptions, its modes of organizing experience—in the individual, in the form of personality. As Durkheim said, personality is the individual socialized. The process of socialization, carried out by the family and secondarily by the school and other agencies of character formation, modifies human nature to conform to the prevailing social norms. Each society tries to solve the universal crises of childhood—the trauma of separation from the mother, the fear of abandonment, the pain of competing with others for the mother's love—in its own way, and the manner in which it deals with these psychic events produces a characteristic form of personality, a characteristic form of psychological deformation, by means of which the individual reconciles himself to instinctual deprivation and submits to the requirements of social existence. Freud's insistence on the continuity between psychic health and psychic sickness makes it possible to see neuroses and psychoses as in some sense the characteristic expression of a given culture. "Psychosis," Jules Henry has written, "is the final outcome of all that is wrong with a culture."

Psychoanalysis best clarifies the connection between society and the individual, culture and personality, precisely when it confines itself to careful examination of individuals. It tells us most about society when it is least determined to do so. Freud's extrapolation of psychoanalytic principles into anthropology, history, and biography can be safely ignored by the student of society, but his clinical investigations constitute a storehouse of indispensable ideas, once it is understood that the unconscious mind represents the modification of nature by culture, the imposition of civilization on instinct.

Freud should not be reproached [wrote T. W. Adorno] for having neglected the concrete social dimension, but for being all too untroubled by the social origin of . . . the rigidity of the unconscious, which he registers with the undeviating objectivity of the natural scientist. . . . In making the leap from psychological images to historical reality, he forgets what he himself discovered—that all reality undergoes modification upon entering the unconscious—and is thus misled into positing such factual events as the murder of the father by the primal horde.*

Those who wish to understand contemporary narcissism as a social and cultural phenomenon must turn first to the growing body of clinical writing on the subject, which makes no claim to social or cultural significance and deliberately repudiates the proposition that "changes in contemporary culture," as Otto Kernberg writes, "have effects on patterns of object relations."† In the clinical literature, narcissism serves as more than a metaphoric term for self-absorption. As a psychic formation in which "love rejected turns back to the self as hatred," narcissism has come to be recognized as an important element in the so-called character disorders that have absorbed much of the clinical attention once given to hysteria and obsessional neuroses. A new

---

* "On . . . its home ground," Adorno added, "psychoanalysis carries specific conviction; the further it removes itself from that sphere, the more its theses are threatened alternately with shallowness or wild over-systematization. If someone makes a slip of the tongue and a sexually loaded word comes out, if someone suffers from agoraphobia or if a girl walks in her sleep, psychoanalysis not merely has its best chances of therapeutic success but also its proper province, the relatively autonomous, monadological individual as arena of the unconscious conflict between instinctual drive and prohibition. The further it departs from this area, the more tyrannically it has to proceed and the more it has to drag what belongs to the dimension of outer reality into the shades of psychic immanence. Its delusion in so doing is not dissimilar from that 'omnipotence of thought' which it itself criticized as infantile."

† Those who argue, in opposition to the thesis of the present study, that there has been no underlying change in the structure of personality, cite this passage to support the contention that although "we do see certain symptom constellations and personality disorders more or less frequently than in Freud's day, . . . this shift in attention has occurred primarily because of a shift in our clinical emphasis due to tremendous advances in our understanding of personality structure."

In light of this controversy, it is important to note that Kernberg adds to his observation a qualification: "This is not to say that such changes in the patterns of intimacy [and of object relations in general] could not occur over a period of several generations, if and when changes in cultural patterns affect family structure to such an extent that the earliest development in childhood would be influenced." This is exactly what I will argue in chapter VII.

theory of narcissism has developed, grounded in Freud's well-known essay on the subject (which treats narcissism—libidinal investment of the self—as a necessary precondition of object love) but devoted not to primary narcissism but to secondary or pathological narcissism: the incorporation of grandiose object images as a defense against anxiety and guilt. Both types of narcissism blur the boundaries between the self and the world of objects, but there is an important difference between them. The newborn infant—the primary narcissist—does not yet perceive his mother as having an existence separate from his own, and he therefore mistakes dependence on the mother, who satisfies his needs as soon as they arise, with his own omnipotence. "It takes several weeks of postnatal development . . . before the infant perceives that the source of his need . . . is within and the source of gratification is outside the self."

Secondary narcissism, on the other hand, "attempts to annul the pain of disappointed [object] love" and to nullify the child's rage against those who do not respond immediately to his needs; against those who are now seen to respond to others beside the child and who therefore appear to have abandoned him. Pathological narcissism, "which cannot be considered simply a fixation at the level of normal primitive narcissism," arises only when the ego has developed to the point of distinguishing itself from surrounding objects. If the child for some reason experiences this separation trauma with special intensity, he may attempt to reestablish earlier relationships by creating in his fantasies an omnipotent mother or father who merges with images of his own self. "Through internalization the patient seeks to recreate a wished-for love relationship which may once have existed and simultaneously to annul the anxiety and guilt aroused by aggressive drives directed against the frustrating and disappointing object."

Narcissism in Recent Clinical Literature   The shifting emphasis in clinical studies from primary to secondary narcissism reflects both the shift in psychoanalytic theory from study of the id to study of the ego and a change in the type of patients seeking

psychiatric treatment. Indeed the shift from a psychology of instincts to ego psychology itself grew partly out of a recognition
that the patients who began to present themselves for treatment
in the 1940s and 1950s "very seldom resembled the classical
neuroses Freud described so thoroughly." In the last twenty-five
years, the borderline patient, who confronts the psychiatrist not
with well-defined symptoms but with diffuse dissatisfactions, has
become increasingly common. He does not suffer from debilitat-
ing fixations or phobias or from the conversion of repressed sexual
energy into nervous ailments; instead he complains "of vague, diffuse dissatisfactions with life" and feels his "amorphous existence
to be futile and purposeless." He describes "subtly experienced
yet pervasive feelings of emptiness and depression," "violent oscillations of self-esteem," and "a general inability to get along."
He gains "a sense of heightened self-esteem only by attaching
himself to strong, admired figures whose acceptance he craves
and by whom he needs to feel supported." Although he carries
out his daily responsibilities and even achieves distinction, happiness eludes him, and life frequently strikes him as not worth living.

Psychoanalysis, a therapy that grew out of experience with
severely repressed and morally rigid individuals who needed to
come to terms with a rigorous inner "censor," today finds itself
confronted more and more often with a "chaotic and impulse-rid-
den character." It must deal with patients who "act out" their
conflicts instead of repressing or sublimating them. These patients, though often ingratiating, tend to cultivate a protective
shallowness in emotional relations. They lack the capacity to
mourn, because the intensity of their rage against lost love objects,
in particular against their parents, prevents their reliving happy
experiences or treasuring them in memory. Sexually promiscuous
rather than repressed, they nevertheless find it difficult to "elaborate the sexual impulse" or to approach sex in the spirit of play.
They avoid close involvements, which might release intense feelings of rage. Their personalities consist largely of defenses against
this rage and against feelings of oral deprivation that originate in
the pre-Oedipal stage of psychic development.

Often these patients suffer from hypochondria and complain

of a sense of inner emptiness. At the same time they entertain fantasies of omnipotence and a strong belief in their right to exploit others and be gratified. Archaic, punitive, and sadistic elements predominate in the superegos of these patients, and they conform to social rules more out of fear of punishment than from a sense of guilt. They experience their own needs and appetites, suffused with rage, as deeply dangerous, and they throw up defenses that are as primitive as the desires they seek to stifle.

On the principle that pathology represents a heightened version of normality, the "pathological narcissism" found in character disorders of this type should tell us something about narcissism as a social phenomenon. Studies of personality disorders that occupy the border line between neurosis and psychosis, though written for clinicians and making no claims to shed light on social or cultural issues, depict a type of personality that ought to be immediately recognizable, in a more subdued form, to observers of the contemporary cultural scene: facile at managing the impressions he gives to others, ravenous for admiration but contemptuous of those he manipulates into providing it; unappeasably hungry for emotional experiences with which to fill an inner void; terrified of aging and death.

The most convincing explanations of the psychic origins of this borderline syndrome draw on the theoretical tradition established by Melanie Klein. In her psychoanalytic investigations of children, Klein discovered that early feelings of overpowering rage, directed especially against the mother and secondarily against the internalized image of the mother as a ravenous monster, make it impossible for the child to synthesize "good" and "bad" parental images. In his fear of aggression from the bad parents—projections of his own rage—he idealizes the good parents who will come to the rescue.

Internalized images of others, buried in the unconscious mind at an early age, become self-images as well. If later experience fails to qualify or to introduce elements of reality into the child's archaic fantasies about his parents, he finds it difficult to distinguish between images of the self and of the objects outside the self. These images fuse to form a defense against the bad representations of the self and of objects, similarly fused in the form of a harsh, punishing superego. Melanie Klein analyzed a ten-year-old boy who unconsciously thought of his mother as a "vampire" or "horrid bird" and internalized this fear as hypochondria. He was afraid that the bad presences inside him would devour the good ones. The rigid separation of good and bad images of the self and of objects, on the one hand, and the fusion of self- and object images on the other, arose from the boy's inability to tolerate ambivalence or anxiety. Because his anger was so intense, he could not admit that he harbored aggressive feelings toward those he loved. "Fear and guilt relating to his destructive phantasies moulded his whole emotional life."

A child who feels so gravely threatened by his own aggressive feelings (projected onto others and then internalized again as inner "monsters") attempts to compensate himself for his experiences of rage and envy with fantasies of wealth, beauty, and omnipotence. These fantasies, together with the internalized images of the good parents with which he attempts to defend himself, become the core of a "grandiose conception of the self." A kind of "blind optimism," according to Otto Kernberg, protects the narcissistic child from the dangers around and within him—particularly from dependence on others, who are perceived as without exception undependable. "Constant projection of 'all bad' self and object images perpetuates a world of dangerous, threatening objects, against which the 'all good' self images are used defensively, and megalomanic ideal self images are built up." The splitting of images determined by aggressive feelings from images that derive from libidinal impulses makes it impossible for the child to acknowledge his own aggression, to experience guilt or concern for objects invested simultaneously with aggression and libido, or to mourn for lost objects. Depression in narcissistic patients takes the form not of mourning with its admixture of guilt, described by Freud in "Mourning and Melancholia," but of impotent rage and "feelings of defeat by external forces."

Because the intrapsychic world of these patients is so thinly populated—consisting only of the "grandiose self," in Kernberg's words, "the devalued, shadowy images of self and others, and potential persecutors"—they experience intense feelings of emptiness and inauthenticity. Although the narcissist can function in the everyday world and often charms other people (not least with his "pseudo-insight into his personality"), his devaluation of others, together with his lack of curiosity about them, impoverishes his personal life and reinforces the "subjective experience of emptiness." Lacking any real intellectual engagement with the world—notwithstanding a frequently inflated estimate of his own intellectual abilities—he has little capacity for sublimation. He therefore depends on others for constant infusions of approval and admiration. He "must attach [himself] to someone, living an almost parasitic" existence. At the same time, his fear of emotional dependence, together with his manipulative, exploitive approach to personal relations, makes these relations bland, superficial, and deeply unsatisfying. "The ideal relationship to me would be a two month relationship," said a borderline patient. "That way there'd be no commitment. At the end of the two months I'd just break it off."

Chronically bored, restlessly in search of instantaneous intimacy—of emotional titillation without involvement and dependence—the narcissist is promiscuous and often pansexual as well, since the fusion of pregenital and Oedipal impulses in the service of aggression encourages polymorphous perversity. The bad images he has internalized also make him chronically uneasy about his health, and hypochondria in turn gives him a special affinity for therapy and for therapeutic groups and movements.

As a psychiatric patient, the narcissist is a prime candidate for interminable analysis. He seeks in analysis a religion or way of life and hopes to find in the therapeutic relationship external support for his fantasies of omnipotence and eternal youth. The strength of his defenses, however, makes him resistant to successful analysis. The shallowness of his emotional life often prevents him from developing a close connection to the analyst, even though he "often uses his intellectual insight to agree verbally with the analyst and recapitulates in his own words what has been analysed in previous sessions." He uses intellect in the service of evasion rather than self-discovery, resorting to some of the same strategies of obfuscation that appear in the confessional writing of recent decades. "The patient uses the analytic interpretations but deprives them quickly of life and meaning, so that only meaningless words are left. The words are then felt to be the patient's own possession, which he idealizes and which give him a sense of superiority." Although psychiatrists no longer consider narcissistic disorders inherently unanalyzable, few of them take an optimistic view of the prospects for success.

According to Kernberg, the great argument for making the attempt at all, in the face of the many difficulties presented by narcissistic patients, is the devastating effect of narcissism on the second half of their lives—the certainty of the terrible suffering that lies in store. In a society that dreads old age and death, aging holds a special terror for those who fear dependence and whose self-esteem requires the admiration usually reserved for youth, beauty, celebrity, or charm. The usual defenses against the ravages of age—identification with ethical or artistic values beyond one's immediate interests, intellectual curiosity, the consoling emotional warmth derived from happy relationships in the past— can do nothing for the narcissist. Unable to derive whatever comfort comes from identification with historical continuity, he finds it impossible, on the contrary, "to accept the fact that a younger generation now possesses many of the previously cherished gratifications of beauty, wealth, power and, particularly, creativity. To be able to enjoy life in a process involving a growing identification with other people's happiness and achievements is tragically beyond the capacity of narcissistic personalities."

Social Influences on Narcissism   Every age develops its own peculiar forms of pathology, which express in exaggerated form its underlying character structure. In Freud's time, hysteria and obsessional neurosis carried to extremes the personality traits associated with the capitalist order at an earlier stage in its development—acquisitiveness, fanatical devotion to work, and a fierce repression of sexuality. In our time, the preschizophrenic, borderline, or personality disorders have attracted increasing attention, along with schizophrenia itself. This "change in the form of neuroses has been observed and described since World War II by an ever-increasing number of psychiatrists." According to Peter

L. Giovacchini, "Clinicians are constantly faced with the seemingly increasing number of patients who do not fit current diagnostic categories" and who suffer not from "definitive symptoms" but from "vague, ill-defined complaints." "When I refer to 'this type of patient,' " he writes, "practically everyone knows to whom I am referring." The growing prominence of "character disorders" seems to signify an underlying change in the organization of personality, from what has been called inner-direction to narcissism.

Allen Wheelis argued in 1958 that the change in "the patterns of neuroses" fell "within the personal experience of older psychoanalysts," while younger ones "become aware of it from the discrepancy between the older descriptions of neuroses and the problems presented by the patients who come daily to their offices. The change is from symptom neuroses to character disorders." Heinz Lichtenstein, who questioned the additional assertion that it reflected a change in personality structure, nevertheless wrote in 1963 that the "change in neurotic patterns" already constituted a "well-known fact." In the seventies, such reports have become increasingly common. "It is no accident," Herbert Hendin notes, "that at the present time the dominant events in psychoanalysis are the rediscovery of narcissism and the new emphasis on the psychological significance of death." "What hysteria and the obsessive neuroses were to Freud and his early colleagues . . . at the beginning of this century," writes Michael Beldoch, "the narcissistic disorders are to the workaday analyst in these last few decades before the next millennium. Today's patients by and large do not suffer from hysterical paralyses of the legs or hand-washing compulsions; instead it is their very psychic selves that have gone numb or that they must scrub and rescrub in an exhausting and unending effort to come clean." These patients suffer from "pervasive feelings of emptiness and a deep disturbance of self-esteem." Burness E. Moore notes that narcissistic disorders have become more and more common. According to Sheldon Bach, "You used to see people coming in with hand-washing compulsions, phobias, and familiar neuroses. Now you see mostly narcissists." Gilbert J. Rose maintains that the psychoanalytic outlook, "inappropriately transplanted from analytic

practice" to everyday life, has contributed to "global permissiveness" and the "over-domestication of instinct," which in turn
contributes to the proliferation of "narcissistic identity disorders." According to Joel Kovel, the stimulation of infantile cravings by advertising, the usurpation of parental authority by the
media and the school, and the rationalization of inner life accompanied by the false promise of personal fulfillment, have created a
new type of "social individual." "The result is not the classical
neuroses where an infantile impulse is suppressed by patriarchal
authority, but a modern version in which impulse is stimulated,
perverted and given neither an adequate object upon which to satisfy itself nor coherent forms of control. . . . The entire complex,
played out in a setting of alienation rather than direct control,
loses the classical form of symptom—and the classical therapeutic
opportunity of simply restoring an impulse to consciousness."

The reported increase in the number of narcissistic patients
does not necessarily indicate that narcissistic disorders are more
common than they used to be, in the population as a whole, or
that they have become more common than the classical conversion neuroses. Perhaps they simply come more quickly to psychiatric attention. Ilza Veith contends that "with the increasing
awareness of conversion reactions and the popularization of psychiatric literature, the 'old-fashioned' somatic expressions of hysteria have become suspect among the more sophisticated classes,
and hence most physicians observe that obvious conversion
symptoms are now rarely encountered and, if at all, only among
the uneducated." The attention given to character disorders in
recent clinical literature probably makes psychiatrists more alert
to their presence. But this possibility by no means diminishes the
importance of psychiatric testimony about the prevalence of narcissism, especially when this testimony appears at the same time
that journalists begin to speculate about the new narcissism and
the unhealthy trend toward self-absorption. The narcissist comes
to the attention of psychiatrists for some of the same reasons that
he rises to positions of prominence not only in awareness movements and other cults but in business corporations, political organizations, and government bureaucracies. For all his inner suffering, the narcissist has many traits that make for success in

bureaucratic institutions, which put a premium on the manipulation of interpersonal relations, discourage the formation of deep personal attachments, and at the same time provide the narcissist with the approval he needs in order to validate his self-esteem. Although he may resort to therapies that promise to give meaning to life and to overcome his sense of emptiness, in his professional career the narcissist often enjoys considerable success. The management of personal impressions comes naturally to him, and his mastery of its intricacies serves him well in political and business organizations where performance now counts for less than "visibility," "momentum," and a winning record. As the "organization man" gives way to the bureaucratic "gamesman"—the "loyalty era" of American business to the age of the "executive success game"—the narcissist comes into his own.

In a study of 250 managers from twelve major companies, Michael Maccoby describes the new corporate leader, not altogether unsympathetically, as a person who works with people rather than with materials and who seeks not to build an empire or accumulate wealth but to experience "the exhilaration of running his team and of gaining victories." He wants to "be known as a winner, and his deepest fear is to be labeled a loser." Instead of pitting himself against a material task or a problem demanding solution, he pits himself against others, out of a "need to be in control." As a recent textbook for managers puts it, success today means "not simply getting ahead" but "getting ahead of others." The new executive, boyish, playful, and "seductive," wants in Maccoby's words "to maintain an illusion of limitless options." He has little capacity for "personal intimacy and social commitment." He feels little loyalty even to the company for which he works. One executive says he experiences power "as not being pushed around by the company." In his upward climb, this man cultivates powerful customers and attempts to use them against his own company. "You need a very big customer," according to his calculations, "who is always in trouble and demands changes from the company. That way you automatically have power in the company, and with the customer too. I like to keep my options open." A professor of management endorses this strategy.

"Overidentification" with the company, in his view, "produces a corporation with enormous power over the careers and destinies of its true believers." The bigger the company, the more important he thinks it is for executives "to manage their careers in terms of their own . . . free choices" and to "maintain the widest set of options possible."*

According to Maccoby, the gamesman "is open to new ideas, but he lacks convictions." He will do business with any régime, even if he disapproves of its principles. More independent and resourceful than the company man, he tries to use the company for his own ends, fearing that otherwise he will be "totally emasculated by the corporation." He avoids intimacy as a trap, preferring the "exciting, sexy atmosphere" with which the modern executive surrounds himself at work, "where adoring, mini-skirted secretaries constantly flirt with him." In all his personal relations, the gamesman depends on the admiration or fear he inspires in others to certify his credentials as a "winner." As he gets older, he finds it more and more difficult to command the kind of attention on which he thrives. He reaches a plateau beyond which he does not advance in his job, perhaps because the very highest positions, as Maccoby notes, still go to "those able to renounce adolescent rebelliousness and become at least to some extent believers in the organization." The job begins to lose its savor. Having little interest in craftsmanship, the new-style executive takes no pleasure in his achievements once he begins to lose the adolescent charm on which they rest. Middle age hits him with the force of a

---

* It is not only the gamesman who "fears feeling trapped." Seymour B. Sarason finds this feeling prevalent among professionals and students training for professional careers. He too suggests a connection between the fear of entrapment and the cultural value set on career mobility and its psychic equivalent, "personal growth." " 'Stay loose,' 'keep your options open,' 'play it cool'—these cautions emerge from the feeling that society sets all kinds of booby traps that rob you of the freedom without which growth is impossible."

This fear of entrapment or stagnation is closely connected in turn with the fear of aging and death. The mobility mania and the cult of "growth" can themselves be seen, in part, as an expression of the fear of aging that has become so intense in American society. Mobility and growth assure the individual that he has not yet settled into the living death of old age.

disaster: "Once his youth, vigor, and even the thrill in winning are lost, he becomes depressed and goalless, questioning the purpose of his life. No longer energized by the team struggle and unable to dedicate himself to something he believes in beyond himself, . . . he finds himself starkly alone." It is not surprising, given the prevalence of this career pattern, that popular psychology returns so often to the "midlife crisis" and to ways of combating it.

In Wilfrid Sheed's novel *Office Politics*, a wife asks, "There are real issues, aren't there, between Mr. Fine and Mr. Tyler?" Her husband answers that the issues are trivial; "the jockeying of ego is the real story." Eugene Emerson Jennings's study of management, which celebrates the demise of the organization man and the advent of the new "era of mobility," insists that corporate "mobility is more than mere job performance." What counts is "style . . . panache . . . the ability to say and do almost anything without antagonizing others." The upwardly mobile executive, according to Jennings, knows how to handle the people around him—the "shelf-sitter" who suffers from "arrested mobility" and envies success; the "fast learner"; the "mobile superior." The "mobility-bright executive" has learned to "read" the power relations in his office and "to see the less visible and less audible side of his superiors, chiefly their standing with their peers and superiors." He "can infer from a minimum of cues who are the centers of power, and he seeks to have high visibility and exposure with them. He will assiduously cultivate his standing and opportunities with them and seize every opportunity to learn from them. He will utilize his opportunities in the social world to size up the men who are centers of sponsorship in the corporate world."

Constantly comparing the "executive success game" to an athletic contest or a game of chess, Jennings treats the substance of executive life as if it were just as arbitrary and irrelevant to success as the task of kicking a ball through a net or of moving pieces over a chessboard. He never mentions the social and economic repercussions of managerial decisions or the power that managers exercise over society as a whole. For the corporate manager on the make, power consists not of money and influence but of "momentum," a "winning image," a reputation as a winner. Power lies in the eye of the beholder and thus has no objective reference at all.*

The manager's view of the world, as described by Jennings, Maccoby, and by the managers themselves, is that of the narcissist, who sees the world as a mirror of himself and has no interest in external events except as they throw back a reflection of his own image. The dense interpersonal environment of modern bureaucracy, in which work assumes an abstract quality almost wholly divorced from performance, by its very nature elicits and often rewards a narcissistic response. Bureaucracy, however, is only one of a number of social influences that are bringing a narcissistic type of personality organization into greater and greater prominence. Another such influence is the mechanical reproduction of culture, the proliferation of visual and audial images in the "society of the spectacle." We live in a swirl of images and echoes that arrest experience and play it back in slow motion. Cameras and recording machines not only transcribe experience but alter its quality, giving to much of modern life the character of an enormous echo chamber, a hall of mirrors. Life presents itself as a succession of images or electronic signals, of impressions recorded and reproduced by means of photography, motion pictures, television, and sophisticated recording devices. Modern life is so thoroughly mediated by electronic images that we cannot help responding to others as if their actions—and our own—were being recorded and simultaneously transmitted to an unseen audience or stored up for close scrutiny at some later time. "Smile, you're on candid camera!" The intrusion into everyday life of this all-seeing eye no longer takes us by surprise or catches us with our defenses down. We need no reminder to smile. A smile is permanently graven on our features, and we already know from which of several angles it photographs to best advantage.

---

* Indeed it has no reference to anything outside the self. The new ideal of success has no content. "Performance means to arrive," says Jennings. Success equals success. Note the convergence between success in business and celebrity in politics or the world of entertainment, which also depends on "visibility" and "charisma" and can only be defined as itself. The only important attribute of celebrity is that it is celebrated; no one can say why.

The proliferation of recorded images undermines our sense of reality. As Susan Sontag observes in her study of photography, "Reality has come to seem more and more like what we are shown by cameras." We distrust our perceptions until the camera verifies them. Photographic images provide us with the proof of our existence, without which we would find it difficult even to reconstruct a personal history. Bourgeois families in the eighteenth and nineteenth centuries, Sontag points out, posed for portraits in order to proclaim the family's status, whereas today the family album of photographs verifies the individual's existence: its documentary record of his development from infancy onward provides him with the only evidence of his life that he recognizes as altogether valid. Among the "many narcissistic uses" that Sontag attributes to the camera, "self-surveillance" ranks among the most important, not only because it provides the technical means of ceaseless self-scrutiny but because it renders the sense of selfhood dependent on the consumption of images of the self, at the same time calling into question the reality of the external world.

By preserving images of the self at various stages of development, the camera helps to weaken the older idea of development as moral education and to promote a more passive idea according to which development consists of passing through the stages of life at the right time and in the right order. Current fascination with the life cycle embodies an awareness that success in politics or business depends on reaching certain goals on schedule; but it also reflects the ease with which development can be electronically recorded. This brings us to another cultural change that elicits a widespread narcissistic response and, in this case, gives it a philosophical sanction: the emergence of a therapeutic ideology that upholds a normative schedule of psychosocial development and thus gives further encouragement to anxious self-scrutiny. The ideal of normative development creates the fear that any deviation from the norm has a pathological source. Doctors have made a cult of the periodic checkup—an investigation carried out once again by means of cameras and other recording instruments—and have implanted in their clients the notion that health depends on eternal watchfulness and the early detection of symptoms, as verified by medical technology. The client no longer feels physically or psychologically secure until his X-rays confirm a "clean bill of health."

Medicine and psychiatry—more generally, the therapeutic outlook and sensibility that pervade modern society—reinforce the pattern created by other cultural influences, in which the individual endlessly examines himself for signs of aging and ill health, for tell-tale symptoms of psychic stress, for blemishes and flaws that might diminish his attractiveness, or on the other hand for reassuring indications that his life is proceeding according to schedule. Modern medicine has conquered the plagues and epidemics that once made life so precarious, only to create new forms of insecurity. In the same way, bureaucracy has made life predictable and even boring while reviving, in a new form, the war of all against all. Our overorganized society, in which large-scale organizations predominate but have lost the capacity to command allegiance, in some respects more nearly approximates a condition of universal animosity than did the primitive capitalism on which Hobbes modeled his state of nature. Social conditions today encourage a survival mentality, expressed in its crudest form in disaster movies or in fantasies of space travel, which allow vicarious escape from a doomed planet. People no longer dream of overcoming difficulties but merely of surviving them. In business, according to Jennings, "The struggle is to survive emotionally"—to "preserve or enhance one's identity or ego." The normative concept of developmental stages promotes a view of life as an obstacle course: the aim is simply to get through the course with a minimum of trouble and pain. The ability to manipulate what Gail Sheehy refers to, using a medical metaphor, as "life-support systems" now appears to represent the highest form of wisdom: the knowledge that gets us through, as she puts it, without panic. Those who master Sheehy's "no-panic approach to aging" and to the traumas of the life cycle will be able to say, in the words of one of her subjects, "I know I can survive . . . I don't panic any more." This is hardly an exalted form of satisfaction, however. "The current ideology," Sheehy writes, "seems a mix of personal survivalism, revivalism, and cynicism"; yet her enormously popular guide to the "predictable crises of adult life," with its superficially optimistic hymn to growth, development, and "self-actualization," does not challenge this ideology, merely restates it in more "humanistic" form. "Growth" has become a euphemism for survival.

The World View of the Resigned   New social forms require new forms of personality, new modes of socialization, new ways of organizing experience. The concept of narcissism provides us not with a ready-made psychological determinism but with a way of understanding the psychological impact of recent social changes—assuming that we bear in mind not only its clinical origins but the continuum between pathology and normality. It provides us, in other words, with a tolerably accurate portrait of the "liberated" personality of our time, with his charm, his pseudo-awareness of his own condition, his promiscuous pansexuality, his fascination with oral sex, his fear of the castrating mother (Mrs. Portnoy), his hypochondria, his protective shallowness, his avoidance of dependence, his inability to mourn, his dread of old age and death.

Narcissism appears realistically to represent the best way of coping with the tensions and anxieties of modern life, and the prevailing social conditions therefore tend to bring out narcissistic traits that are present, in varying degrees, in everyone. These conditions have also transformed the family, which in turn shapes the underlying structure of personality. A society that fears it has no future is not likely to give much attention to the needs of the next generation, and the ever-present sense of historical discontinuity—the blight of our society—falls with particularly devastating effect on the family. The modern parent's attempt to make children feel loved and wanted does not conceal an underlying coolness—the remoteness of those who have little to pass on to the next generation and who in any case give priority to their own right to self-fulfillment. The combination of emotional detachment with attempts to convince a child of his favored position in the family is a good prescription for a narcissistic personality structure.

Through the intermediary of the family, social patterns reproduce themselves in personality. Social arrangements live on in the individual, buried in the mind below the level of consciousness, even after they have become objectively undesirable and unnecessary—as many of our present arrangements are now widely acknowledged to have become. The perception of the world as a dangerous and forbidding place, though it originates in a realistic awareness of the insecurity of contemporary social life, receives reinforcement from the narcissistic projection of aggressive impulses outward. The belief that society has no future, while it rests on a certain realism about the dangers ahead, also incorporates a narcissistic inability to identify with posterity or to feel oneself part of a historical stream.

The weakening of social ties, which originates in the prevailing state of social warfare, at the same time reflects a narcissistic defense against dependence. A warlike society tends to produce men and women who are at heart antisocial. It should therefore not surprise us to find that although the narcissist conforms to social norms for fear of external retribution, he often thinks of himself as an outlaw and sees others in the same way, "as basically dishonest and unreliable, or only reliable because of external pressures." "The value systems of narcissistic personalities are generally corruptible," writes Kernberg, "in contrast to the rigid morality of the obsessive personality."

The ethic of self-preservation and psychic survival is rooted, then, not merely in objective conditions of economic warfare, rising rates of crime, and social chaos but in the subjective experience of emptiness and isolation. It reflects the conviction—as much a projection of inner anxieties as a perception of the way things are—that envy and exploitation dominate even the most intimate relations. The cult of personal relations, which becomes increasingly intense as the hope of political solutions recedes, conceals a thoroughgoing disenchantment with personal relations, just as the cult of sensuality implies a repudiation of sensuality in all but its most primitive forms. The ideology of personal growth, superficially optimistic, radiates a profound despair and resignation. It is the faith of those without faith.

III

Changing Modes of Making It:
From Horatio Alger to the Happy Hooker

American society is marked by a central stress upon personal achievement, especially secular occupational achievement. The "success story" and the respect accorded to the self-made man are distinctly American if anything is. . . . [American society] has endorsed Horatio Alger and has glorified the rail splitter who became president.

ROBIN WILLIAMS

The man of ambition is still with us, as in all times, but now he needs a more subtle initiative, a deeper capacity to manipulate the democracy of emotions, if he is to maintain his separate identity and significantly augment it with success. . . . The sexual problems of the neurotic competing for some ephemeral kudos in mid-century Manhattan are very different from the problems of the neurotic in turn-of-the-century Vienna. History changes the expression of neurosis even if it does not change the underlying mechanisms.

PHILIP RIEFF

The Original Meaning of the Work Ethic   Until recently, the Protestant work ethic stood as one of the most important underpinnings of American culture. According to the myth of capitalist enterprise, thrift and industry held the key to material success and spiritual fulfillment. America's reputation as a land of opportunity rested on its claim that the destruction of hereditary obstacles to advancement had created conditions in which social mobility depended on individual initiative alone. The self-made

52

man, archetypical embodiment of the American dream, owed his advancement to habits of industry, sobriety, moderation, self-discipline, and avoidance of debt. He lived for the future, shunning self-indulgence in favor of patient, painstaking accumulation; and as long as the collective prospect looked on the whole so bright, he found in the deferral of gratification not only his principal gratification but an abundant source of profits. In an expanding economy, the value of investments could be expected to multiply with time, as the spokesman for self-help, for all their celebration of work as its own reward, seldom neglected to point out.

In an age of diminishing expectations, the Protestant virtues no longer excite enthusiasm. Inflation erodes investments and savings. Advertising undermines the horror of indebtedness, exhorting the consumer to buy now and pay later. As the future becomes menacing and uncertain, only fools put off until tomorrow the fun they can have today. A profound shift in our sense of time has transformed work habits, values, and the definition of success. Self-preservation has replaced self-improvement as the goal of earthly existence. In a lawless, violent, and unpredictable society, in which the normal conditions of everyday life come to resemble those formerly confined to the underworld, men live by their wits. They hope not so much to prosper as simply to survive, although survival itself increasingly demands a large income. In earlier times, the self-made man took pride in his judgment of character and probity; today he anxiously scans the faces of his fellows not so as to evaluate their credit but in order to gauge their susceptibility to his own blandishments. He practices the classic arts of seduction and with the same indifference to moral niceties, hoping to win your heart while picking your pocket. The happy hooker stands in place of Horatio Alger as the prototype of personal success. If Robinson Crusoe embodied the ideal type of economic man, the hero of bourgeois society in its ascendancy, the spirit of Moll Flanders presides over its dotage.

The new ethic of self-preservation has been a long time taking shape; it did not emerge overnight. In the first three centuries of our history, the work ethic constantly changed its meaning; these vicissitudes, often imperceptible at the time, foreshadowed its eventual transformation into an ethic of personal survival. For the Puritans, a godly man worked diligently at his calling not so much in order to accumulate personal wealth as to add to the comfort and convenience of the community. Every Christian had a "general calling" to serve God and a "personal calling," in the words of Cotton Mather, "by which his Usefulness, in his Neighborhood, is distinguished." This personal calling arose from the circumstance that "God hath made man a Sociable Creature." The Puritans recognized that a man might get rich at his calling, but they saw personal aggrandizement as incidental to social labor—the collective transformation of nature and the progress of useful arts and useful knowledge. They instructed men who prospered not to lord it over their neighbors. The true Christian, according to Calvinist conceptions of an honorable and godly existence, bore both good fortune and bad with equanimity, contenting himself with what came to his lot. "This he had learned to doe," said John Cotton, "if God prosper him, he had learned not to be puffed up, and if he should be exposed to want, he could do it without murmuring. It is the same act of unbeleefe, that makes a man murmure in crosses, which puffes him up in prosperity."

Whatever the moral reservations with which Calvinism surrounded the pursuit of wealth, many of its practitioners, especially in New England, waxed fat and prosperous on the trade in rum and slaves. As the Puritan gave way to the Yankee, a secularized version of the Protestant ethic emerged. Whereas Cotton Mather advised against going into debt on the grounds that it injured the creditor ("Let it be uneasy unto you, at any time to think, *I have so much of another mans Estate in my Hands, and I to his damage detain it from him*"), Benjamin Franklin argued that indebtedness injured the debtor himself, putting him into his creditors' hands. Puritan sermons on the calling quoted copiously from the Bible; Franklin codified popular common sense in the sayings of Poor Richard. *God helps them that help themselves. Lost time is never found again. Never leave that till to-morrow which you can do today. If you would know the value of money, go and try to borrow some; for he that goes a borrowing goes a sorrowing.*

The Puritans urged the importance of socially useful work;

the Yankee stressed self-improvement. Yet he understood self-improvement to consist of more than money-making. This important concept also implied self-discipline, the training and cultivation of God-given talents, above all the cultivation of reason. The eighteenth-century ideal of prosperity included not only material comfort but good health, good temper, wisdom, usefulness, and the satisfaction of knowing that you had earned the good opinion of others. In the section of his *Autobiography* devoted to "The Art of Virtue," Franklin summed up the results of a lifelong program of moral self-improvement:

To Temperance he ascribes his long-continu'd Health, and what is still left to him of a good Constitution. To Industry and Frugality, the early Easiness of his Circumstances, and Acquisition of his Fortune, with all that Knowledge which enabled him to be an useful Citizen, and obtain'd for him some Degree of Reputation among the Learned. To Sincerity and Justice the Confidence of his Country, and the honourable Employs it conferr'd upon him. And to the joint influence of the whole Mass of the Virtues, evenness of Temper, and that Cheerfulness in Conversation which makes his Company still sought for, and agreeable even to his younger Acquaintance.

Virtue pays, in the eighteenth-century version of the work ethic; but what it pays cannot be measured simply in money. The real reward of virtue is to have little to apologize for or to repent of at the end of your life. Wealth is to be valued, but chiefly because it serves as one of the necessary preconditions of moral and intellectual cultivation.*

* Efforts to reduce Franklin's "art of virtue" to a purely prudential ethic of money-getting and self-advancement miss its finer shadings. "All Franklin's moral attitudes," wrote Max Weber in *The Protestant Ethic and the Spirit of Capitalism,* "are coloured with utilitarianism. . . . Virtues . . . are only in so far virtues as they are actually useful to the individual. . . . Man is dominated by the making of money, by acquisition as the ultimate purpose of his life." D. H. Lawrence expressed a somewhat similar opinion in *Studies in Classic American Literature.* These interpretations ignore the connections, so important in the bourgeois outlook of the eighteenth century, between money-making, sociability, and the progress of the useful arts; between the spirit of capitalism and the spirit of invention and workmanship. Self-improvement is not the same thing as self-advancement, in Franklin's eyes; indeed, ambition, in the eighteenth century, was a Hamiltonian much more than a Franklinian or Jeffersonian virtue.

From "Self-Culture" to Self-Promotion through "Winning Images" In the nineteenth century, the ideal of self-improvement degenerated into a cult of compulsive industry. P. T. Barnum, who made a fortune in a calling the very nature of which the Puritans would have condemned ("Every calling, whereby God will be Dishonored; every Calling whereby none but the Lusts of men are Nourished: . . . every such Calling is to be Rejected"), delivered many times a lecture frankly entitled "The Art of Money-Getting," which epitomized the nineteenth-century conception of worldly success. Barnum quoted freely from Franklin but without Franklin's concern for the attainment of wisdom or the promotion of useful knowledge. "Information" interested Barnum merely as a means of mastering the market. Thus he condemned the "false economy" of the farm wife who douses her candle at dusk rather than lighting another for reading, not realizing that the "information" gained through reading is worth far more than the price of the candles. "Always take a trustworthy newspaper," Barnum advised young men on the make, "and thus keep thoroughly posted in regard to the transactions of the world. He who is without a newspaper is cut off from his species."

Barnum valued the good opinion of others not as a sign of one's usefulness but as a means of getting credit. "Uncompromising integrity of character is invaluable." The nineteenth century attempted to express all values in monetary terms. Everything had its price. Charity was a moral duty because "the liberal man will command patronage, while the sordid, uncharitable miser will be avoided." The sin of pride was not that it offended God but that it led to extravagant expenditures. "A spirit of pride and vanity, when permitted to have full sway, is the undying cankerworm which gnaws the very vitals of a man's worldly possessions."

The eighteenth century made a virtue of temperance but did not condemn moderate indulgence in the service of sociability. "Rational conversation," on the contrary, appeared to Franklin and his contemporaries to represent an important value in its own right. The nineteenth century condemned sociability itself, on the grounds that it might interfere with business. "How many good opportunities have passed, never to return, while a man was sipping a 'social glass' with his friend!" Preachments on self-help now breathed the spirit of compulsive enterprise. Henry Ward Beecher defined "the *beau ideal* of happiness" as a state of mind in which "a man [is] so busy that he does not know whether he is or is not happy." Russell Sage remarked that "work has been the chief, and, you might say, the only source of pleasure in my life."

Even at the height of the Gilded Age, however, the Protestant ethic did not completely lose its original meaning. In the success manuals, the McGuffey readers, the Peter Parley Books, and the hortatory writings of the great capitalists themselves, the Protestant virtues—industry, thrift, temperance—still appeared not merely as stepping-stones to success but as their own reward.

The spirit of self-improvement lived on, in debased form, in the cult of "self-culture"—proper care and training of mind and body, nurture of the mind through "great books," development of "character." The social contribution of individual accumulation still survived as an undercurrent in the celebration of success, and the social conditions of early industrial capitalism, in which the pursuit of wealth undeniably increased the supply of useful objects, gave some substance to the claim that "accumulated capital means progress." In condemning speculation and extravagance, in upholding the importance of patient industry, in urging young men to start at the bottom and submit to "the discipline of daily life," even the most unabashed exponents of self-enrichment clung to the notion that wealth derives its value from its contribution to the general good and to the happiness of future generations.

The nineteenth-century cult of success placed surprisingly little emphasis on competition. It measured achievement not against the achievements of others but against an abstract ideal of discipline and self-denial. At the turn of the century, however, preachments on success began to stress the will to win. The bureaucratization of the corporate career changed the conditions of self-advancement; ambitious young men now had to compete with their peers for the attention and approval of their superiors The struggle to surpass the previous generation and to provide for the next gave way to a form of sibling rivalry, in which men of approximately equal abilities jostled against each other in competition for a limited number of places. Advancement now depended on "will-power, self-confidence, energy, and initiative"—the qualities celebrated in such exemplary writings as George Lorimer's *Letters from a Self-Made Merchant to His Son.* "By the end of the nineteenth century," writes John Cawelti in his study of the success myth, "self-help books were dominated by the ethos of salesmanship and boosterism. Personal magnetism, a quality which supposedly enabled a man to influence and dominate others, became one of the major keys to success." In 1907, both Lorimer's *Saturday Evening Post* and Orison Swett Marden's *Success* magazine inaugurated departments of instruction in the "art of conversation," fashion, and "culture." The management of interpersonal relations came to be seen as the essence of self-advancement. The captain of industry gave way to the confidence man, the master of impressions. Young men were told that they had to sell themselves in order to succeed.

At first, self-testing through competition remained almost indistinguishable from moral self-discipline and self-culture, but the difference became unmistakable when Dale Carnegie and then Norman Vincent Peale restated and transformed the tradition of Mather, Franklin, Barnum, and Lorimer. As a formula for success, winning friends and influencing people had little in common with industry and thrift. The prophets of positive thinking disparaged "the old adage that hard work alone is the magic key that will unlock the door to our desires." They praised the love of money, officially condemned even by the crudest of Gilded Age materialists, as a useful incentive. "You can never have riches in great quantities," wrote Napoleon Hill in his *Think and Grow Rich,* "unless you can work yourself into a white heat of *desire* for money." The pursuit of wealth lost the few shreds of moral meaning that still clung to it. Formerly the Protestant virtues appeared to have an independent value of their own. Even when they became purely instrumental, in the second half of the nineteenth century, success itself retained moral and social overtones, by virtue of its contribution to the sum of human comfort and progress. Now success appeared as an end in its own right, the victory over your competitors that alone retained the capacity to instill a sense of self-approval. The latest success manuals differ from earlier ones—even surpassing the cynicism of Dale Carnegie and Peale—in their frank acceptance of the need to exploit and intimidate others, in their lack of interest in the substance of success, and in the candor with which they insist that appearances—"winning images"—count for more than performance, ascription for more than achievement. One author seems to imply that the self consists of little more than its "image" reflected in others' eyes. "Although I'm not being original when I say it, I'm sure you'll agree that the way you see yourself will reflect the image you portray to others." Nothing succeeds like the appearance of success.

The Eclipse of Achievement   In a society in which the dream of success has been drained of any meaning beyond itself, men have nothing against which to measure their achievements except the achievements of others. Self-approval depends on public recognition and acclaim, and the quality of this approval has undergone important changes in its own right. The good opinion of friends and neighbors, which formerly informed a man that he had lived a useful life, rested on appreciation of his accomplishments. Today men seek the kind of approval that applauds not their actions but their personal attributes. They wish to be not so much esteemed as admired. They crave not fame but the glamour and excitement of celebrity. They want to be envied rather than respected. Pride and acquisitiveness, the sins of an ascendant capitalism, have given way to vanity. Most Americans would still define success as riches, fame, and power, but their actions show that they have little interest in the substance of these attainments. What a man does matters less than the fact that he has "made it." Whereas fame depends on the performance of notable deeds acclaimed in biography and works of history, celebrity—the reward of those who project a vivid or pleasing exterior or have otherwise attracted attention to themselves—is acclaimed in the news media, in gossip columns, on talk shows, in magazines devoted to "personalities." Accordingly it is evanescent, like news itself, which loses its interest when it loses its novelty. Worldly success has always carried with it a certain poignancy, an awareness that "you can't take it with you"; but in our time, when success is so largely a function of youth, glamour, and novelty, glory is more fleeting than ever, and those who win the attention of the public worry incessantly about losing it.

Success in our society has to be ratified by publicity. The tycoon who lives in personal obscurity, the empire builder who controls the destinies of nations from behind the scenes, are vanishing types. Even nonelective officials, ostensibly preoccupied with questions of high policy, have to keep themselves constantly on view; all politics becomes a form of spectacle. It is well known that Madison Avenue packages politicians and markets them as if they were cereals or deodorants; but the art of public relations penetrates even more deeply into political life, transforming policy making itself. The modern prince does not much care that "there's a job to be done"—the slogan of American capitalism at an earlier and more enterprising stage of its development; what interests him is that "relevant audiences," in the language of the Pentagon Papers, have to be cajoled, won over, seduced. He confuses successful completion of the task at hand with the impression he makes or hopes to make on others. Thus American officials blundered into the war in Vietnam because they could not distinguish the country's military and strategic interests from "our reputation as a guarantor," as one of them put it. More concerned with the trappings than with the reality of power, they convinced themselves that failure to intervene would damage American "credibility." They borrowed the rhetoric of games theory to dignify their obsession with appearances, arguing that American policy in Vietnam had to address itself to "the relevant 'audiences' of U.S. actions"—the communists, the South Vietnamese, "our allies (who must trust us as 'underwriters')," and the American public.

When policy making, the search for power, and the pursuit of wealth have no other objects than to excite admiration or envy, men lose the sense of objectivity, always precarious under the best of circumstances. Impressions overshadow achievements.

Public men fret about their ability to rise to crisis, to project an image of decisiveness, to give a convincing performance of executive power. Their critics resort to the same standards: when doubts began to be raised about the leadership of the Johnson administration, they focused on the "credibility gap." Public relations and propaganda have exalted the image and the pseudoevent. People "talk constantly," Daniel Boorstin has written, "not of things themselves, but of their images."

In the corporate structure as in government, the rhetoric of achievement, of single-minded devotion to the task at hand—the rhetoric of performance, efficiency, and productivity—no longer provides an accurate description of the struggle for personal survival. "Hard work," according to Eugene Emerson Jennings, ". . . constitutes a necessary but not sufficient cause of upward mobility. It is not a route to the top." A newspaper man with experience both in journalism and in the Southern Regional Council has reported that "in neither, I realized, did it matter to the people in charge how well or how badly I performed. . . . Not the goals, but keeping the organization going, became the important thing." Even the welfare of the organization, however, no longer excites the enthusiasm it generated in the fifties. The "self-sacrificing company man," writes Jennings, has become "an obvious anachronism."* The upwardly mobile corporate executive "does not view himself as an organization man." His "anti-organizational posture," in fact, has emerged as his "chief characteristic." He advances through the corporate ranks not by serving the organization but by convincing his associates that he possesses the attributes of a "winner."

As the object of the corporate career shifts "from task-orientation and task-mastery to the control of the other player's moves,"

---

* In the 1950s, the organization man thought of an attractive, socially gifted wife as an important asset to his career. Today executives are warned of the "apparent serious conflict between marriage and a management career." A recent report compares the "elite corps of professional managers" to the Janissaries, elite soldiers of the Ottoman empire who were taken from their parents as children, raised by the state, and never allowed to marry. "A young man considering [a managerial] career might well think of himself as a modern-day Janissary—and consider very, very carefully whether marriage in any way conforms to his chosen life."

in the words of Thomas Szasz, success depends on "information about the personality of the other players." The better the corporate executive or bureaucrat understands the personal characteristics of his subordinates, the better he can exploit their mistakes in order to control them and to reassert his own supremacy. If he knows that his subordinates lie to him, the lie communicates the important information that they fear and wish to please him. "By accepting the bribe, as it were, of flattery, cajolery, or sheer subservience implicit in being lied to, the recipient of the lie states, in effect, that he is willing to barter these items for the truth." On the other hand, acceptance of the lie reassures the liar that he will not be punished, while reminding him of his dependence and subordination. "In this way, both parties gain a measure . . . of security." In Joseph Heller's novel *Something Happened*, the protagonist's boss makes it clear that he wants from his subordinates not "good work" but "spastic colitis and nervous exhaustion."

God dammit, I want the people working for me to be worse off than I am, not better. That's the reason I pay you so well. I want to see you right on the verge. I want it right out in the open. I want to be able to hear it in a stuttering, flustered, tongue-tied voice. . . . Don't trust me. I don't trust flattery, loyalty, and sociability. I don't trust deference, respect, and cooperation. I trust fear.

According to Jennings, the "loyalty ethic" has declined in American business among other reasons because loyalty can "be too easily simulated or feigned by those most desirous of winning."

The argument that bureaucratic organizations devote more energy to the maintenance of hierarchical relations than to industrial efficiency gains strength from the consideration that modern capitalist production arose in the first place not because it was necessarily more efficient than other methods of organizing work but because it provided capitalists with greater profits and power. The case for the factory system, according to Stephen Marglin, rested not on its technological superiority over handicraft production but on the more effective control of the labor force it allowed the employer. In the words of Andrew Ure, the philosopher of manufactures, introduction of the factory system enabled the capitalist to "subdue the refractory tempers of work people." As the hierarchical organization of work invades the managerial function itself, the office takes on the characteristics of the factory, and the enforcement of clearly demarcated lines of dominance and subordination within management takes on as much importance as the subordination of labor to management as a whole. In the "era of corporate mobility," however, the lines of superiority and subordination constantly fluctuate, and the successful bureaucrat survives not by appealing to the authority of his office but by establishing a pattern of upward movement, cultivating upwardly mobile superiors, and administering "homeopathic doses of humiliation" to those he leaves behind in his ascent to the top.

The Art of Social Survival   The transformation of the myth of success—of the definition of success and of the qualities believed to promote it—is a long-term development arising not from particular historical events but from general changes in the structure of society: the shifting emphasis from capitalist production to consumption; the growth of large organizations and bureaucracies; the increasingly dangerous and warlike conditions of social life. More than twenty-five years have passed since David Riesman argued that the transition from the "invisible hand" to the "glad hand" marked a fundamental change in the organization of personality, from the inner-directed type dominant in the nineteenth century to the other-directed type of today. Other scholars at that time, when interest in culture and personality studies was stronger than it is now, proposed similar descriptions of the changing character structure of advanced capitalist society. William H. Whyte's "organization man;" Erich Fromm's "market-oriented personality," Karen Horney's "neurotic personality of our time," and the studies of American national character by Margaret Mead and Geoffrey Gorer all captured essential aspects of the new man: his eagerness to get along well with others; his need to organize even his private life in accordance with the requirements of large organizations; his attempt to sell himself as if his own personality were a commodity with an assignable market value; his neurotic need for affection, reassurance, and oral gratification; the corruptibility of his values. In one respect, however, these studies of American culture and personality created a misleading impression of the changes that were taking place beneath what Riesman called the "bland surface of American sociability." The critics of the forties and fifties mistook this surface for the deeper reality.

According to Erich Fromm, Americans had lost the capacity for spontaneous feeling, even for anger. One of "the essential aims of the educational process" was to eliminate antagonism, to cultivate a "commercialized friendliness." "If you do not smile you are judged lacking in a 'pleasing personality'—and you need a pleasing personality if you want to sell your services, whether as a waitress, a salesman, or a physician." Like many social scientists, Fromm exaggerated the degree to which aggressive impulses can be socialized; he saw man as entirely a product of socialization, not as a creature of instinct whose partially repressed or sublimated drives always threaten to break out in all their original ferocity. The American cult of friendliness conceals but does not eradicate a murderous competition for goods and position; indeed this competition has grown more savage in an age of diminishing expectations.

In the fifties, affluence, leisure, and the "quality of life" loomed as major issues. The welfare state had allegedly eradicated poverty, gross economic inequalities, and the conflicts to which they formerly gave rise. The seeming triumphs of American capitalism left social critics little to worry about except the decline of individualism and the menace of conformity. Arthur Miller's Willy Loman, the salesman who wants no more out of life than to be "well liked," symbolized the issues that troubled the postwar period. In the seventies, a harsher time, it appears that the prostitute, not the salesman, best exemplifies the qualities indispensable to success in American society. She too sells herself for a living, but her seductiveness hardly signifies a wish to be well liked. She craves admiration but scorns those who provide it and thus derives little gratification from her social successes. She attempts to move others while remaining unmoved herself. The fact that she lives in a milieu of interpersonal rela tions does not make her a conformist or an "other-directed" type. She remains a loner, dependent on others only as a hawk depends on chickens. She exploits the ethic of pleasure that has replaced the ethic of achievement, but her career more than any other reminds us that contemporary hedonism, of which she is the supreme symbol, originates not in the pursuit of pleasure but in a war of all against all, in which even the most intimate encounters become a form of mutual exploitation.

It is not merely that pleasure, once it is defined as an end in itself, takes on the qualities of work, as Martha Wolfenstein observed in her essay on "fun morality"—that play is now "measured by standards of achievement previously applicable only to work." The measurement of sexual "performance," the insistence that sexual satisfaction depends on proper "technique," and the widespread belief that it can be "achieved" only after coordinated effort, practice, and study all testify to the invasion of play by the rhetoric of achievement. But those who deplore the transformation of play into performance confine their attention to the surface of play, in this case to the surface of sexual encounters. Beneath the concern for performance lies a deeper determination to manipulate the feelings of others to your own advantage. The search for competitive advantage through emotional manipulation increasingly shapes not only personal relations but relations at work as well; it is for this reason that sociability can now function as an extension of work by other means. Personal life, no longer a refuge from deprivations suffered at work, has become as anarchical, as warlike, and as full of stress as the marketplace itself. The cocktail party reduces sociability to social combat. Experts write tactical manuals in the art of social survival, advising the status-seeking partygoer to take up a commanding position in the room, surround himself with a loyal band of retainers, and avoid turning his back on the field of battle.

The recent vogue of "assertiveness therapy," a counterprogram designed to equip the patient with defenses against manipulation, appeals to the growing recognition that agility in interpersonal relations determines what looks on the surface like achievement. Assertiveness training seeks to rid the patient of "feelings of anxiety, ignorance, and guilt that . . . are used efficiently by other people to get us to do what they want." Other forms of game therapy alert patients to the "games people play" and thus attempt to promote "game-free intimacy." The importance of such programs, however, lies not so much in their objectives as in the anxiety to which they appeal and the vision of reality that informs them—the perception that success depends on psychological manipulation and that all of life, even the ostensibly achievement-oriented realm of work, centers on the struggle for interpersonal advantage, the deadly game of intimidating friends and seducing people.

The Apotheosis of Individualism   The fear that haunted the social critics and theorists of the fifties—that rugged individualism had succumbed to conformity and "low-pressure sociability"—appears in retrospect to have been premature. In 1960, David Riesman complained that young people no longer had much social "presence," their education having provided them not with "a polished personality but [with] an affable, casual, adaptable one, suitable to the loose-jointed articulation and heavy job turnover in the expanding organizations of an affluent society." It is true that "a present-oriented hedonism," as Riesman went on to argue, has replaced the work ethic "among the very classes which in the earlier stages of industrialization were oriented toward the future, toward distant goals and delayed gratification." But this hedonism is a fraud; the pursuit of pleasure disguises a struggle for power. Americans have not really become more sociable and cooperative, as the theorists of other-direction and conformity would like us to believe; they have merely become more adept at exploiting the conventions of interpersonal relations for their own benefit. Activities ostensibly undertaken purely for enjoyment often have the real object of doing others in. It is symptomatic of the underlying tenor of American life that vulgar terms for sexual intercourse also convey the sense of getting the better of someone, working him over, taking him in, imposing your will through guile, deception, or superior force. Verbs associated with sexual pleasure have acquired more than the usual overtones of violence and psychic exploitation. In the violent world of the ghetto, the language of which now pervades American society as a whole, the violence associated with sexual intercourse is directed with special intensity by men against women, specifically against their mothers. The language of ritualized aggression and abuse reminds those who use it that exploitation is the general rule and some form of dependence the common fate; that "the individual," in Lee Rainwater's words, "is not strong enough or adult enough to achieve his goal in a legitimate way, but is rather like a child, dependent on others who tolerate his childish maneuvers"; accordingly males, even adult males, often depend on women for support and nurture. Many of them have to pimp for a living, ingratiating themselves with a woman in order to pry money from her; sexual relations thus become manipulative and predatory. Satisfaction depends on taking what you want instead of waiting for what is rightfully yours to receive. All this enters everyday speech in language that connects sex with aggression and sexual aggression with highly ambivalent feelings about mothers.*

In some ways middle-class society has become a pale copy of the black ghetto, as the appropriation of its language would lead us to believe. We do not need to minimize the poverty of the ghetto or the suffering inflicted by whites on blacks in order to see that the increasingly dangerous and unpredictable conditions of middle-class life have given rise to similar strategies for survival. Indeed the attraction of black culture for disaffected whites sug-

---

* In the late sixties, white radicals enthusiastically adopted the slogan, "Up against the Wall, Motherfucker!" But the term has long since lost its revolutionary associations, like other black idioms first popularized among whites by political radicals and spokesmen for the counterculture, and in slightly expurgated form has become so acceptable that the term "mother" has everywhere become, even among teeny-boppers, a term of easygoing familiarity or contempt. Similarly the Rolling Stones and other exponents of hard or acid rock, who used the obscenity of the ghetto to convey a posture of militant alienation, have given way to groups that sing more sweetly, but still in ghetto accents, of a world where you get only what you're prepared to take. The pretense of revolutionary solidarity having evaporated, as the zonked-out lovefest of the "Woodstock Nation" deteriorated into the murderous chaos of Altamont, the underlying cynicism surfaces more clearly than ever. Every mother for himself!

gests that black culture now speaks to a general condition, the most important feature of which is a widespread loss of confidence in the future. The poor have always had to live for the present, but now a desperate concern for personal survival, sometimes disguised as hedonism, engulfs the middle class as well. Today almost everyone lives in a dangerous world from which there is little escape. International terrorism and blackmail, bombings, and hijackings arbitrarily affect the rich and poor alike. Crime, violence, and gang wars make cities unsafe and threaten to spread to the suburbs. Racial violence on the streets and in the schools creates an atmosphere of chronic tension and threatens to erupt at any time into full-scale racial conflict. Unemployment spreads from the poor to the white-collar class, while inflation eats away the savings of those who hoped to retire in comfort. Much of what is euphemistically known as the middle class, merely because it dresses up to go to work, is now reduced to proletarian conditions of existence. Many white-collar jobs require no more skill and pay even less than blue-collar jobs, conferring little status or security. The propaganda of death and destruction, emanating ceaselessly from the mass media, adds to the prevailing atmosphere of insecurity. Far-flung famines, earthquakes in remote regions, distant wars and uprisings attract the same attention as events closer to home. The impression of arbitrariness in the reporting of disaster reinforces the arbitrary quality of experience itself, and the absence of continuity in the coverage of events, as today's crisis yields to a new and unrelated crisis tomorrow, adds to the sense of historical discontinuity—the sense of living in a world in which the past holds out no guidance to the present and the future has become completely unpredictable.

Older conceptions of success presupposed a world in rapid motion, in which fortunes were rapidly won and lost and new opportunities unfolded every day. Yet they also presupposed a certain stability, a future that bore some recognizable resemblance to the present and the past. The growth of bureaucracy, the cult of consumption with its immediate gratifications, but above all the severance of the sense of historical continuity have transformed the Protestant ethic while carrying the underlying principles of capitalist society to their logical conclusion. The pursuit of self-interest, formerly identified with the rational pursuit of gain and the accumulation of wealth, has become a search for pleasure and psychic survival. Social conditions now approximate the vision of republican society conceived by the Marquis de Sade at the very outset of the republican epoch. In many ways the most farsighted and certainly the most disturbing of the prophets of revolutionary individualism, Sade defended unlimited self-indulgence as the logical culmination of the revolution in property relations—the only way to attain revolutionary brotherhood in its purest form. By regressing in his writings to the most primitive level of fantasy, Sade uncannily glimpsed the whole subsequent development of personal life under capitalism, ending not in revolutionary brotherhood but in a society of siblings that has outlived and repudiated its revolutionary origins.

Sade imagined a sexual utopia in which everyone has the right to everyone else, where human beings, reduced to their sexual organs, become absolutely anonymous and interchangeable. His ideal society thus reaffirmed the capitalist principle that human beings are ultimately reducible to interchangeable objects. It also incorporated and carried to a surprising new conclusion Hobbes's discovery that the destruction of paternalism and the subordination of all social relations to the market had stripped away the remaining restraints and the mitigating illusions from the war of all against all. In the resulting state of organized anarchy, as Sade was the first to realize, pleasure becomes life's only business—pleasure, however, that is indistinguishable from rape, murder, unbridled aggression. In a society that has reduced reason to mere calculation, reason can impose no limits on the pursuit of pleasure—on the immediate gratification of every desire no matter how perverse, insane, criminal, or merely immoral. For the standards that would condemn crime or cruelty derive from religion, compassion, or the kind of reason that rejects purely instrumental applications; and none of these outmoded forms of thought or feeling has any logical place in a society based on commodity production. In his misogyny, Sade perceived that bourgeois en-

lightenment, carried to its logical conclusions, condemned even
the sentimental cult of womanhood and the family, which the
bourgeoisie itself had carried to unprecedented extremes.

At the same time, he saw that condemnation of "woman-
worship" had to go hand in hand with a defense of woman's sexual rights—their right to dispose of their own bodies, as feminists
would put it today. If the exercise of that right in Sade's utopia
boils down to the duty to become an instrument of someone else's
pleasure, it was not so much because Sade hated women as because he hated humanity. He perceived, more clearly than the
feminists, that all freedoms under capitalism come in the end to
the same thing, the same universal obligation to enjoy and be enjoyed. In the same breath, and without violating his own logic,
Sade demanded for women the right "fully to satisfy all their
desires" and "all parts of their bodies" and categorically stated
that "all women must submit to our pleasure." Pure individualism thus issued in the most radical repudiation of individuality. "All men, all women resemble each other," according to
Sade; and to those of his countrymen who would become republicans he adds the ominous warning: "Do not think you can make
good republicans so long as you isolate in their families the children who should belong to the republic alone." The bourgeois
defense of privacy culminates—not just in Sade's thought but in
the history to come, so accurately foreshadowed in the very excess, madness, infantilism of his ideas—in the most thoroughgoing attack on privacy; the glorification of the individual, in his
annihilation.

IV

The Banality of Pseudo-Self-Awareness:
Theatrics of Politics and Everyday Existence

The death of conscience is not the death of self-consciousness.

HARRY CROSBY

The Propaganda of Commodities   In the early days of industrial capitalism, employers saw the workingman as no more than a beast of burden—"a man of the type of the ox," in the words of the efficiency expert Frederick W. Taylor. Capitalists considered the worker purely as a producer; they cared nothing for the worker's activities in his leisure time—the little leisure that was left to him after twelve or fourteen hours in the factory. Employers attempted to supervise the worker's life on the job, but their control ended when the worker left the factory at closing time. Even when Henry Ford established a Sociological Department at the Ford Motor Works in 1914, he regarded the supervision of the workers' private lives merely as a means of making the men sober, thrifty, industrious producers. Ford's sociologists attempted to impose an old-fashioned Protestant morality on the labor force; they inveighed against tobacco, liquor, and dissipation.

Only a handful of employers at this time understood that the worker might be useful to the capitalist as a consumer; that he needed to be imbued with a taste for higher things; that an economy based on mass production required not only the capitalistic organization of production but the organization of consumption and leisure as well. "Mass production," said the Boston department store magnate Edward A. Filene in 1919, "demands the education of the masses; the masses must learn to behave like human beings in a mass production world. . . . They must achieve, not mere literacy, but culture." In other words, the modern manufacturer has to "educate" the masses in the culture of consumption. The mass production of commodities in every-increasing abundance demands a mass market to absorb them.

The American economy, having reached the point where its technology was capable of satisfying basic material needs, now relied on the creation of new consumer demands—on convincing people to buy goods for which they are unaware of any need until the "need" is forcibly brought to their attention by the mass media. Advertising, said Calvin Coolidge, "is the method by which the desire is created for better things." The attempt to "civilize" the masses has now given rise to a society dominated by appearances—the society of the spectacle. In the period of primitive accumulation, capitalism subordinated being to having, the use value of commodities to their exchange value. Now it subordinates possession itself to appearance and measures exchange value as a commodity's capacity to confer prestige—the illusion of prosperity and well-being. "When economic necessity yields to the necessity for limitless economic development," writes Guy Debord, "the satisfaction of basic and generally recognized human needs gives way to an uninterrupted fabrication of pseudo-needs."

In a simpler time, advertising merely called attention to the product and extolled its advantages. Now it manufactures a product of its own: the consumer, perpetually unsatisfied, restless, anxious, and bored. Advertising serves not so much to advertise products as to promote consumption as a way of life. It "educates" the masses into an unappeasable appetite not only for goods but for new experiences and personal fulfillment. It upholds consumption as the answer to the age-old discontents of loneliness, sickness, weariness, lack of sexual satisfaction; at the same time it creates new forms of discontent peculiar to the modern age. It plays seductively on the malaise of industrial civilization. Is your job boring and meaningless? Does it leave you with feelings of futility and fatigue? Is your life empty? Consumption promises to fill the aching void; hence the attempt to surround commodities with an aura of romance; with allusions to exotic places and vivid experiences; and with images of female breasts from which all blessings flow.

The propaganda of commodities serves a double function. First, it upholds consumption as an alternative to protest or rebellion. Paul Nystrom, an early student of modern marketing, once noted that industrial civilization gives rise to a "philosophy of futility," a pervasive fatigue, a "disappointment with achievements" that finds an outlet in changing the "more superficial things in which fashion reigns." The tired worker, instead of attempting to change the conditions of his work, seeks renewal in brightening his immediate surroundings with new goods and services.

In the second place, the propaganda of consumption turns alienation itself into a commodity. It addresses itself to the spiritual desolation of modern life and proposes consumption as the cure. It not only promises to palliate all the old unhappiness to which flesh is heir; it creates or exacerbates new forms of unhappiness—personal insecurity, status anxiety, anxiety in parents about their ability to satisfy the needs of the young. Do you look dowdy next to your neighbors? Do you own a car inferior to theirs? Are your children as healthy? as popular? doing as well in school? Advertising institutionalizes envy and its attendant anxieties.

The servant of the status quo, adveritising has nevertheless identified itself with a sweeping change in values, a "revolution in manners and morals" that began in the early years of the twentieth century and has continued until the present. The demands of the mass-consumption economy have made the work ethic obsolete even for workers. Formerly the guardians of public health and morality urged the worker to labor as a moral obligation; now they teach him to labor so that he can partake of the fruits of consumption. In the nineteenth century, elites alone obeyed the laws of fashion, exchanging old possessions for new ones for no other reason than that they had gone out of style. Economic orthodoxy condemned the rest of society to a life of drudgery and mere subsistence. The mass production of luxury items now extends aristocratic habits to the masses. The apparatus of mass promotion attacks ideologies based on the postponement of gratification; it allies itself with sexual "revolution"; it sides or seems to side with women against male oppression and with the young against the authority of their elders. The logic of demand creation requires that women smoke and drink in public, move about freely, and assert their right to happiness instead of living for others. The advertising industry thus encourages the pseudo-emancipation of women, flattering them with its insinuating reminder, "You've come a long way, baby," and disguising the freedom to consume as genuine autonomy. Similarly it flatters and glorifies youth in the hope of elevating young people to the status of full-fledged consumers in their own right, each with a telephone, a television set, and a hi-fi in his own room. The "education" of the masses has altered the balance of forces within the family, weakening the authority of the husband in relation to the wife and parents in relation to their children. It emancipates women and children from patriarchal authority, however, only to subject them to the new paternalism of the advertising industry, the industrial corporation, and the state.*

Truth and Credibility   The role of the mass media in the manipulation of public opinion has received a great deal of anguished but misguided attention. Much of this commentary assumes that the problem is to prevent the circulation of obvious untruths; whereas it is evident, as the more penetrating critics of mass culture have pointed out, that the rise of mass media makes the categories of truth and falsehood irrelevant to an evaluation of their influence. Truth has given way to credibility, facts to statements that sound authoritative without conveying any authoritative information.

---

* Family life, according to Nystrom, inherently tends to promote custom, the antithesis of fashion. "Private home life is more effectively ruled by custom than public or semi-public life." On the other hand, "the conflict of youth with convention" encourages rapid changes in dress and styles of consumption. In general, Nystrom argues, rural life, illiteracy, social hierarchy, and inertia support custom, whereas fashion—the culture of consumption—derives from the progressive forces at work in modern society: public education, free speech, circulation of ideas and information, the "philosophy of progress."

Statements announcing that a given product is preferred by leading authorities without saying what it is preferred to, statements claiming a product's superiority to unspecified competitors, statements implying that a given characteristic belongs uniquely to the product in question when in fact it belongs to its rivals as well all serve to blur the distinction between truth and falsehood in a fog of plausibility. Such claims are "true" yet radically misleading. President Nixon's press secretary, Ron Ziegler, once demonstrated the political use of these techniques when he admitted that his previous statements on Watergate had become "inoperative." Many commentators assumed that Ziegler was groping for a euphemistic way of saying that he had lied. What he meant, however, was that his earlier statements were no longer believable. Not their falsity but their inability to command assent rendered them "inoperative." The question of whether they were true or not was beside the point.

Advertising and Propaganda　　As Daniel Boorstin has pointed out, we live in a world of pseudo-events and quasi information, in which the air is saturated with statements that are neither true nor false but merely credible. But even Boorstin minimizes the degree to which appearances—"images"—dominate American society. Backing away from the more disturbing implications of his study, he draws a false distinction between advertising and propaganda, which allows him to posit a sphere of technological rationality—one that includes the operations of the state and much of the routine of modern industry—into which the irrationality of image making cannot penetrate. Propaganda, which he identifies exclusively with totalitarian régimes, consists of "information intentionally biased," according to Boorstin; information, moreover, that "depends primarily on its emotional appeal"—whereas a pseudo-event represents an "ambiguous truth" that appeals to "our honest desire to be informed." This distinction will not stand up. It rests on a crude conception of modern propaganda, an art which long ago incorporated the most advanced techniques of modern advertising.

The master propagandist, like the advertising expert, avoids obvious emotional appeals and strives for a tone that is consistent with the prosaic quality of modern life—a dry, bland matter-of-factness. Nor does the propagandist circulate "intentionally biased" information. He knows that partial truths serve as more effective instruments of deception than lies. Thus he tries to impress the public with statistics of economic growth that neglect to give the base year from which growth is calculated, with accurate but meaningless facts about the standard of living—with raw and uninterpreted data, in other words, from which the audience is invited to draw the inescapable conclusion that things are getting better and the present régime therefore deserves the people's confidence, or on the other hand that things are getting worse so rapidly that the present régime should be given emergency powers to deal with the developing crisis. By using accurate details to imply a misleading picture of the whole, the artful propagandist, it has been said, makes truth the principal form of falsehood.

In propaganda as in advertising, the important consideration is not whether information accurately describes an objective situation but whether it sounds true. It sometimes becomes necessary to suppress information even when it reflects credit on the government, for no other reason than that the facts sound implausible. Jacques Ellul explains in his study of propaganda why, in 1942, the Germans did not reveal that the invincible General Rommel had been absent from North Africa at the moment of Montgomery's victory: "Everybody would have considered it a lie to explain the defeat and prove that Rommel had not really been beaten." The Office of War Information in the United States, eager to use atrocities to inflame public opinion against Germany, deliberately avoided the most horrifying atrocity of all, the extermination of the Jews, on the ground that the story would be "confusing and misleading if it appears to be simply affecting the Jewish people." Truth has to be suppressed if it sounds like propaganda. "The only reason to suppress a piece of news," says an Allied handbook used in World War II, "is if it is unbelievable."

It is true that propaganda subtly appeals to the emotions.

Ellul notes that propaganda uses facts not to support an argument but to exert emotional pressure. The same thing is true of advertising, however. In both cases, the emotional appeal remains muted and indirect; it inheres in the facts themselves; nor is it inconsistent with the "honest desire to be informed." Knowing that an educated public craves facts and cherishes nothing so much as the illusion of being well informed, the modern progagandist avoids using high-sounding slogans; he rarely appeals to a higher destiny; he seldom calls for heroism and sacrifice or reminds his audience of the glorious past. He sticks to the "facts." Propaganda thus merges with "information."

One of the principal functions of the greatly enlarged federal bureaucracy is to satisfy the demand for this kind of information. The bureaucracy not only provides supposedly reliable information to high officials; it provides misinformation to the public. The more technical and recondite this product, the more convincing it sounds. Hence the pervasiveness, in our culture, of the obfuscatory jargon of pseudo-science. This language surrounds the claims of administrators and advertisers alike with an aura of scientific detachment. More important, it is calculatedly obscure and unintelligible—qualities that commend it to a public that feels informed in proportion as it is befuddled. In one of his characteristic pronouncements, at a press conference in May 1962, John F. Kennedy proclaimed the end of ideology in words that appealed to both these public needs—the need to believe that political decisions are in the hands of dispassionate, bipartisan experts and the need to believe that the problems experts deal with are unintelligible to laymen.

Most of us are conditioned for many years to have a political viewpoint—Republican or Democratic, liberal, conservative, or moderate. The fact of the matter is that most of the problems . . . that we now face are technical problems, are administrative problems. They are very sophisticated judgments, which do not lend themselves to the great sort of passionate movements which have stirred this country so often in the past. [They] deal with questions which are now beyond the comprehension of most men. . . .

Politics as Spectacle   Systems analysts and "social accountants" take it as an article of faith that "with the growth of the complexity of society," as one of them, Albert Biderman, once put it, "immediate experience with its events plays an increasingly smaller role as a source of information and basis of judgment in contrast to symbolically mediated information about these events." But the substitution of symbolically mediated information for immediate experience—of pseudo-events for real events—has not made government more rational and efficient, as both the technocrats and their critics assume. On the contrary, it has given rise to a pervasive air of unreality, which ultimately befuddles the decision makers themselves. The contagion of unintelligibility spreads through all levels of government. It is not merely that propagandists fall victim to their own propaganda; the problem goes deeper. When politicians and administrators have no other aim than to sell their leadership to the public, they deprive themselves of intelligible standards by which to define the goals of specific policies or to evaluate success or failure. It was because prestige and credibility had become the only measure of effectiveness that American policy in Vietnam could be conducted without regard to the strategic importance of Vietnam or the political situation in that country. Since there were no clearly defined objectives in view, it was not even possible to say how defeat or victory was to be recognized, except that American prestige must not suffer as a result. The object of American policy in Vietnam was defined from the outset as the preservation of American credibility. This consideration, which amounted to an obsession, repeatedly overrode such elementary principles of statecraft as avoidance of excessive risks, assessment of the likelihood of success and failure, and calculation of the strategic and political consequences of defeat.

The art of crisis management, now widely acknowledged to be the essence of statecraft, owes its vogue to the merger of politics and spectacle. Propaganda seeks to create in the public a chronic sense of crisis, which in turn justifies the expansion of executive power and the secrecy surrounding it. The executive then asserts his "presidential" qualities by conveying his determination to rise to crisis, whatever the crisis of the moment happens to be—to run risks, to test his mettle, to shrink from no danger, to resort to bold and decisive action even when the occasion calls for prudence and caution. The careers of both Kennedy and Nixon testify to the prevailing obsession with crisis management and the management of impressions. Kennedy, in his eagerness to overcome the impression of weakness left by the Bay of Pigs fiasco—itself the product of a haunting fear that the Cuban revolution had undermined American prestige in Latin America—blustered against Nikita Khruschchev in Vienna, proclaimed Berlin "the great testing-place of Western courage and will," and risked nuclear war over the Cuban missile crisis, even though Soviet missiles in Cuba, deliberately provocative as they were, in no way altered the military balance of power. In many ways the most important event of the Kennedy administration, however—its high point, from which everything else was a decline—was the inaugural, a spectacle that solidified the myth of Camelot before Camelot had even come into being. "The torch has been passed to a new generation of Americans, born in this century, tempered by war, disciplined by a hard and bitter peace. . . ." In these words Kennedy invoked his preoccupation with discipline, testing, and tempering on behalf of a whole generation's belief—so soon shattered—that it stood poised on the brink of greatness. "Ask not what your country can do for you; ask what you can do for your country." No other president exemplified so completely the subordination of policy to national prestige, to the appearance and illusion of national greatness.

With Nixon, the politics of spectacle reached a tragicomic climax. Uninterested in principles and programs, driven only by ambition and by a vague resentment against the Eastern liberal establishment, Nixon devoted most of his career to the art of impressing an unseen audience with his powers of leadership. The turning points of his career, the "crises" of which he has written so revealingly, presented themselves as occasions on which he was tempted to quit the field but survived—in each case through a public performance—by demonstrating his ability to rise to the occasion. With his theatrical conception of politics, Nixon prided himself on his ability to distinguish a convincing performance from a poor one, as in the Hiss case, when he became certain that Whittaker Chambers was telling the truth because "I did not feel that [his performance] was an act." After watching the Army-McCarthy hearings on television, he remarked scornfully, "I prefer professionals to amateur actors." During his famous kitchen debate with Nikita Khruschchev, Nixon was sure that Khruschchev "was going through an act," and he later reproached Marshal Georgi Zhukov with underestimating the intelligence of the Soviet people. "They aren't dumb. They know when somebody is acting and when it's the real thing—particularly when the acts have been so amateurish."

In one of his televised debates with Kennedy in 1960, Nixon denounced Kennedy for demanding more active support of the anti-Castro forces in Cuba—the very strategy that was secretly being carried out, partly at Nixon's own instigation, by the Eisenhower administration. Even more remarkable than this performance itself, in which Nixon formulated the most telling criticisms of a policy with which he himself was in complete agreement, is the detachment with which Nixon discusses it in *Six Crises*. He comments on his own performance with the same objectivity with which he comments on the performance of Hiss and Chambers, noting with some pleasure—but with complete indifference to the irony of the situation—that he spoke "the exact opposite of the truth" so effectively that several liberal papers strongly commended him and even forced Kennedy to modify his own position.

As president, Nixon inherited the domestic tensions and confusion that had been generated by the culminating spectacle of the sixties, the war in Vietnam. He did not limit himself, however, to attempts to stifle opposition and destroy the left. Instead he mounted a full-scale attack on a single individual (Daniel Ellsberg), instituted an elaborate security program to prevent further leaks of what was regarded as vital security information, and convinced himself that Ellsberg was somehow in league with the leading Democratic contender for the presidency. These "security" measures, though highly irrational, probably originated in the not unreasonable belief that presidential power had come to rest on the ability to manipulate information and that this power, in order to be completely effective, had to be recognized by everyone else as indivisible. Once Watergate became a full-fledged "crisis," Nixon devoted himself to convincing the nation that he would by all means prove equal to the emergency. To the end, he approached his mounting difficulties as a problem in public relations. In long conversations with his chief adviser, himself a public relations man, both Nixon and H. R. Haldeman showed an indifference to truth that goes beyond cynicism—an indifference that can be explained only on the assumption that the concept of truth, for men exercising irresponsible powers, has lost most of its meaning. "I think we have to find a way to make statements," Nixon said at one point," . . . any kind of statement . . . as general as possible . . . just so somebody can say that . . . a statement has been made through the President upon which he has based his statement to the effect that he has confidence in his staff. . . . I didn't do this, I didn't do that, da da da da, da da da da, da da da da, da da da da. Haldeman didn't do this, Erlichman didn't do that. Colson didn't do that." Haldeman's reply—"I wouldn't say that this is the whole truth"—evinces a lingering capacity to distinguish between truth and falsehood but does not alter the fact that words chosen purely for their public effect quickly lose all reference to reality. Political discussion founded on such principles degenerates into meaningless babble, even when it is carried on behind closed doors.

Radicalism as Street Theater   The degeneration of politics into spectacle has not only transformed policy making into publicity, debased political discourse, and turned elections into sporting events in which each side claims the advantage of "momentum," it has also made it more difficult than ever to organize a political opposition. When the images of power overshadow the reality, those without power find themselves fighting phantoms. Particularly in a society where power likes to present itself in the guise of benevolence—where government seldom resorts to the naked use of force—it is hard to identify the oppressor, let alone to personify him, or to sustain a burning sense of grievance in the masses. In the sixties, the new left attempted to overcome this insubstantiality of the establishment by resorting to politics of confrontation. By deliberately provoking violent repression, it hoped to forestall the co-optation of dissent. The attempt to dramatize official repression, however, imprisoned the left in a politics of theater, of dramatic gestures, of style without substance—a mirror-image of the politics of unreality which it should have been the purpose of the left to unmask.

Theoreticians of the cold war saw the tactics of "escalation" as a means of impressing "relevant audiences" with the nation's strength of purpose; the strategists of the left, equally obsessed with appearances, believed that gestures of escalating opposition would eventually bring the establishment to its knees. In both cases, politics appeared as a game the object of which was to communicate to the opponent the escalating cost of his own policies. When he was sufficiently impressed with the cost, on this assumption, he would abandon intransigence in favor of conciliation. Thus opponents of the war in Vietnam announced in 1967, with great fanfare, that they intended to move "from dissent to resistance," expecting that resistance would have to be countered by repressive measures intolerable to liberal opinion. "It will be bloody," said one radical in defense of a particularly futile protest, "but blood makes the liberals mad." Far from provoking a liberal reaction, however, the politics of street theater solidified opposition to the left and created a mounting demand for law and order. The escalation of militant tactics fragmented the left and drew the more "revolutionary" elements into suicidal confrontations with the police and the National Guard. "We are working to build a guerrilla force in an urban environment," the national secretary of SDS announced in 1967. In fact, SDS was laying the groundwork for its own collapse two years later.

The delusion that street theater represented the newest form of guerrilla warfare helped to ward off an uneasy realization that it represented no more than a form of self-promotion, by means of which the media stars of the left brought themselves to national attention with its concomitant rewards. One exponent of "guerrilla theater," after exhorting his followers to live by their wits, quickly explained that "to live by your wits is not to imitate the hustler who is a low-class capitalist, but rather the Latin American guerrilla who is a low-class socialist." Such talk served not only to reassure the faithful but to play up to the "relevant audience" of black and third-world militants, to which the white left had become unduly sensitive and which it desperately wanted to impress with its revolutionary machismo. The rhetoric of black power corrupted the white left and the black left alike, substituting a politics of the media for the civil rights struggles earlier waged in deadly earnest in the South. As the black power rhetoreticians co-opted the civil rights movement, they also captivated white liberals who sought to appease the guilt associated with "white skin privilege" by adopting the gestures and language of black militancy. Both whites and blacks embraced radical style in place of radical substance.

By 1968, when the new left gathered for its "festival of life" outside the Democratic National Convention in Chicago, the prominence of the Youth International led by Jerry Rubin and Abbie Hoffman made it clear that a theatrical conception of politics had driven more rational conceptions from the field. "Yippie is gestalt theater of the streets," Rubin has claimed, "compelling people by example to change their awareness. Entering a Congressional hearing room in a Paul Revere costume or wearing judicial robes to a court proceeding is a way of acting out fantasies and ending repressions." Acting out fantasies does not end repressions, however; it merely dramatizes the permissible limits of antisocial behavior. In the sixties and early seventies, radicals who transgressed these limits, under the illusion that they were fomenting insurrection or "doing gestalt therapy on the nation," in Rubin's words, often paid a heavy price: clubbing, imprisonment, police harassment, or death itself, in the case of the terrorists—the Weathermen and the recruits to the Symbionese Liberation Army—who followed the logic of guerrilla theater to its inevitable ending. Yet these radicals had so few practical results to show for their sacrifices that we are driven to conclude that they embraced radical politics in the first place not because it promised practical results but because it served as a new mode of self-dramatization.

Hero Worship and Narcissistic Idealization   On the fringes of the radical movement, many tortured spirits actively sought a martyrdom made doubly attractive by the glamour of modern publicity. The left, with its vision of social upheaval, has always attracted more than its share of lunatics, but the media have conferred a curious sort of legitimacy on antisocial acts merely by reporting them. The streaker at a football game becomes for a moment the center of all eyes. The criminal who murders or kidnaps a celebrity takes on the glamour of his victim. The Manson gang with their murder of Sharon Tate and her friends, the Symbionese Liberation Army with its abduction of Patty Hearst, share with the presidential assassins and would-be assassins of recent years a similar psychology. Such people display, in exaggerated form, the prevailing obsession with celebrity and a determination to achieve it even at the cost of rational self-interest and personal safety. The narcissist divides society into two groups: the rich, great, and famous on the one hand and the common herd on the other. Narcissistic patients, according to Kernberg, "are afraid of not belonging to the company of the great, rich, and powerful, and of belonging instead to the 'mediocre,' by which they mean worthless and despicable rather than 'average' in the ordinary sense of the term." They worship heroes only to turn against them when their heroes disappoint them. "Unconsciously fixated on an idealized self-object for which they continue to yearn, . . . such persons are forever searching for external omnipotent powers from whose support and approval they attempt to derive strength." Thus the presidential assassin establishes with his victim a deadly intimacy, follows his movements, attaches himself to his rising star. The machinery of mass promotion encourages this identification by simultaneously exalting and humanizing the Olympians, endowing them with the same appetites and eccentricities that we recognize in our neighbors. Through his desperate act, the assassin or would-be assassin joins their exalted company. Assassination itself becomes a form of spectacle, and the inner lives of assassins—Oswald's difficulties with Marina, the state of Bremer's soul as recorded in his diary—

provide the same popular entertainment as the private lives of their victims or near-victims.

Narcissistic patients, according to Kernberg, "often admire some hero or outstanding individual" and "experience themselves as part of that outstanding person." They see the admired individual as "merely an extension of themselves." If the person rejects them, "they experience immediate hatred and fear, and react by devaluing the former idol." Just as heroism differs in subtle ways from celebrity, so hero worship, which esteems the hero's actions and hopes to emulate them or at least to prove worthy of his example, must be distinguished from narcissistic idealization. The narcissist admires and identifies himself with "winners" out of his fear of being labeled a loser. He seeks to warm himself in their reflected glow; but his feelings contain a strong admixture of envy, and his admiration often turns to hatred if the object of his attachment does something to remind him of his own insignificance. The narcissist lacks the confidence in his own abilities that would encourage him to model himself on another person's exalted example. Thus the narcissistic fascination with celebrity, so rampant in our society, coincides historically with what Jules Henry calls "the erosion of the capacity for emulation, loss of the ability to model one's self consciously after another person." One of the high school students interviewed by Henry said flatly, "I think a person shouldn't mold himself after someone else."

To pick a person after whom to model one's self [Henry writes] is an aggressive act of will, and Bill is much too anxious and passive to do it. . . . When cynicism, resignation, and passivity enter life the first makes all emulative choice of properties seem vain, and passivity and resignation sap the will necessary to the emulative decision. But positively, in order for a morally sound emulative choice to be made there must be present some faith in one's self; a certain amount of naive optimism and a certain quantity of will.

When the superego consists not so much of conscious ego ideals but of unconscious, archaic fantasies about parents of superhuman size, emulation becomes almost entirely unconscious and expresses not the search for models but the emptiness of self-images. The protagonist of Heller's *Something Happened*, who completely lacks "naive optimism" and a sense of self, experiences an "almost enslaving instinct to be like just about everyone I find myself with. It happens not only in matters of speech, but with physical actions as well. . . . It operates unconsciously, . . . with a determination of its own, in spite of my vigilance and aversion, and usually I do not realize I have slipped into someone else's personality until I am already there."

The narcissist cannot identify with someone else without seeing the other as an extension of himself, without obliterating the other's identity. Incapable of identification, in the first instance with parents and other authority figures, he is therefore incapable of hero worship or of the suspension of disbelief that makes it possible to enter imaginatively into the lives of others while acknowledging their independent existence. A narcissistic society worships celebrity rather than fame and substitutes spectacle for the older forms of theater, which encouraged identification and emulation precisely because they carefully preserved a certain distance between the audience and the actors, the hero worshipper and the hero.

Narcissism and the Theater of the Absurd   At the same time that public life and even private life take on the qualities of spectacle, a countermovement seeks to model spectacle, theater, all forms of art, on reality—to obliterate the very distinction between art and life. Both developments popularize a sense of the absurd, that hallmark of the contemporary sensibility. Note the close connection between a surfeit of spectacles, the cynical awareness of illusion it creates even in children, the imperviousness to shock or surprise, and the resulting indifference to the distinction between illusion and reality.

We are cynics [writes Joyce Maynard of herself and a four-year-old child she took to the circus], who see the trap door in the magic show, the pillow stuffing in Salvation Army Santa Clauses, the camera tricks in TV commercials ("That isn't really a genie's hand coming out of the washing machine," Hanna tells me, "it's just an actor with gloves on."). So at the circus . . . she leaned back on her padded seat, my four-year-old, . . . anticipating pratfalls, toughly, smartly, sadly, wisely, agedly unenthralled, more wrapped up in the cotton candy than in the Greatest Show on Earth. . . . We had seen greater spectacles, unmoved, our whole world was a visual glut, a ten-ring circus even Ringling Brothers couldn't compete with. A man stuck his head into a tiger's mouth and I pointed it out, with more amazement than I really felt, to my cool, unfazed friend, and when she failed to look . . . turned her head for her, forced her to take the sight in. The tiger could have bitten the tamer's head off, I think, swallowed him whole and turned into a monkey and she wouldn't have blinked. We watched what must have been two dozen clowns pile out of a Volkswagen without Hanna's knowing what the point of all that was. It isn't just the knowledge that they emerge from a trap door in the sawdust that keeps Hanna from looking up, either. Even if she didn't know the trick involved, she wouldn't care.

Overexposure to manufactured illusions soon destroys their representational power. The illusion of reality dissolves, not in a hightened sense of reality as we might expect, but in a remarkable indifference to reality. Our sense of reality appears to rest, curiously enough, on our willingness to be taken in by the staged illusion of reality. Even a rational understanding of the techniques by means of which a given illusion is produced does not necessarily destroy our capacity to experience it as a representation of reality. The urge to understand a magician's tricks, like the recent interest in the special effects behind a movie like *Star Wars*, shares with the study of literature a willingness to learn from the masters of illusion lessons about reality itself. But a complete indifference even to the mechanics of illusion announces the collapse of the very idea of reality, dependent at every point on the distinction between nature and artifice, reality and illusion. This indifference betrays the erosion of the capacity to take any interest in anything outside the self. Thus the worldly child, unmoved, stuffs herself with cotton candy and "wouldn't care" even if she knew how twenty-four clowns managed to fit into a single car.

The history of theatrical innovation illustrates the principle that a sense of reality thrives on the conventions of formalized illusion and shrivels when those conventions collapse. The experimental theater has for a long time waged a war against illusion, attempting to undermine the theatrical conventions that encourage the spectator to accept the play as a depiction of reality. Ibsen, a master of those conventions, said of his work: "The illusion I wished to create was that of reality." Avant-garde playwrights in the twentieth century, on the other hand, believe that reality is itself an illusion and thus make no attempt to sustain illusions in their work. The plays of Pirandello explored the relation between fact and illusion and "questioned the right of the ordinary world to be considered more real than the fabricated world of the play." Brecht, instead of attempting to disguise the conventions of the stage, deliberately called attention to them in order to subvert the suspension of disbelief. In the same way, experimental novelists have done whatever they can to alienate the reader, to make it impossible for him to identify with the characters in their works, and to remind him at every opportunity that art—like life itself—is a fiction: the arbitrary imposition of meaning on experiences otherwise meaningless. Modern writers have reversed Ibsen's formula: the reality they wish to re-create in their works is that of illusion.

Nineteenth-century realists understood that verisimilitude depended in part on the artist's ability to keep a distance between the audience and the work of art. This distance, most clearly exemplified in the physical separation of actors and audience in the theater, paradoxically enabled the spectator to observe events on stage as if they were scenes from real life. "The effect of the play," Ibsen wrote, "depends a great deal on making the spectator feel as if he were actually sitting, listening and looking at events happening in real life." He complained that a production of *Ghosts* in 1883 left too little room between the spectators and the stage. At Beyreuth, Wagner built a second proscenium arch over the edge of the orchestra pit, in addition to the arch over the stage, so as to create a "mystic gulf" between the audience and the stage. "It makes the spectator imagine the stage is quite far away, though he sees it in all the clearness of its actual proximity; and this in turn gives rise to the illusion that the persons appearing on it are of larger, superhuman stature."

As art abandons the attempt to weave illusions around the audience and to present a heightened version of reality, it tries to close the gap between audience and actors. Sometimes it justifies this procedure by invoking theories tracing the origins of drama to religious ritual, orgiastic communion. Unfortunately the attempt to restore a sense of collective worship cannot restore the unity of belief that once gave life to such forms. The merging of actors and audience does not make the spectator into a communicant; it merely provides him—if it does not drive him out of the theater altogether—with a chance to admire himself in the new role of pseudo-performer, an experience not qualitatively different (even when clothed in the rhetoric of the avant-garde) from that of the studio audience at television performances, which dotes on images of itself periodically flashed across the monitors. In the performances of the Living Theater, in the much-acclaimed production *Dionysus '69*, and in other short-lived sensations of the late sixties, actors alternately insulted the spectators and made love to them, exhorting them to join the actors onstage in pseudo-orgies or gestures of political solidarity. "I don't want to play Antigone," said Judith Malina, "I want to play Judith Malina." Such strategies abolish the audience, Eric Bentley has observed, only to enlarge the acting company.

The rise of the theater of the absurd, it has been argued, "seems to mirror the change in the predominant form of mental disorders which has been observed and described since World War II by an ever-increasing number of psychiatrists." Whereas the "classical" drama of Sophocles, Shakespeare, and Ibsen turned on conflicts associated with classical neuroses, the absurdist theater of Albee, Beckett, Ionesco, and Genet centers on the emptiness, isolation, loneliness, and despair experienced by the borderline personality. The affinity between the theater of the absurd and the borderline's "fear of close relationships," "attendant feelings of helplessness, loss, and rage," "fear of destructive impulses," and "fixation to early omnipotence" inheres not only in the content of these plays but—more to the point of the present discussion—in their form. The contemporary playwright abandons the effort to portray coherent and generally recognized truths and presents the poet's personal intuition of truth. The characteristic devaluation of language, vagueness as to time and place, sparse scenery, and lack of plot development evoke the barren world of the borderline, his lack of faith in the growth or development of object relations, his "oft-stated remark that words do not matter, only action is important," and above all his belief that the world consists of illusions. "Instead of the neurotic character with well-structured conflicts centering around forbidden sex, authority, or dependence and independence within a family setting, we see characters filled with uncertainty about what is real." This uncertainty now invades every form of art and crystallizes in an imagery of the absurd that reenters daily life and encourages a theatrical approach to existence, a kind of absurdist theater of the self.

The Theater of Everyday Life   A number of historical currents have converged in our time to produce not merely in artists but in ordinary men and women an escalating cycle of self-consciousness—a sense of the self as a performer under the constant scrutiny of friends and strangers. Erving Goffman, the sociologist of the performing self, writes in a characteristic passage: "As human beings we are presumably creatures of variable impulse with moods and energies that change from one moment to the next. As characters put on for an audience, however, we must not be subject to ups and downs. . . . A certain bureaucratization of the spirit is expected so that we can be relied upon to give a perfectly homogeneous performance at every appointed time." This "bureaucratization of the spirit" has become more and more oppressive and is now widely recognized, thanks to Goffman, as an important element in the contemporary malaise.

   The self-consciousness that mocks all attempts at spontaneous action or enjoyment derives in the last analysis from the waning belief in the reality of the external world, which has lost its immediacy in a society pervaded by "symbolically mediated information." The more man objectifies himself in his work, the more reality takes on the appearance of illusion. As the workings of the modern economy and the modern social order become increasingly inaccessible to everyday intelligence, art and philosophy abdicate the task of explaining them to the allegedly objective sciences of society, which themselves have retreated from the effort to master reality into the classification of trivia. Reality thus presents itself, to laymen and "scientists" alike, as an impenetrable network of social relations—as "role playing," the "presentation of self in everyday life." To the performing self, the only reality is the identity he can construct out of materials furnished by advertising and mass culture, themes of popular film and fiction, and fragments torn from a vast range of cultural traditions, all of them equally contemporaneous to the contemporary mind.* In order to polish and perfect the part he has devised for himself, the new Narcissus gazes at his own reflection, not so much in admiration as in unremitting search of flaws, signs of fatigue, decay. Life becomes a work of art, while "the first art work in an artist," in Norman Mailer's pronouncement, "is the shaping of his own personality." The second of these principles has now been adopted not only by those who write "advertise-

---

* In *Slaughterhouse-Five*, a novel written "somewhat in the telegraphic schizophrenic manner of tales" (i.e., in deliberate disregard of the conventional sense of time), Kurt Vonnegut makes a passing observation that illustrates the eclecticism with which the modern sensitivity approaches the culture of the past. "What we love in our books are the depths of many marvelous moments seen all at one time." The fragmentizing impact of the mass media, according to Marshall McLuhan, "makes all civilizations contemporary with our own."

It is interesting to compare these cheerful expressions of the contemporary sensibility with the contention of two Marxist critics of literature, William Phillips and Philip Rahv, that the critical sense is necessarily rooted in the historical sense, the sense of continuity. "Lacking a continuity of development, criticism becomes unconscious of its own history, and regards all past criticism as a simultaneous order of ideas. In any critical essay one may find the ideas of Aristotle, Hegel, and Croce, for example, blandly reposing side by side. . . . Within this chaos social necessity asserts itself, of course [that is, fashions change; consciousness changes; new generations grow up and are influenced by the accumulated weight of the past], but only as an unpredictable, blind force, itself adding to the confusion of critics unable to fathom the currents of never-flagging change." Though these reflections were addressed to the literary humanism of the twenties and thirties, they apply with equal force to the postmodernist revolt against time.

"People aren't supposed to look back," Vonnegut writes. "I'm certainly not going to do it anymore." According to the study of the borderline personality and the theater of the absurd, already cited, "Clinically, many of the borderline patients express just such an inability to integrate past experiences with the present, and have almost panic-like feelings when forced to do so."

ments for myself" for publication but by the everyday artist in the street.

All of us, actors and spectators alike, live surrounded by mirrors. In them, we seek reassurance of our capacity to captivate or impress others, anxiously searching out blemishes that might detract from the appearance we intend to project. The advertising industry deliberately encourages this preoccupation with appearances. In the twenties, "the women in ads were constantly observing themselves, ever self-critical. . . . A noticeable proportion of magazine ads directed at women depicted them looking into mirrors. . . . Ads of the 1920s were quite explicit about this narcissistic imperative. They unabashedly used pictures of veiled nudes, and women in auto-erotic stances to encourage self-comparison and to remind women of the primacy of their sexuality." A booklet advertising beauty aids depicted on its cover a nude with the caption: "Your Masterpiece—Yourself."

Today the treatment of such themes is more explicit than ever; moreover, advertising encourages men as well as women to see the creation of the self as the highest form of creativity. In an earlier stage of capitalist development, industrialization reduced the artisan or peasant to a proletarian, stripped him of his land and tools, and stranded him in the marketplace with nothing to sell but his labor power. In our time, the elimination of skills not only from manual work but from white-collar jobs as well has created conditions in which labor power takes the form of personality rather than strength or intelligence. Men and women alike have to project an attractive image and to become simultaneously role players and connoisseurs of their own performance.

Changes in the social relations of production, which have given society the appearance of something opaque and impenetrable, have also given rise to the new idea of personality described by Richard Sennett in *The Fall of Public Man*. Whereas the eighteenth-century concept of character stressed the elements common to human nature, the nineteenth century began to see personality as the unique and idiosyncratic expression of individual traits. Outward appearances, in this view, involuntarily expressed the inner man. People soon became obsessed, according to Sennett, with the fear of inadvertently giving themselves away through their actions, facial expressions, and details of dress. In the same century, as Edgar Wind has shown, the art critic Giovanni Morelli propounded the theory that original paintings could be distinguished from forgeries by close examination of insignificant details—the characteristic rendering of an ear or an eye—that betrayed the hand of the master. "Every painter," Morelli insisted, "has his own peculiarities which escape him without his being aware of them."

Naturally these discoveries about personality and its involuntary expression had the effect, not only on artists and critics but on laymen as well, of encouraging self-conscious self-scrutiny. Artists could never again become unconscious of details; indeed the new attention to detail, as one critic has pointed out, obliterated the very notion of detail. Similarly, in everyday life the average man became a connoisseur of his own performance and that of others, bringing the skills of a novelist to the task of "decoding isolated details of appearance," as Sennett writes of Balzac, "magnifying the detail into an emblem of the whole man." But the mastery of these new social skills, while increasing esthetic satisfaction, has created new forms of uneasiness and anxiety. Imprisoned in his self-awareness, modern man longs for the lost innocence of spontaneous feeling. Unable to express emotion without calculating its effects on others, he doubts the authenticity of its expression in others and therefore derives little comfort from audience reactions to his own performance, even when the audience claims to be deeply moved. Andy Warhol complains:

Day after day I look in the mirror and I still see something—a new pimple. . . . I dunk a Johnson and Johnson cotton ball into Johnson and Johnson rubbing alcohol and rub the cotton ball against the pimple. . . . And while the alcohol is drying I think about nothing. How it's always in style. Always in good taste. . . . When the alcohol is dry, I'm ready to apply the flesh-colored acne-pimple medication. . . . So now the pimple's covered. But am I covered? I have to look into the mirror for some more clues. Nothing is missing. It's all there. The affectless gaze. . . . The bored languor, the wasted pallor. . . . The graying lips. The shaggy silver-white hair, soft and metallic. . . . Nothing is missing. I'm everything my scrapbook says I am.

The sense of security provided by the mirror proves fleeting. Each new confrontation with the mirror brings new risks. Warhol confesses that he is "still obsessed with the idea of looking into the mirror and seeing no one, nothing."

The analysis of interpersonal relations in the theater of everyday life—an analysis which deliberately sticks to the surface of social intercourse and makes no attempt to uncover its psychological depths—leads to conclusions similar to those of psychoanalysis. The psychoanalytic description of the pathological narcissist, whose sense of selfhood depends on the validation of others whom he nevertheless degrades, coincides in many particulars with the description of the performing self in literary criticism and in the sociology of everyday life. The developments that have created a new awareness of motive and involuntary expression—not least among which is the popularization of psychiatric modes of thought—cannot be disentangled from the historical changes that have produced not merely a new concept of personality, but a new form of personality organization. The pathological narcissist reveals, at a deeper level, the same anxieties which in milder form have become so common in everyday intercourse. The prevailing forms of social life, as we have seen, encourage many forms of narcissistic behavior. Moreover, they have altered the process of socialization—as we shall find in chapter VII—in ways that give further encouragement to narcissistic patterns by rooting them in the individual's earliest experience.

Ironic Detachment as an Escape from Routine   We have not yet exhausted, however, what can be learned from role theory alone. In our society, anxious self-scrutiny (not to be confused with critical self-examination) not only serves to regulate information signaled to others and to interpret signals received; it also establishes an ironic distance from the deadly routine of daily life. On the one hand, the degradation of work makes skill and competence increasingly irrelevant to material success and thus encourages the presentation of the self as a commodity; on the other hand, it discourages commitment to the job and drives people, as the only alternative to boredom and despair, to view work with self-critical detachment. When jobs consist of little more than meaningless motions, and when social routines, formerly dignified as ritual, degenerate into role playing, the worker—whether he toils on an assembly line or holds down a high-paying job in a large bureaucracy—seeks to escape from the resulting sense of inauthenticity by creating an ironic distance from his daily routine. He attempts to transform role playing into a symbolic elevation of daily life. He takes refuge in jokes, mockery, and cynicism. If he is asked to perform a disagreeable task, he makes it clear that he doesn't believe in the organization's objectives of increased efficiency and greater output. If he goes to a party, he shows by his actions that it's all a game—false, artificial, insincere; a grotesque travesty of sociability. In this way he attempts to make himself invulnerable to the pressures of the situation. By refusing to take seriously the routines he has to perform, he denies their capacity to injure him. Although he assumes that it is impossible to alter the iron limits imposed on him by society, a detached awareness of those limits seems to make them matter less. By demystifying daily life, he conveys to himself and others the impression that he has risen beyond it, even as he goes through the motions and does what is expected of him.

As more and more people find themselves working at jobs that are in fact beneath their abilities, as leisure and sociability themselves take on the qualities of work, the posture of cynical detachment becomes the dominant style of everyday intercourse. Many forms of popular art appeal to this sense of knowingness and thereby reinforce it. They parody familiar roles and themes, inviting the audience to consider itself superior to its surroundings. Popular forms begin to parody themselves: Westerns take off on Westerns; soap operas like *Fernwood, Soap,* and *Mary Hartman, Mary Hartman* assure the viewer of his own sophistication by mocking the conventions of soap opera. Yet much popular art remains romantic and escapist, eschews this theater of the absurd, and promises escape from routine instead of ironic detachment from it. Advertising and popular romance dazzle their audience with visions of rich experience and adventure. They promise not cynical detachment but a piece of the action, a part in the drama instead of cynical spectatorship. Emma Bovary, prototypical consumer of mass culture, still dreams; and her dreams, shared by millions, intensify dissatisfaction with jobs and social routine.

Unreflective accommodation to routine becomes progressively more difficult to achieve. While modern industry condemns people to jobs that insult their intelligence, the mass culture of romantic escape fills their heads with visions of experience beyond their means—beyond their emotional and imaginative capacities as well—and thus contributes to a further devaluation of routine. The disparity between romance and reality, the world of the beautiful people and the workaday world, gives rise to an ironic detachment that dulls pain but also cripples the will to change social conditions, to make even modest improvements in work and play, and to restore meaning and dignity to everyday life.

No Exit   Escape through irony and critical self-awareness is in any case itself an illusion; at best it provides only momentary relief. Distancing soon becomes a routine in its own right. Awareness commenting on awareness creates an escalating cycle of self-consciousness that inhibits spontaneity. It intensifies the feeling of inauthenticity that rises in the first place out of resentment against the meaningless roles prescribed by modern industry. Self-created roles become as constraining as the social roles from which they are meant to provide ironic detachment. We long for the suspension of self-consciousness, of the pseudoanalytic attitude that has become second nature; but neither art nor religion, historically the great emancipators from the prison of the self, retain the power to discourage disbelief. In a society based so largely on illusions and appearances, the ultimate illusions, art and religion, have no future. *Credo quia absurdum*, the paradox of religious experience in the past, has little meaning in a world where everything seems absurd, not merely the miracles associated with religious faith and practice.

As for art, it not only fails to create the illusion of reality but suffers from the same crisis of self-consciousness that afflicts the man in the street. Novelists and playwrights call attention to the artificiality of their own creations and discourage the reader from identifying with the characters. By means of irony and eclecticism, the writer withdraws from his subject but at the same time becomes so conscious of these distancing techniques that he finds it more and more difficult to write about anything except the difficulty of writing. Writing about writing then becomes in itself an object of self-parody, as when Donald Barthelme inserts into one of his stories the wry reflection: "Another story about writing a story! Another regressus in infinitum! Who doesn't prefer art that at least overtly imitates something other than its own processes? That doesn't continually proclaim 'Don't forget I'm an artifice!' "

In the same vein, John Barth asks, in the course of writing a novella: "How does one write a novella? How find the channel, bewildered in these creeks and crannies? Storytelling isn't my cup of wine; isn't somebody's; my plot doesn't rise and fall in meaningful stages but . . . digresses, retreats, hesitates, groans from its utter et cetera, collapses, dies." The experimental writer's "emotional withdrawal," according to Morris Dickstein, threatens to disintegrate into catatonia. Giving up the effort to "master reality," the writer retreats into a superficial self-analysis which blots out not only the external world but the deeper subjectivity "that enables the imagination to take wing. . . . His incursions into the self are as hollow as his excursus into the world."

Psychological analysis once again reinforces what we learn from the sociology of art and the sociology of role playing in everyday life. Although the inability to suspend disbelief originates in changing artistic conventions and in the self-consciousness through which we try to distance ourselves from everyday life (and which imprisons us in its own right), this vigilant self-scrutiny often has a psychological basis as well. Those who feel secure in the ego's ability to control the id, according to Kohut, take pleasure in occasionally suspending the secondary process (for example, in sleep or in sexual activity), since they know they can regain it when they wish to. The narcissist, on the other hand, finds his own desires so threatening that he often experiences the utmost difficulty in sleeping, in elaborating the sexual impulse in fantasy ("the foremost proving ground for a person's capacity to decathect the secondary processes"), or in suspending current reality during psychoanalytic sessions. The narrator of Heller's *Something Happened* confesses: "I am often aghast upon awakening from a sound, dreamless sleep to realize how far away from life I have been, and how defenseless I was while I was there. . . . I might be unable to return. I don't like to lose touch with consciousness entirely."

In psychiatric sessions as in the theater, conventions surrounding the psychoanalytic encounter normally support "decathexis of current reality": the "diminution of stimuli from the immediate surroundings" makes it possible to turn "toward a world of imaginatively and artistically worked over memories." With some patients, however, the "inability to tolerate the decathexis of current reality and to accept the ambiguity of the analytic situation" becomes itself the central problem of analysis. As usual, Kohut adds, it does no good to confront the patient with a moral argument against this incapacity or to persuade or exhort him to change his ways.

The recent attack on theatrical illusion, which undermines the twentieth-century religion of art as effectively as the attack on religious illusions in the nineteenth century undermined religion itself, participates in the fear of fantasy associated with resistance to the "decathexis of current reality." When art, religion, and finally even sex lose their power to provide an imaginative release from everyday reality, the banality of pseudo-self-awareness becomes so overwhelming that men finally lose the capacity to envision any release at all except in total nothingness, blankness. Warhol provides a good description of the resulting state of mind:

The best love is not-to-think-about .it love. Some people can have sex and really let their minds go blank and fill up with the sex; other people can never let their minds go blank and fill up with the sex, so while they're having the sex they're thinking, "Can this really be me? Am I really doing this? This is very strange. Five minutes ago I wasn't doing this. In a little while I won't be doing it. What would Mom say? How did people ever think of doing this?" So the first type of person . . . is better off. The other type has to find something else to relax with and get lost in.

Imprisoned in his pseudo-awareness of himself, the new Narcissus would gladly take refuge in an *idée fixe*, a neurotic compulsion, a "magnificent obsession"—anything to get his mind off his own mind. Even unreflecting acquiescence in the daily grind, as the possibility of achieving it recedes into the historical distance, comes to seem like an almost enviable state of mind. It is a tribute to the peculiar horror of contemporary life that it makes the worst features of earlier times—the stupefaction of the masses, the obsessed and driven lives of the bourgeoisie—seem attractive by comparison. The nineteenth-century capitalist, compulsively industrious in the attempt to deliver himself from temptation, suffered torments inflicted by inner demons. Contemporary man, tortured on the other hand by self-consciousness, turns to new cults and therapies not to free himself from obsessions but to find meaning and purpose in life, to find something to live for, precisely to embrace an obsession, if only the *passion maîtresse* of therapy itself. He would willingly exchange his self-consciousness for oblivion and his freedom to create new roles for some form of external dictation, the more arbitrary the better. The hero of a recent novel renounces free choice and lives according to the dictation of dice: "I established in my mind at that moment and for all time, the never questioned principle that what the dice dictates, I will perform." Men used to rail against the irony of fate; now they prefer it to the irony of unceasing self-consciousness. Whereas earlier ages sought to substitute reason for arbitrary dictation both from without and within, the twentieth century finds reason, in the debased contemporary form of ironic self-consciousness, a harsh master; it seeks to revive earlier forms of enslavement. The prison life of the past looks in our own time like liberation itself.

V

The Degradation of Sport

The Spirit of Play versus the Rage for National Uplift
Among the activities through which men seek release from
everyday life, games offer in many ways the purest form of escape. Like sex, drugs, and drink, they obliterate awareness of
everyday reality, but they do this not by dimming awareness but
by raising it to a new intensity of concentration. Moreover, they
have no side effects, hangovers, or emotional complications.
Games simultaneously satisfy the need for free fantasy and the
search for gratuitous difficulty; they combine childlike exuber-
ance with deliberately created complications. By establishing
conditions of equality among the players, according to Roger
Caillois, games attempt to substitute ideal conditions for "the normal confusion of everyday life." They re-create the freedom, the
remembered perfection of childhood, and mark it off from ordinary life with artificial boundaries, within which the only constraints are the rules to which the players freely submit. Games
enlist skill and intelligence, the utmost concentration of purpose,
on behalf of activities utterly useless, which make no contribution
to the struggle of man against nature, to the wealth or comfort of
the community, or to its physical survival.

The uselessness of games makes them offensive to social reformers, improvers of public morals, or functionalist critics of society like Veblen, who saw in the futility of upper-class sports
anachronistic survivals of militarism and prowess. Yet the "futility" of play, and nothing else, explains its appeal—its artificiality,
the arbitrary obstacles it sets up for no other purpose than to
challenge the players to surmount them, the absence of any utilitarian or uplifting object. Games quickly lose their charm when
forced into the service of education, character development, or
social improvement.

Today the official view of the beneficial, wholesome effects of sport, which has replaced the various utilitarian ideologies of the past, stresses their contribution to health, fitness, and hence to the national well-being, considered as the sum of the nation's "human resources." The "socialist" version of this ideology hardly differs from the capitalist version promulgated, for example, by John F. Kennedy in his tiresome pronouncements on physical fitness. Attempting to justify the creation of his President's Council on Youth Fitness (headed by the Oklahoma football coach, Bud Wilkinson), Kennedy cited the consistent decline of strength and fitness as measured by standard tests. "Our growing softness, our increasing lack of physical fitness, is a menace to our security." This attack on "softness" goes hand in hand with a condemnation of spectatorship.

Socialist pronouncements sound depressingly similar. The Cuban government announced in 1967 that sport should be considered part of the "inseparable element of education, culture, health, defense, happiness and the development of people and a new society." In 1925, the central committee of the Soviet Communist party declared that sport should be consciously used "as a means of rallying the broad masses of workers and peasants around the various Party Soviet and Trade Union organizations through which the masses of workers and peasants are to be drawn into social and political activity." Fortunately, people of all nations intuitively tend to resist such exhortations. They know that games remain gloriously pointless and that watching an exciting athletic contest, moreover, can be emotionally almost as exhausting as participation itself—hardly the "passive" experience it is made out to be by the guardians of public health and virtue.

Huizinga on Homo Ludens Modern industry having reduced most jobs to a routine, games take on added meaning in our society. Men seek in play the difficulties and demands—both intellectual and physical—they no longer find in work. It is not perhaps monotony and routine in themselves that take the enjoyment out of work, for any job worth doing entails a certain amount of drudgery, but the peculiar conditions that prevail in large bureau-cratic organizations and increasingly in the modern factory as well. When work loses its tangible, palpable quality, loses the character of the transformation of matter by human ingenuity, it becomes wholly abstract and interpersonal. The intense subjec-tivity of modern work, exemplified even more clearly in the office than in the factory, causes men and women to doubt the reality of the external world and to imprison themselves, as noted in the previous chapter, in a shell of protective irony. Work now retains so few traces of play, and the daily routine affords so few oppor-tunities to escape from the ironic self-consciousness that has itself assumed the qualities of a routine, that people seek abandon in play with more than the usual intensity. "At a time when *image* is one of the most frequently used words in American speech and writing," Joseph Epstein notes in a recent essay on sports, "one does not too often come upon the real thing."

The history of culture, as Huizinga showed in his classic study of play, *Homo Ludens*, appears from one perspective to con-sist of the gradual eradication of the play element from all cultural forms—from religion, from the law, from warfare, above all from productive labor. The rationalization of these activities leaves little room for the spirit of arbitrary invention or the disposition to leave things to chance. Risk, daring, and uncertainty—impor-tant components of play—have no place in industry or in activi-ties infiltrated by industrial standards, which seek precisely to predict and control the future and to eliminate risk. Games ac-cordingly have assumed an importance unprecedented even in an-cient Greece, where so much of social life revolved around con-tests. Sports, which satisfy also the starved need for physical exertion—for a renewal of the sense of the physical basis of life—have become an enthusiasm not just of the masses but of those who set themselves up as a cultural elite.

The rise of spectator sports to their present importance coin-cides historically with the rise of mass production, which inten-sifies the needs sport satisfies while creating the technical and promotional capacity to market athletic contests to a vast audi-ence. But according to a common criticism of modern sport, these same developments have destroyed the value of athletics. Com-mercialization has turned play into work, subordinated the athlete's pleasure to the spectator's, and reduced the spectator himself to a state of vegetative passivity—the very antithesis of the health and vigor sport ideally promotes. The mania for winning has encouraged an exaggerated emphasis on the competitive side of sport, to the exclusion of the more modest but more satisfying experiences of cooperation and competence. The cult of victory, proclaimed by such football coaches as Vince Lombardi and George Allen, has made savages of the players and rabid chauvinists of their followers. The violence and partisanship of modern sports lead some critics to insist that athletics impart militaristic values to the young, irrationally inculcate local and national pride in the spectator, and serve as one of the strongest bastions of male chauvinism.

Huizinga himself, who anticipated some of these arguments but stated them far more persuasively, argued that modern games and sports had been ruined by a "fatal shift toward over-seriousness." At the same time, he maintained that play had lost its element of ritual, had become "profane," and consquently had ceased to have any "organic connection whatever with the structure of society." The masses now crave "trivial recreation and crude sensationalism" and throw themselves into these pursuits with an intensity far beyond their intrinsic merit. Instead of playing with the freedom and intensity of children, they play with the "blend of adolescence and barbarity" that Huizinga calls puerilism, investing games with patriotic and martial fervor while treating serious pursuits like games. "A far-reaching contamination of play and serious activity has taken place," according to Huizinga. "The two spheres are getting mixed. In the activities of an outwardly serious nature hides an element of play. Recognized play, on the other hand, is no longer able to maintain its true play-character as a result of being taken too seriously and being technically over-organised. The indispensable qualities of detachment, artlessness, and gladness are thus lost."

The Critique of Sport   An analysis of the critique of modern sport, in its vulgar form as well as in Huizinga's more refined version, brings to light a number of common misconceptions about modern society and clarifies some of the central issues of this study, especially the nature of spectacle and the difference between spectacle and other kinds of performance, ritual, and contest. A large amount of writing on sports has accumulated in recent years, and the sociology of sport has even entrenched itself as a minor branch of social science. Much of this commentary has no higher purpose than to promote athletics or to exploit the journalistic market they have created, but some of it aspires to social criticism. Those who have formulated the now familiar indictment of organized sport include the sociologist Harry Edwards; psychologist and former tennis player Dorcas Susan Butt, who thinks sport should promote competence instead of competition; disillusioned professional athletes like Dave Meggyesy and Chip Oliver; and radical critics of culture and society, notably Paul Hoch and Jack Scott.

A discussion of their work helps to isolate what is historically specific to the present cultural malaise. The critics of sport, in their eagerness to uncover evidence of corruption and decline, attack intrinsic elements of athletics, elements essential to their appeal in all periods and places, on the erroneous assumption that spectatorship, violence, and competition reflect conditions peculiar to modern times. On the other hand, they overlook the distinctive contribution of contemporary society to the degradation of sport and therefore misconceive the nature of that degradation. They concentrate on issues, such as "over-seriousness," which are fundamental to an understanding of sport, indeed to the very definition of play, but peripheral or irrelevant to their historical development and contemporary transformation.

Take the common complaint that modern sports are "spectator-oriented rather than participant-oriented." Spectators, in this view, are irrelevant to the success of the game. What a naïve theory of human motivation this implies! The attainment of certain skills unavoidably gives rise to an urge to show them off. At a higher level of mastery, the performer no longer wishes merely to display his virtuosity—for the true connoisseur can easily distinguish between the performer who plays to the crowd and the superior artist who matches himself against the full rigor of his art itself—but to ratify a supremely difficult accomplishment; to give pleasure; to forge a bond between himself and his audience, which consists in their shared appreciation of a ritual executed flawlessly, with deep feeling and a sense of style and proportion.*

In all games, particularly in athletic contests, display and representation constitute a central element—a reminder of the former connections between play, ritual, and drama. The players not only compete; they enact a familiar ceremony that reaffirms common values. Ceremony requires witnesses: enthusiastic spectators conversant with the rules of the performance and its underlying meaning. Far from destroying the value of sports, the attendance of spectators makes them complete. Indeed one of the virtues of contemporary sports lies in their resistance to the erosion of standards and their capacity to appeal to a knowledgeable audience. Norman Podhoretz has argued that the sports public remains more discriminating than the public for the arts and that "excellence is relatively uncontroversial as a judgment of performance." More important, everyone agrees on the standards

---

* This does not mean that virtuosity is the principal component of sport. In implying a comparison, here and elsewhere, between athletic and musical performances, I wish to make just the opposite point. A performer who seeks merely to dazzle the audience with feats of technical brilliance plays to the lowest level of understanding, forgoing the risks that come from intense emotional engagement with the material itself. In the most satisfying kind of performance, the performer becomes unconscious of the audience and loses himself in his part. In sport, the moment that matters is what a former basketball player describes as the moment "when all those folks in the stands don't count." The player in question, now a scholar, left big-time sport when he discovered he was expected to have no life outside it, but he retains more insight into the nature of games than Dave Meggyesy, Chip Oliver, and other ex-athletes. Rejecting the simple-minded radicalism according to which "commercialization" has corrupted sports, he says: "Money [in professional sports] has nothing to do with capitalism, owners, or professionalism. It's the moment in some games where it doesn't matter who's watching, all that counts is that instant where how you play determines which team wins and which team loses."

If virtuosity were the essence of sport, we could dispense with basketball and content ourselves with displays of dunking and dribbling. But to say that real artistry consists not of dazzling technique but of teamwork, timing, a sense of the moment, an understanding of the medium, and the capacity to lose oneself in play does not of course mean that games would have the same significance if no one watched them. It means simply that the superior performance has the quality of being unobserved.

against which excellence should be measured. The public for sports still consists largely of men who took part in sports during boyhood and thus acquired a sense of the game and a capacity to distinguish among many levels of excellence.

The same can hardly be said for the audience for artistic performance, even though amateur musicians, dancers, actors, and painters may still comprise a small nucleus of the audience. Constant experimentation in the arts has created so much confusion about standards that the only surviving measure of excellence is novelty and shock value, which in a jaded time often resides in a work's sheer ugliness and banality. In sport, on the other hand, novelty and rapid shifts of fashion play a small part in games' appeal to a discriminating audience.

Yet even here, the contamination of standards has already begun. Faced with rising costs, owners seek to increase attendance at sporting events by installing exploding scoreboards, broadcasting recorded cavalry charges, giving away helmets and bats, and surrounding the spectator with cheerleaders, usherettes, and ball girls. Television has enlarged the audience for sports while lowering the level of its understanding; at least this is the operating assumption of sports commentators, who direct at the audience an interminable stream of tutelage in the basics of the game, and of the promoters who reshape one game after another to conform to the tastes of an audience supposedly incapable of grasping their finer points. The American League's adoption of the designated-hitter rule, which relieves pitchers of the need to bat and diminishes the importance of managerial strategy, provides an especially blatant example of the dilution of sports by the requirements of mass promotion. Another is the "Devil-Take-the-Hindmost Mile," a track event invented by the San Francisco *Examiner*, in which the last runner in the early stages of the race has to drop out—a rule that encourages an early scramble to avoid disqualification but lowers the general quality of the event. When the television networks discovered surfing, they insisted that events be held according to a prearranged schedule, without regard to weather conditions. One surfer complained, "Television is destroying our sport. The TV producers are turning a sport and an art form into a circus." The same practices produce the same effects on other sports, forcing baseball players, for example, to play World Series games on freezing October evenings. The substitution of artificial surfaces for grass in tennis, which has slowed the pace of the game, placed a premium on reliability and patience, and reduced the element of tactical brilliance and overpowering speed, commends itself to television producers because it makes tennis an all-weather game and even permits it to be played indoors, in sanctuaries of sport like Caesar's Palace in Las Vegas. Television has rearranged the athletic calendar and thus deprived sports of their familiar connection with the seasons, diminishing their power of allusiveness and recall.

As spectators become less knowledgeable about the games they watch, they become sensation-minded and bloodthirsty. The rise of violence in ice hockey, far beyond the point where it plays any functional part in the game, coincided with the expansion of professional hockey into cities without any traditional attachment to the sport—cities in which weather conditions, indeed, had always precluded any such tradition of local play. But the significance of such changes is not that sports ought to be organized, as a number of recent critics imagine, solely for the edification of the players and that corruption sets in when sports begin to be played to spectators for a profit. No one denies the desirability of participation in sports—not because it builds strong bodies but because it brings joy and delight. It is by watching those who have mastered a sport, however, that we derive standards against which to measure ourselves. By entering imaginatively into their world, we experience in heightened form the pain of defeat and the triumph of persistence in the face of adversity. An athletic performance, like other performances, calls up a rich train of associations and fantasies, shaping unconscious perceptions of life. Spectatorship is no more "passive" than daydreaming, provided the performance is of such quality that it elicits an emotional response.

It is a mistake to suppose that organized athletics ever serve the interests of the players alone or that professionalization inevitably corrupts all who take part in it. In glorifying amateurism, equating spectatorship with passivity, and deploring competition, recent criticism of sport echoes the fake radicalism of the counterculture, from which so much of its derives. It shows its contempt for excellence by proposing to break down the "elitist" distinction between players and spectators. It proposes to replace competitive professional sports, which notwithstanding their shortcomings uphold standards of competence and bravery that might otherwise become extinct, with a bland regimen of cooperative diversions in which everyone can join regardless of age or ability—"new sports for the noncompetitive," having "no object, really," according to a typical effusion, except to bring "people together to enjoy each other." In its eagerness to remove from athletics the element that has always underlain their imaginative appeal, the staged rivalry of superior ability, this "radicalism" proposes merely to complete the degradation already begun by the very society the cultural radicals profess to criticize and subvert. Vaguely uneasy about the emotional response evoked by competitive sports, the critics of "passive" spectatorship wish to enlist sport in the service of healthy physical exercise, subduing or eliminating the element of fantasy, make-believe, and play-acting that has always been associated with games. The demand for greater participation, like the distrust of competition, seems to originate in a fear that unconscious impulses and fantasies will overwhelm us if we allow them expression.*

The Trivialization of Athletics What corrupts an athletic performance, as it does any other performance, is not professionalism or competition but a breakdown of the conventions surrounding the game. It is at this point that ritual, drama, and sports all degenerate into spectacle. Huizinga's analysis of the secularization of sport helps to clarify this point. In the degree to which athletic events lose the element of ritual and public festiv-

---

* In any case, the fashionable chatter about the need for greater participation in sports is entirely irrelevant to a discussion of their cultural significance. We might just as well assess the future of American music by counting the number of amateur musicians. In both cases, participation can be an eminently satisfying experience; but in neither case does the level of participation tell us much about the status of the art.

ity, according to Huizinga, they deteriorate into "trivial recreation and crude sensationalism." Even Huizinga misunderstands the cause of this development, however. It hardly lies in the "fatal shift towards over-seriousness." Huizinga himself, when he is writing about the theory of play rather than the collapse of "genuine play" in our own time, understands very well that play at its best is always serious; indeed that the essence of play lies in taking seriously activities that have no purpose, serve no utilitarian ends. He reminds us that "the majority of Greek contests were fought out in deadly earnest" and discusses under the category of play duels in which contestants fight to the death, water sports in which the object is to drown your opponent, and tournaments the training and preparation for which consume the athletes' entire existence.

The degradation of sport, then, consists not in its being taken too seriously but in its trivialization. Games derive their power from the investment of seemingly trivial activity with serious intent. By submitting without reservation to the rules and conventions of the game, the players (and the spectators too) cooperate in creating an illusion of reality. In this way the game becomes a representation of life, and play takes on the character of play-acting as well. In our time, games—sports in particular—are rapidly losing the quality of illusion. Uneasy in the presence of fantasy and illusion, our age seems to have resolved on the destruction of the harmless substitute gratifications that formerly provided charm and consolation. In the case of sports, the attack on illusion comes from players, promoters, and spectators alike. The players, eager to present themselves as entertainers (partly in order to justify their inflated salaries), deny the seriousness of sport. Promoters urge fans to become rabid partisans, even in sports formerly ruled by decorum, such as tennis. Television creates a new audience at home and makes "live" spectators into participants who mug for the camera and try to attract its attention by waving banners commenting on the action not on the field but in the press box. Sometimes fans interject themselves into the game more aggressively, by dashing onto the field or tearing up the stadium after an important victory.

The rising violence of crowds, routinely blamed on the violence of modern sports and the habit of taking them too seriously, arises, on the contrary, out of a failure to take them seriously enough—to abide by the conventions that should bind spectators as well as players. After the exciting match between Vilas and Connors, in the 1977 finals of the U.S. Open at Forest Hills, an unruly crowd spilled onto the court immediately after the last point and thus broke the hours of tension that should have been broken by the traditional handshake between the players themselves—incidentally allowing Connors to escape from the stadium without acknowledging his rival's victory or taking part in the closing ceremonies. Repeated transgressions of this kind undermine the illusion games create. To break the rules is to break the spell. The merging of players and spectators, here as in the theater, prevents the suspension of disbelief and thus destroys the representational value of organized athletics.

Imperialism and the Cult of the Strenuous Life   The recent history of sports is the history of their steady submission to the demands of everyday reality. The nineteenth-century bourgeoisie suppressed popular sports and festivals as part of their campaign to establish the reign of sobriety. Fairs and football, bullbaiting, cockfighting and boxing offended middle-class reformers because of their cruelty and because they blocked up public thoroughfares, disrupted the daily routine of business, distracted the people from their work, encouraged habits of idleness, extravagance, and insubordination, and gave rise to licentiousness and debauchery. In the name of rational enjoyment and the spirit of improvement, these reformers exhorted the laboring man to forsake his riotous public sports and wakes and to stay at his hearth, in the respectable comfort of the domestic circle. When exhortation failed, they resorted to political action. In early nineteenth-century England, they were opposed by a conservative coalition that crossed class lines, the commoners having been joined in the defense of their "immemorial" enjoyments by traditionalists among the gentry, especially the provincial gentry not yet infected with evangelical piety, sentimental humanitarianism, and the dogma of enterprise. "What would be the Consequence," they asked, "if all such Diversions were entirely banished? The common People seeing themselves cut off from all Hope of this enjoyment, would become dull and spiritless . . . : And not only so, but thro' the absolute Necessity of diverting themselves at Times, they would addict themselves rather to less warrantable Pleasures."

In the United States, the campaign against popular amusements, closely associated with the crusade against liquor and the movement for more strict observance of the Sabbath, took on the character of an ethnic as well as a class conflict. The working class, largely immigrant and Catholic, struggled, often in uneasy alliance with the "sporting element" and with "fashionable society," to defend its drink and its gambling against the assault of middle-class respectability. In mid-nineteenth-century New York, for example, the Whig party identified itself with enterprise, improvement, sobriety, piety, thrift, "steady habits," "book-learning," and strict observance of the Sabbath; while the Democrats, at once the party of rural reaction and the party of the immigrant masses, appealed among other constituencies to the sporting set—in Lee Benson's characterization, to lovers of "hard liquor, fast women and horses, and strong, racy language." The passage of blue laws, which rendered many popular amusements illegal and drove them underground, testifies to the political failure of the alliance between sport and fashion. Middle-class reformers enjoyed the advantage not merely of superior access to political power but of a burning sense of moral purpose. The spirit of early bourgeois society was deeply antithetical to play. Not only did games contribute nothing to capital accumulation, not only did they encourage gambling and reckless expenditure, but they contained an important element of pretense, illusion, mimicry, and make-believe. The bourgeois distrust of games reflected a deeper distrust of fancy, of histrionics, of elaborate dress and costume. Veblen, whose satire against middle-class society incorporated many of its own values, including its hatred of useless and unproductive play, condemned upper-class sports on the grounds of their "futility"; nor did he miss the connection between sport and histrionic display: "It is noticeable, for instance, that even very mild-mannered and matter-of-fact men who go out shooting are apt to carry an excess of arms and accoutrements in order to impress upon their own imagination the seriousness of their undertaking. These huntsmen are also prone to a histrionic, prancing gate and to an elaborate exaggeration of the motions, whether of stealth or of onslaught, involved in their deeds of exploit."

Veblen's satire against the "leisure class" miscarried; in America, where leisure found its only justification in the capacity to renew mind and body for work, the upper class refused to become a leisure class at all. Fearful of being displaced by the rising robber barons, it mastered the art of mass politics, asserted its control over the emerging industrial corporations, and embraced the ideal of the "strenuous life." Sports played an important part in this moral rehabilitation of the ruling class. Having suppressed or driven to the margins of society many of the recreations of the people, the *haute bourgeoisie* proceeded to adapt the games of its class enemies to its own purposes. In the private schools that prepared its sons for the responsibilities of business and empire, sports were placed at the service of character building. The new ideology of imperialism, both in England and in the United States, glorified the playing field as the source of qualities essential to national greatness and martial success. Far from cultivating sport as a form of display and splendid futility, the new national bourgeoisie—which at the end of the century replaced the local elites of an earlier day—celebrated precisely their capacity to instill the "will to win."*

At a time when popular preachers of success were redefining the work ethic to stress the element of competition, athletic com-

---

* The founder of the modern Olympics, Pierre de Coubertin, admired the English and attributed their imperial success to the character-building influence of athletics. "Is Arnoldism applicable in France?" he wondered. Philip Goodhart and Christopher Chataway, in their account of the rise of this new cult of sports, character development, and empire, make it clear that the new view of sports was a middle-class view that unfolded in opposition to both aristocratic and popular traditions. Whereas cricket, boxing, and horse racing had been identified with gambling, the middle class attempted to use sports to promote respectability, patriotism, and manly vigor.

petition took on new importance as a preparation for the battle of life. In a never-ending stream of books turned out to satisfy the rising demand for sports fiction, popular authors upheld Frank Merriwell and other athletes as models for American youth. The young man on the make, formerly advised to go into business at an early age and to master it from top to bottom, now learned the secret of success on the playing field, in fierce but friendly competition with his peers. Proponents of the new strenuousness insisted that athletics trained the courage and manliness that would promote not only individual success but upper-class ascendancy. "In most countries," according to Theodore Roosevelt, "the 'Bourgeoisie'—the moral, respectable, commercial, middle class—is looked upon with a certain contempt which is justified by their timidity and unwarlikeness. But the minute a middle class produces men like Hawkins and Frobisher on the seas, or men such as the average Union soldier in the civil war, it acquires the hearty respect of others which it merits." Roosevelt believed that sports would help to produce such leaders; at the same time he warned his sons not to regard football, boxing, riding, shooting, walking, and rowing as "the end to which *all* your energies must be devoted, or even the major portion of your energies."

Athletic competition also laid the foundations of national greatness, according to ideologues of the new imperialism. Walter Camp, whose tactical innovations at Yale brought into being the modern game of football, argued during World War I that the "grand do-or-die spirit that holds the attack on the one yard line was what made Chateau-Thierry." General Douglas MacArthur echoed these platitudes in World War II: "Upon the fields of friendly strife are sown the seeds which, on other days, on other fields, will bear the seeds of victory." By this time, however, the cult of the strenuous life was as obsolete as the explicit racism that once informed imperialist ideology. MacArthur himself was an anachronism in his flamboyance and his reactionary faith in clean living and high thinking. As American imperialism allied itself with more liberal values, the cult of "manly arts" survived as an important theme only in the ideology of the far right. In the sixties, reactionary ideologues extolled athletics as "a fortress that has held the wall against radical elements," in the words of the head football coach at Washington State University; or as Spiro Agnew put it, "one of the few bits of glue that holds society together." Max Rafferty, California superintendent of schools, defended the view that "a coach's job was to make men out of wet-behind-the-ears boys" and tried to reassure himself that "the love of clean, competitive sports is too deeply imbedded in the American matrix, too much a part of the warp and woof of our free people, ever to surrender to the burning-eyed, bearded draft-card-burners who hate and envy the athlete because he is something they can never be—a *man*."

Corporate Loyalty and Competition Left-wing critics of sport have made such statements the focus of their attack—another sample of the way in which cultural radicalism, posing as a revolutionary threat to the status quo, in reality confines its criticism to values already obsolescent and to patterns of American capitalism that have long ago been superseded. Left-wing criticism of sport provides one of the most vivid examples of the essentially conformist character of the "cultural revolution" with which it identifies itself. According to Paul Hoch, Jack Scott, Dave Meggyesy, and other cultural radicals, sport is a "mirror reflection" of society that indoctrinates the young with the dominant values. In America, organized athletics teach militarism, authoritarianism, racism, and sexism, thereby perpetuating the "false consciousness" of the masses. Sports serve as an "opiate" of the people, diverting the masses from their real problems with a "dream world" of glamour and excitement. They promote sexual rivalry among males—with "vestal virgins" leading the cheers from the sidelines—and thus prevent the proletariat from achieving revolutionary solidarity in the face of its oppressors. Competitive athletics force the "pleasure oriented id" to submit to "the hegemony of the repressed ego" in order to shore up the nuclear family—the basic form of authoritarianism—and to divert sexual energy into the service of the work ethic. For all these reasons, organized competition should give way to "intramural sports aimed at making everyone a player." If everyone "had fulfilling, creative jobs, they wouldn't need to look for the pseudo satisfactions of being fans."

This indictment, offensive in the first place in its assumption that cultural radicals understand the needs and interests of the masses better than the masses themselves, also offends every principle of social analysis. It confuses socialization with indoctrination and takes the most reactionary pronouncements at face value, as if athletes automatically imbibed the right-wing opinions of some of their mentors and spokesmen. Sport does play a role in socialization, but the lessons it teaches are not necessarily the ones that coaches and teachers of physical education seek to impart. The mirror theory of sport, like all reductionist interpretations of culture, makes no allowance for the autonomy of cultural traditions. In sport, these traditions come down from one generation of players to another, and although athletics do reflect social values, they can never be completely assimilated to those values. Indeed they resist assimilation more effectively than many other activities, since games learned in youth exert their own demands and inspire loyalty to the game itself, rather than to the programs ideologues seek to impose on them.

In any case, the reactionary values allegedly perpetuated by sport no longer reflect the dominant needs of American capitalism at all. If a society of consumers has no need of the Protestant work ethic, neither does it need the support of an ideology of racism, manliness, and martial valor. Racism once provided ideological support for colonialism and for backward labor systems based on slavery or peonage. These forms of exploitation rested on the direct, unconcealed appropriation of surplus value by the master class, which justified its domination on the grounds that the lower orders, disqualified for self-government by virtue of racial inferiority or lowly birth, needed and benefited from their masters' protection. Racism and paternalism were two sides of the same coin, the "white man's burden."

Capitalism has gradually substituted the free market for direct forms of domination. Within advanced countries, it has converted the serf or slave into a free worker. It has also revolutionized colonial relations. Instead of imposing military rule on their colonies, industrial nations now govern through client states, ostensibly sovereign, which keep order in their stead. Such changes have made both racism and the ideology of martial conquest, appropriate to an earlier age of empire building, increasingly anachronistic.

In the United States, the transition from Theodore Roosevelt's jingoism to Woodrow Wilson's liberal neocolonialism already spelled the obsolescence of the older ideology of Anglo-Saxon supremacy. The collapse of "scientific" racism in the twenties and thirties, the integration of the armed forces in the Korean War, and the attack on racial segregation in the fifties and sixties marked a deep-seated ideological shift, rooted in changing modes of exploitation. Of course the relation between material life and ideology is never simple, least of all in the case of an ideology as irrational as racism. In any case, de facto racism continues to flourish without a racial ideology. Indeed it is precisely the collapse of de jure racism in the South and the discovery of de facto racism in the North, sheltering under the ideology of tolerance, that distinguishes the most recent phase of the race problem in the United States. The ideology of white supremacy, however, no longer appears to serve any important social function.

"Martial machismo," as Paul Hoch calls it, is equally irrelevant to an age of technological warfare. The military ethic, moreover, required the athlete or soldier to submit to a common discipline, to sacrifice himself for the good of a higher cause; and it thus suffers the general erosion of organizational allegiance in a society where men and women perceive the organization as an enemy, even the organizations in which they work. In sport as in business, group loyalties no longer temper competition. Individuals seek to exploit the organization to their own advantage and to advance their interests not merely against rival organizations but against their own teammates. The team player, like the organization man, has become an anachronism. The contention that sport fosters an unhealthy spirit of competition needs to be refined. Insofar as sport measures individual achievement against abstract standards of excellence, encourages cooperation among teammates, and enforces rules of fair play, it gives expression to the competitive urge but also helps to discipline it. The crisis of athletic competition today derives not from the persistence of a martial ethic, the cult of victory, or the obsession with achievement (which some critics still see as the "dominant sports creed"), but from the collapse of conventions that formerly restrained rivalry even as they glorified it.

George Allen's dictum—"winning isn't the most important thing, it's the only thing"—represents a last-ditch defense of team spirit in the face of its deterioration. Such pronouncements, usually cited as evidence of an exaggerated stress on competition, may help to keep it within bounds. The intrusion of the market into every corner of the sporting scene, however, re-creates all the antagonisms characteristic of late capitalist society. With the free-agent draft, the escalation of athletic salaries, and the instantaneous stardom conferred by the media on athletic success, competition among rival organizations has degenerated into a free-for-all. It is no wonder that criticism of competition has emerged as the principal theme in the rising criticism of sport. People today associate rivalry with boundless aggression and find it difficult to conceive of competition that does not lead directly to thoughts of murder. Kohut writes of one of his patients: "Even as a child he had become afraid of emotionally cathected competitiveness for fear of the underlying (near delusional) fantasies of exerting absolute, sadistic power." Herbert Hendin says of the students he analyzed and interviewed at Columbia that "they could conceive of no competition that did not result in someone's annihilation."

The prevalence of such fears helps to explain why Americans have become uneasy about rivalry unless it is accompanied by the disclaimer that winning and losing don't matter or that games are unimportant anyway. The identification of competition with the wish to annihilate opponents inspires Dorcas Butt's accusation that competitive sports have made us a nation of militarists, fascists, and predatory egoists; have encouraged "poor sportsmanship" in all social relations; and have extinguished cooperation and compassion. It inspires Paul Hoch's plaintive cry: "Why bother scoring or winning the game at all? Wouldn't it be enough just to enjoy it?" In all likelihood, the same misgivings lie behind Jack Scott's desire to find a proper "balance" between competition and cooperation. "Competitive sport is in trouble," Scott says, "when the balance is tipped toward competition." An athlete should strive for accomplishment, according to Scott, but not "at the expense of himself or others." These words express a belief that excellence usually *is* achieved at the expense of others, that competition tends to become murderous unless balanced by cooperation, and that athletic rivalry, if it gets out of hand, gives expression to the inner rage contemporary man desperately seeks to stifle.

Bureaucracy and "Teamwork" The prevalent mode of social interaction today is antagonistic cooperation (as David Riesman called it in *The Lonely Crowd*), in which a cult of teamwork conceals the struggle for survival within bureaucratic organizations. In sport, the rivalry among teams, now drained of its capacity to call up local or regional loyalties, reduces itself (like the rivalry among business corporations) to a struggle for shares of the market. The professional athlete does not care whether his team wins or loses (since losers share in the pot), as long as it stays in business.

The professionalization of sport and the extension of professional athletics into the universities, which now serve as a farm system for the major leagues, have undercut the old "school spirit" and have given rise among athletes to a thoroughly businesslike approach to their craft. Athletes now regard the inspirational appeals of old-fashioned coaches with amused cynicism; nor do they readily submit to authoritarian discipline. The proliferation of franchises and the frequency with which they move from one locality to another undermines local loyalties, both among participants and spectators, and discourages attempts to model "team spirit" on patriotism. In a bureaucratic society, all forms of corporate loyalty lose their force, and although athletes still make a point of subordinating their own achievements to those of the team, they do so in order to promote easy relations with their colleagues, not because the team as a corporate entity transcends individual interests. On the contrary, the athlete as a professional entertainer seeks above all to further his own interests and willingly sells his services to the highest bidder. The better athletes become media celebrities and supplement their salaries with endorsements that often exceed the salaries themselves.

All these developments make it difficult to think of the athlete as a local or national hero, as the representative of his class or race, or in any way as the embodiment of some larger corporate unit. Only the recognition that sports have come to serve as a form of entertainment justifies the salaries paid to star athletes and their prominence in the media. As Howard Cosell has candidly acknowledged, sports can no longer be sold to the public as "just sports or as religion. . . . Sports aren't life and death. They're entertainment." Even as the television audience demands the presentation of sports as a form of spectacle, however, the widespread resentment of star athletes among followers of sport—a resentment directed against the inflated salaries negotiated by their agents and against their willingness to become hucksters, promoters, and celebrities—indicates the persistence of a need to believe that sport represents something more than entertainment, something that, though neither life nor death in itself, retains some lingering capacity to dramatize and clarify those experiences.

Sports and the Entertainment Industry

The secularization of sport, which began as soon as athletics were pressed into the cause of patriotism and character building, became complete only when sport became an object of mass consumption. The first stage in this process was the establishment of big-time athletics in the university and their spread from the Ivy League to the large public and private schools, thence downward into the high schools. The bureaucratization of the business career, which placed unprecedented emphasis on competition and the will to win, stimulated the growth of sports in another way. It made the acquisition of educational credentials essential to a business or professional career and thus created in large numbers a new kind of student, utterly indifferent to higher learning but forced to undergo it for purely economic reasons. Large-scale athletic programs helped colleges to attract such students, in competitive bidding for enrollments, and to entertain them once they enrolled. In the closing years of the nineteenth century, according to Donald Meyer, the development of an "alumni culture" centering on clubs, fraternities, alumni offices, money drives, homecoming ceremonies, and football, grew out of the colleges' need not only to raise money in large amounts but to attract "a clientele for whom the classroom had no real meaning but who were by no means ready to send their sons out into the world at age eighteen." At Notre Dame, as Frederick Rudolph has pointed out, "intercollegiate athletics . . . were consciously developed in the 1890s as an agency of student recruitment." As early as 1878, President McCosh of Princeton wrote to an alumnus in Kentucky: "You will confer a great favor on us if you will get . . . the college noticed in the Louisville papers. . . . We must persevere in our efforts to get students from your region. . . . Mr. Brand Ballard has won us great reputation as captain of the football team which has beaten both Harvard and Yale."

In order to accommodate the growing hordes of spectators, the colleges and universities, sometimes aided by local business interests, built lavish athletic facilities—enormous field houses, football stadiums in the pretentious imperial style of the early twentieth century. Growing investment in sports led in turn to a growing need to maintain a winning record: a new concern with system, efficiency, and the elimination of risk. Camp's innovations at Yale emphasized drill, discipline, teamwork. As in industry, the attempt to coordinate the movements of many men created a demand for "scientific management" and for the expansion of managerial personnel. In many sports, trainers, coaches, doctors, and public relations experts soon outnumbered the players. The accumulation of elaborate statistical records arose from management's attempt to reduce winning to a routine, to measure efficient performance. The athletic contest itself, surrounded by a vast apparatus of information and promotion, now appeared almost incidental to the expensive preparation required to stage it.

The rise of a new kind of journalism—the yellow journalism pioneered by Hearst and Pulitzer, which sold sensations instead of reporting news—helped to professionalize amateur athletics, to assimilate sport to promotion, and to make professional athletics into a major industry. Until the twenties, professional sports, where they existed at all, attracted little of the public attention lavished on college football. Even baseball, the oldest and most highly organized of professional sports, suffered from faintly unsavory associations—its appeal to the working class and the sporting crowd, its rural origins. When a Yale alumnus complained to Walter Camp about the overemphasis on football, he could think of no better way of dramatizing the danger than to cite the example of baseball: "The language and scenes which are too often witnessed [in football games] are such as to degrade the college student and bring him down to a par with or even lower than the average professional baseball player."

The World Series scandal of 1919 confirmed baseball's bad reputation, but it also set in motion the reforms of Kenesaw Mountain Landis, the new commissioner brought in by the owners to clean up the game and give it a better public image. Landis's régime, the success of the eminently respectable and efficient New York Yankees, and the idolization of Babe Ruth soon made professional baseball "America's number-one pastime." Ruth became the first modern athlete to be sold to the public as much for his color, personality, and crowd appeal as for his remarkable abilities. His press agent, Christy Walsh, developer of a syndicate of ghost writers who sold books and articles under the names of sports heroes, arranged barnstorming tours, endorsements, and movie roles and thus helped to make the "Sultan of Swat" a national celebrity.

In the quarter-century following World War II, entrepreneurs extended the techniques of mass promotion first perfected in the marketing of college football and professional baseball to other professional sports, notably hockey, basketball, and football. Television did for these games what mass journalism and radio had done for baseball, elevating them to new heights of popularity and at the same time reducing them to entertainment. In his recent study of sport, Michael Novak notes that television has lowered the quality of sports reporting, freeing announcers from the need to describe the course of play and encouraging them instead to adopt the style of professional entertainers. The invasion of sport by the "entertainment ethic," according to Novak, breaks down the boundaries between the ritual world of play and the sordid reality from which it is designed to provide escape. Broadcasters like Howard Cosell, who embody the "virulent passion for debunking in the land," mistakenly import critical standards more appropriate to political reporting into the coverage of sports. Newspapers report the "business side" of sports on the sports page, instead of confining it to the business section where it belongs. "It is important," Novak argues, ". . . to keep sports as insulated as we can from business, entertainment, politics, and even gossip. . . . The preservation of parts of life not drawn up into politics and work is essential for the human spirit." Especially when politics has become "a brutal, ugly business" and work (not sport) the opiate of the people, athletics alone, in Novak's view, offer a glimpse of the "real thing." They take place in a "world outside of time," which must be sealed off from the surrounding corruption.

Leisure as Escape   The anguished outcry of the true fan, who brings to sports a proper sense of awe only to find them corrupted from within by the spread of the "entertainment ethic," sheds more light on the degradation of sports than the strictures of left-wing critics, who wish to abolish competition, emphasize the value of sports as health-giving exercise, and promote a more "co-operative" conception of athletics—in other words, to make sports an instrument of personal and social therapy. Novak's analysis, however, minimizes the extent of the problem and misconstrues its cause. In a society dominated by the production and consumption of images, no part of life can long remain immune from the invasion of spectacle. Nor can this invasion be blamed on the spirit of debunking. It arises, in a paradoxical fashion, precisely out of the attempt to set up a separate sphere of leisure uncontaminated by the world of work and politics. Play has always, by its very nature, set itself off from workaday life; yet it retains an organic connection with the life of the community, by virtue of its capacity to dramatize reality and to offer a convincing representation of the community's values. The ancient connections between games, ritual, and public festivity suggest that although games take place within arbitrary boundaries, they are nevertheless rooted in shared traditions to which they give objective expression. Games and athletic contests offer a dramatic commentary on reality rather than an escape from it—a heightened reenactment of communal traditions, not a repudiation of them. It is only when games and sports come to be valued purely as a form of escape that they lose the capacity to provide this escape.

The appearance in history of an escapist conception of "leisure" coincides with the organization of leisure as an extension of commodity production. The same forces that have organized the factory and the office have organized leisure as well, reducing it to an appendage of industry. Accordingly sport has come to be dominated not so much by an undue emphasis on winning as by the desperate urge to avoid defeat. Coaches, not quarterbacks, call the plays, and the managerial apparatus makes every effort to eliminate the risk and uncertainty that contribute so centrally to the ritual and dramatic success of any contest. When sports can no longer be played with appropriate abandon, they lose the capacity to raise the spirits of players and spectators, to transport them into a higher realm of existence. Prudence, caution, and calculation, so prominent in everyday life but so inimical to the spirit of games, come to shape sports as they shape everything else.

While he deplores the subordination of sport to entertainment, Novak takes for granted the separation of work and leisure that gives rise in the first place to this invasion of play by the standards of the workaday world. He does not see that the degradation of play originates in the degradation of work, which creates both the need and the opportunity for commercialized "recreation." As Huizinga has shown, it is precisely when the play element disappears from law, statecraft, and other cultural forms that men turn to play not to witness a dramatic reenactment of their common life but to find diversion and sensation. At that point, games and sport, far from taking themselves too seriously, as Huizinga mistakenly concluded, become, on the contrary, a "thing of no consequence." As Edgar Wind shows in his analysis of modern art, the trivialization of art was already implicit in the modernist exaltation of art, which assumed that "the experience of art will be more intense if it pulls the spectator away from his ordinary habits and preoccupations." The modernist esthetic guarantees the socially marginal status of art at the same time that it opens art to the invasion of commercialized esthetic fashion—a process that culminates, by a curious but inexorable logic, in the postmodernist demand for the abolition of art and its assimilation to reality.

The development of sport follows the same pattern. The attempt to create a separate realm of pure play, totally isolated from work, gives rise to its opposite—the insistence, in Cosell's words, that "sports are not separate and apart from life, a special 'Wonderland' where everything is pure and sacred and above criticism," but a business subject to the same standards and open to the same scrutiny as any other. The positions represented by Novak and Cosell are symbiotically related and arise out of the same historical development: the emergence of the spectacle as the dominant form of cultural expression. What began as an attempt to invest sport with religious significance, indeed to make it into a surrogate religion in its own right, ends with the demystification of sport, the assimilation of sport to show business.

VI

Schooling and the New Illiteracy

The Spread of Stupefaction   The extension of formal schooling to groups formerly excluded from it is one of the most striking developments in modern history. The experience of western Europe and the United States in the last 200 years suggests that mass education provides one of the principal foundations of economic development, and modernizers throughout the rest of the world have tried to duplicate the achievement of the West in bringing education to the masses. Faith in the wonder-working powers of education has proved to be one of the most durable components of liberal ideology, easily assimilated by ideologies hostile to the rest of liberalism. Yet the democratization of education has accomplished little to justify this faith. It has neither improved popular understanding of modern society, raised the quality of popular culture, nor reduced the gap between wealth and poverty, which remains as wide as ever. On the other hand, it has contributed to the decline of critical thought and the erosion of intellectual standards, forcing us to consider the possibility that mass education, as conservatives have argued all along, is intrinsically incompatible with the maintenance of educational quality.

Conservative and radical critics of the educational system agree on a central contention—that intellectual standards are inherently elitist. Radicals attack the school system on the grounds that it perpetuates an obsolescent literary culture, the "linear" culture of the written word, and imposes it on the masses. Efforts to uphold standards of literary expression and logical coherence, according to this view, serve only to keep the masses in their place. Educational radicalism unwittingly echoes the conservatism which assumes that common people cannot hope to master

125

the art of reasoning or achieve clarity of expression and that forcibly exposing them to high culture ends, inevitably, in abandonment of academic rigor. Cultural radicals take the same position, in effect, but use it to justify lower standards as a step toward the cultural emancipation of the oppressed.

Forced to choose between these positions, those who believe in critical thought as an indispensable precondition of social or political progress might well renounce the very possibility of progress and side with the conservatives, who at least recognize intellectual deterioration when they see it and do not attempt to disguise it as liberation. But the conservative interpretation of the collapse of standards is much too simple. Standards are deteriorating even at Harvard, Yale, and Princeton, which can hardly be described as institutions of mass education. A faculty committee at Harvard reports, "The Harvard faculty does not care about teaching." According to a study of general education at Columbia, teachers have lost "their common sense of what kind of ignorance is unacceptable." As a result, "Students reading Rabelais's description of civil disturbances ascribe them to the French Revolution. A class of twenty-five had never heard of the Oedipus complex—or of Oedipus. Only one student in a class of fifteen could date the Russian Revolution within a decade."

In any case, the decline of literacy cannot be attributed solely to the failure of the educational system. Schools in modern society serve largely to train people for work, but most of the available jobs, even in the higher economic range, no longer require a high level of technical or intellectual competence. Indeed most jobs consist so largely of routine, and depend so little on enterprise and resourcefulness, that anyone who successfully completes a given course of study soon finds himself "overqualified" for most of the positions available. The deterioration of the educational system thus reflects the waning social demand for initiative, enterprise, and the compulsion to achieve.

Contrary to the pronouncements of most educational theorists and their allies in the social sciences, advanced industrial society no longer rests on a population primed for achievement. It requires instead a stupefied population, resigned to work that is trivial and shoddily performed, predisposed to seek its satisfaction in the time set aside for leisure. Such at least is the belief held, though not always avowed, by those who wield most of the power in America. "The crisis of our culture," as R. P. Blackmur noted in 1954, "rises from the false belief that our society requires only enough mind to create and tend the machines together with enough of the new illiteracy for other machines—those of our mass media—to exploit. This is perhaps the form of society most expensive and wasteful in human talent mankind has yet thrown off." Blackmur's analysis has gained cogency with the passage of time. Writing on the eve of an unprecedented expansion of academic facilities, he saw beyond the academic boom, predicted the academic depression of the seventies, and connected this depression to the surplus of talent endemic to modern industrial society. "The existing surplus of talent in the academic proletariat in Western Europe [i.e., the growing number of people turned out by institutions of higher learning who find that 'there is nothing serious for them to do with their training'] is only an advance form of the surplus which will appear in 1970, at latest, in America."

Not only has the American economy outlived the need for large numbers of highly trained workers—a fact to which the rising levels of unemployment among Ph.D.s and college graduates eloquently attest—but political power no longer seeks to surround itself with philosophical justifications. Even patriotism, the inculcation of which once constituted one of the school's most important tasks, has become superfluous to the defense of the status quo. The deterioration of training in history, government, and philosophy reflects their increasingly marginal status as part of the apparatus of social control.

The Atrophy of Competence   Sweeping social changes, reflected in academic practice, thus underlie the deterioration of the school system and the consequent spread of stupidity. Mass education, which began as a promising attempt to democratize the higher culture of the privileged classes, has ended by stupefying the privileged themselves. Modern society has achieved unprecedented rates of formal literacy, but at the same time it has produced new forms of illiteracy. People increasingly find themselves unable to use language with ease and precision, to recall the basic facts of their country's history, to make logical deductions, to understand any but the most rudimentary written texts, or even to grasp their constitutional rights. The conversion of popular traditions of self-reliance into esoteric knowledge administered by experts encourages a belief that ordinary competence in almost any field, even the art of self-government, lies beyond reach of the layman. Standards of teaching decline, the victims of poor teaching come to share the experts' low opinion of their capacities, and the teaching profession complains of unteachable students.

One study after another documents the steady decline of basic intellectual skills. In 1966, high school seniors scored an average of 467 points on the verbal section of the Scholastic Aptitude Test—hardly cause for celebration. Ten years later they scored only 429. Scores on the mathematical part of the test dropped from an average of 495 to 470. Many publishers have simplified textbooks in response to complaints that a new generation of students, raised on television, movies, and what one educator calls "the antilanguage assumptions of our culture," find existing textbooks unintelligible. The decline of intellectual competence cannot be accounted for, as some observers would have it, on the reactionary assumption that more students from minority- and low-income groups are taking tests, going to college, and thus dragging down the scores. The proportion of these students has remained unchanged over the last ten years; meanwhile the decline of academic achievement has extended to elite schools as well as to community colleges, junior colleges, and public high schools. Every year, 40 to 60 percent of the students at the University of California find themselves required to enroll in remedial English. At Stanford, only a quarter of the students in the class entering in 1975 managed to pass the university's English placement test, even though these students had achieved high scores on the Scholastic Aptitude Test. At private high schools, average test scores in math and English dropped by eight and ten points in a single year, between 1974 and 1975.

Such studies merely confirm what everyone knows who has taught high school or college students in the last ten or fifteen years. Even at the top schools in the country, students' ability to use their own language, their knowledge of foreign languages, their reasoning powers, their stock of historical information, and their knowledge of the major literary classics have all undergone a relentless process of deterioration. According to the dean of the University of Oregon, "They don't read as much, they haven't been given enough practice in thinking and composition. The net result is that when you walk into a classroom you can't expect as much from a student as you could say fifteen years ago. That is a fact of professional life." A professor of psychology at UCLA reports "almost universal faculty concern about composition, the very poor essays and the tremendous amount of students who need remedial work." An English professor at Ohio State has observed "an increase in complaints in the last three years," among faculty throughout the university, "about the functional illiteracy of lower division students." Nor is this functional illiteracy confined to freshmen and sophomores. Scores on the Graduate Record Examination have also declined.

In view of all this evidence, it should not surprise us that Americans are becoming increasingly ignorant about their own rights as citizens. Forty-seven percent of a sample of seventeen-year-olds, on the verge of becoming eligible voters, did not know the simple fact, according to a recent survey, that each state elects two United States senators. More than half of the seventeen-year-olds and more than three-fourths of the thirteen-year-olds in the survey could not explain the significance of the Fifth Amendment protection against self-incrimination. One of every eight seventeen-year-olds believed that the president does not have to obey the law, and one of every two students at both ages believed that the president appoints members of Congress. Half the thirteen-year-olds thought that the law forbids anyone to start a new political party. Hardly any of the students in either group could explain what steps the Constitution entitles Congress to take in order to stop a president from fighting a war without congressional approval. If an educated electorate is the best defense against arbitrary government, the survival of political freedom appears uncertain at best. Large numbers of Americans now believe that the Constitution sanctions arbitrary executive power, and recent political history, with its steady growth of presidential power, can only have reinforced such an assumption. What has become of the early republican dream? Universal public education, instead of creating a community of self-governing citizens, has contributed to the spread of intellectual torpor and political passivity. The reasons for this anomaly lie in the peculiar historical conditions in which the modern educational system developed.

Historical Origins of the Modern School System   The democratization of education took place for two reasons: to provide the modern state with enlightened citizens and to train an efficient work force. In the nineteenth century, political considerations predominated; educational reform went hand in hand with the broadening of the suffrage, the disestablishment of religion, and the establishment of republican institutions. Like these other innovations, the common school system grew out of the democratic revolution, which created a new type of citizenship based on equality before the law and limited government—a "government of laws, not men." The model citizen of early republican theory knew what his rights were and defended them from infringement by his fellow citizens and by the state. He could not be fooled by demagogues or overawed by the learned obfuscations of professional wise men. Appeals to authority left him unimpressed. Always on the alert for forgery, he had, moreover, enough worldly wisdom about men's motives, understanding of the principles of critical reasoning, and skill in the use of language to detect intellectual fraud in whatever form it presented itself.

Training such exemplary citizens obviously required a new system of education—though far more important, in the minds of early republican theorists, was the consideration that it presupposed a nation of small-property holders and a fairly equal distribution of wealth. Republican education had as its object, in Jefferson's words, "to diffuse knowledge more generally through the mass of the people." It stressed what the eighteenth century would have called useful knowledge, especially ancient and modern history, which Jefferson hoped might teach the young to judge "the actions and designs of men, to know ambition under every disguise it may assume; and knowing it, to defeat its views."

The contrast between early American society and politically more backward states clarifies the conditions republican education was designed to overcome. In France, for example, even the revolution did not put an end to the vegetative stupor of the masses, which social reformers saw as a major obstacle to further progress. In their eyes, the rural population remained not only illiterate but irrationally attached to traditional ways, steeped in superstition. Michael Chevalier ended his study of American society, written in the 1830s, with a series of observations that vividly crystallizes the issue. The progress of the human race, according to Chevalier, could be conceived as a progressive "initiation" of the masses into the intellectual discoveries, the "conquests of the human mind," that began with the Reformation. In America "the great discoveries of science and art" had already been "exposed to the vulgar gaze and placed within the reach of all." France, on the other hand, especially the French countryside, presented the depressing picture of age-old ignorance.

Examine the population of our rural districts, sound the brains of our peasants, and you will find that the spring of all their actions is a confused medley of biblical parables with the legends of gross superstition. Try the same operation on an American farmer and you will find that the great scriptural traditions are harmoniously combined in his mind with the principles of modern science as taught by Bacon and Descartes, with the doctrine of moral and religious independence proclaimed by Luther, and with the still more recent notions of political freedom. He is one of the initiated.

After commenting on the superior sexual morality and more settled domestic habits of the American farmer, Chevalier went on to note that in political affairs as well, "the American mass has reached a much higher degree of initiation than the European mass, for it does not need to be governed; every man here [in the United States] has in himself the principle of self-government in a much higher degree and is more fit to take a part in public affairs." The difference extended to economic life as well, according to Chevalier: the American mechanic was a better workman, largely because he was self-reliant and "full of self-respect."

From Industrial Discipline to Manpower Selection Ironically, these observations appeared at the very moment European conditions were about to reproduce themselves in the United States, in the form of a mass migration of European workers and peasants. Beginning with the Irish in the 1840s, the immigration of politically backward elements, as they were commonly regarded, sharpened the fear, already an undercurrent in American social thought, that the United States would regress to a hated old-world pattern of class conflict, hereditary poverty, and political despotism. In the climate of such anxieties, educational reformers like Horace Mann and Henry Barnard won a hearing for proposals to set up a national system of compulsory education and to broaden the curriculum beyond the purely intellectual training envisioned by earlier reformers. From this time on, the problem of acculturating the immigrant population never wandered far from the center of the American educational enterprise. "Americanization" became the specifically American model for education conceived as initiation into modern culture. Because the task of initiation presented itself in this form, the American school, in contrast to the European, placed heavy emphasis on the nonacademic side of the curriculum. The democratic aim of bringing the fruits of modern culture to the masses gave way in practice to a concern with education as a form of social control. Even in the 1830s, the common school already commended itself, in part, as a means of subtly discouraging the masses from aspiring to "culture."

In soliciting public support, nineteenth-century reformers appealed to the belief that schools under proper professional leadership would facilitate social mobility and the gradual eradication of poverty or, alternately, to the quite different hope that the system would promote order by discouraging ambitions incommensurate with the students' stations and prospects. The latter argument probably appealed more strongly to wealthy benefactors and public officials than the first. Both led to the same conclusions: that the best interests of society lay in a system of universal compulsory education which would isolate the student from other influences and subject him to a regular regimen, and that the system must be operated by a centralized professional bureaucracy.

The differences between American and European systems of public education should not be exaggerated. European systems too gave much attention to moral instruction. Both served the same general purposes—to train self-reliant citizens, to diffuse the elementary principles of modern culture, to overcome provincial backwardness, and also—what was not always easy to distinguish from these objectives—to unify modern nations by eliminating linguistic and regional variations, inculcating patriotism, and instilling loyalty to the principles of '89, '76, the Glorious Revolution, or some other event symbolizing the birth of the state. Both systems from the beginning thus combined democratic and undemocratic features; as the political objectives of public education gave way to a growing preoccupation with industrial objectives, the undemocratic features became more and more pronounced.

At first, nineteenth-century students of society saw a close connection between political and economic "initiation." They conceived of industrial training as an extension of the training required for republican citizenship. The same habits of mind that made good citizens—self-reliance, self-respect, versatility—appeared to be essential to good workmanship. By bringing modern culture to the masses, the school system would also inculcate industrial discipline in the broadest sense of the term. To speak of industrial discipline today has unfortunate connotations of regimentation, the subordination of men to machines, the substitution of the laws of the marketplace for the laws of nature. What industrial discipline meant to an earlier and now almost extinct democratic tradition was best expressed by one of its last exponents, Veblen, who believed that modern industry nourished in the producing classes "iconoclastic" habits of mind—skepticism, a critical attitude toward authority and tradition, a "materialistic" and scientific outlook, and a development of the "instinct of work-manship" beyond anything possible in earlier forms of society. An efficient labor force, from the point of view of this tradition, did not imply docile and subservient workers; on the contrary, it implied a labor force, in Chevalier's terms, that did not need to be governed.

During the period around the turn of the century—the same period in which "Americanization" became the semiofficial slogan of American educators—a second and much cruder form of in-dustrial education, stressing manual training and vocational edu-cation, crept into the public schools under the watchword of "efficiency." According to educators and industrial spokesmen, the schools had a responsibility to instruct the lower orders in the manual skills that would make them productive workers and use-ful citizens. George Eastman, after complaining that black people were "densely ignorant," concluded that "the only hope of the Negro race and the settlement of this problem is through proper education of the Hampton-Tuskegee type, which is directed al-most wholly toward making them useful citizens through educa-tion on industrial lines." In 1908, a group of businessmen urged the National Education Association to introduce more courses in commercial and industrial subjects into the elementary cur-riculum. Seventy percent of the pupils in elementary schools, they pointed out, never went on to high school, and the best training for these students was "utilitarian first, and cultural af-terward."

Manpower training bore the same relation to "industrial dis-cipline" in Veblen's sense that political indoctrination—"training for citizenship," as it now came to be called—bore to political "initiation." Both innovations represented debased versions of democratic practice, attractive to those who resented what they regarded as the school's overemphasis on "culture." Both reforms belonged to a broader movement to make the school more "ef-ficient." In response to a public outcry about the high rate of aca-demic failure in the schools, an outcry that swelled to a chorus around 1910, educators introduced systems of testing and track-ing that had the effect of relegating academic "failures" to pro-grams of manual and industrial training (where many of them continued to fail). Protests against genteel culture, overemphasis on academic subjects, "gentleman's education," and the "cultured ease in the classroom, of drawing room quiet and refinement," frequently coincided with an insistence that higher education and "culture" should not in any case be "desired by the mob." The progressive period thus saw the full flowering of the school as a major agency of industrial recruitment, selection, and certification. Of the three ways in which the schools train an efficient labor force—inculcation of industrial discipline, vocational training, and selection—the third henceforth became by far the most important: "fitting the man to the job," in the jargon of educational reformers at the time of World War I.

From Americanization to "Life Adjustment"   Even in the twentieth century, however, the school system by no means had a universally demoralizing effect on those who passed through it. Down into the thirties and forties, those groups with a cultural tradition that valued formal learning, notably the Jews, managed to make use of the system, even a system increasingly geared to the purpose of industrial recruitment, as a lever of collective self-advancement. Under favorable conditions, the school's emphasis on "Americanism" and its promotion of universal norms had a liberating effect, helping individuals to make a fruitful break with parochial ethnic traditions. Recent criticism of the school, which sometimes equates mass education with a rigid form of indoctrination and totalitarian conditioning, partakes of the prevailing sentimentality about ethnicity. It deplores the distintegration of folk culture and pays no attention to the degree to which disintegration was often the price paid for intellectual emancipation. When Randolph Bourne (a favorite of radical historians, who believe his critique of education anticipates their own) extolled cultural pluralism, he had in mind as a model not the intact immigrant cultures of the ghettos but the culture of the twice-uprooted immigrant intellectuals he met at Columbia. One of those immigrant intellectuals, Mary Antin, wrote an account of her schooling that shows how Americanization could lead, in some cases, to a new sense of dignity. Learning about George Washington taught her, she says, "that I was more nobly related than I had ever supposed. I had relatives and friends who were notable people by the old standards,—I had never been ashamed of my family,—but this George Washington, who died long before I was born, was like a king in greatness, and he and I were Fellow Citizens." More recently, Norman Podhoretz has described his introduction to literary culture, in the 1940s, at the hands of a teacher who exemplified all the limitations of the genteel sensibility yet conveyed to her student an indispensable sense of the world beyond his experience.

The reforms of the progressive period gave rise to an unimaginative educational bureaucracy and a system of industrial recruitment that eventually undermined the ability of the school to serve as an agency of intellectual emancipation; but it was a long time before the bad effects of these changes became pervasive. As educators convinced themselves, with the help of intelligence tests, that most of the students could never master an academic curriculum, they found it necessary to devise other ways of keeping them busy. The introduction of courses in homemaking, health, citizenship, and other nonacademic subjects, together with the proliferation of athletic programs and extracurricular activities, reflected the dogma that schools had to educate the "whole child"; but it also reflected the practical need to fill up the students' time and to keep them reasonably contented. Such programs spread rapidly through the public schools in the twenties and thirties, often justified by the need to make "good citizenship," in the words of the dean of Teachers College, "a dominant aim of the American public school." The Lynds reported in Middletown that vocational education, bookkeeping, stenography, "commercial English," home economics, physical education, and extracurricular activities—skills and pastimes formerly centered in the home or taught by means of apprenticeship—occupied much of the time formerly devoted to Greek, Latin, history, grammar, and rhetoric.

Educational reformers brought the family's work into the school in the hope of making the school an instrument not merely of education but of socialization as well. Dimly recognizing that in many areas—precisely those that lie outside the formal curriculum—experience teaches more than books, educators then proceeded to do away with books: to import experience into the academic setting, to re-create the modes of learning formerly associated with the family, to encourage students to "learn by doing." Having imposed a deadening academic curriculum on every phase of the child's experience, they demanded, too late, that education be brought into contact with "life." Two educators wrote in 1934, without any awareness of the irony of their prescriptions:

By bringing into the school those who are practical doers from the world . . . to supplement and stimulate the teaching of those whose training has been in the normal school, education can be vitalized. How can we expect an individual to achieve "mastery of his tools" if he is never exposed to the example of mastery? By some such means education may be brought much more closely in touch with life and may approximate the advantages of the practical education of an earlier day.

In practice, this advice dictated a continuing search for undemanding programs of study. The search reached new heights in the forties, when the educational establishment introduced another in a series of panaceas—education for "life adjustment." In Illinois, proponents of life adjustment urged schools to give more attention to such "problems of high school youth" as "improving one's personal appearance," "selecting a family dentist," and "developing and maintaining wholesome boy-girl relationships." Elsewhere, observers reported hearing classroom discussions on such topics as "How can I be popular?" "Why are my parents so strict?" "Should I follow my crowd or obey my parents' wishes?"

Given the underlying American commitment to the integral high school—the refusal to specialize college preparation and technical training in separate institutions—make-work programs, athletics, extracurricular activities, and the pervasive student emphasis on sociability corrupted not merely the vocational and life-adjustment programs but the college preparatory course as well. The concept of industrial discipline deteriorated to the point where intellectual and even manual training became incidental to the inculcation of orderly habits. According to a report of the National Manpower Council issued in 1954, "The school enforces a regular schedule by setting hours of arrival and attendance; assigns tasks that must be completed; rewards diligence, responsibility, and ability; corrects carelessness and ineptness; encourages ambition." The more closely education approximated this empty ideal, however, the more effectively it discouraged ambition of any sort, except perhaps the ambition to get away from school by one expedient or another. By draining the curriculum not merely of academic but of practical content, educators deprived students of challenging work and forced them to find other means of filling time which the law nevertheless required them to spend in school. The compulsive sociability of high school students, formerly concentrated on what Willard Waller called the "rating and dating complex," more recently on drugs, arose in part from sheer boredom with the prescribed course of study. Though teachers and administrators often deplored their students' obsession with popularity, they themselves encouraged it by giving so much attention to the need to get along with others—to master the cooperative habits considered indispensable to industrial success.

Basic Education versus National Defense Education　By the fifties, the trivialization of the high school curriculum had become unmistakable. Two groups of critics emerged. The first, led by Arthur Bestor, Albert Lynd, Mortimer Smith, and the Council for Basic Education, attacked the imperialistic expansion of the school system. They denied that the school should socialize the "whole child," assume the functions of the family and the church, or serve as an agency of industrial recruitment. They argued that the school's only responsibility was to provide basic intellectual training and to extend this training to everyone. They deplored antiintellectualism but also condemned the tracking system. According to Smith, educators had used Dewey's idea that the school should serve the child's needs as an excuse for avoiding their responsibility to extend a basic education to every child. This dogma enabled the teacher "who finds Johnny or Mary a little dull-witted in the academic subjects to ease up on them on the basis of supposed lack of interest and ability and to shove them into more courses in manual training or industrial arts or home economics, where mechanical skill takes precedence over thinking."

A second group of critics attacked American education not because it was both antiintellectual and undemocratic but because it failed to turn out enough scientists and high-level technicians. Educational reformers like Vannevar Bush, James B. Conant, and Vice-Admiral Hyman G. Rickover insisted that the United States lagged behind the Soviet Union in the arms race because the schools had failed to provide an efficient system of manpower selection. After the Russians launched a space capsule in 1957, this kind of criticism forced educators to institute new methods of training in science and mathematics, which stressed assimilation of basic concepts rather than memorization of facts. Although Conant, Rickover, and their followers called for a return to basics, their program had little in common with the reforms advocated by the Council of Basic Education. They did not question the school's function as an instrument of military and industrial recruitment, they merely sought to make the selection process more efficient.

Both Conant and Bush favored a system of universal military service in debates over that issue in the late forties. They saw such a system both as a means of enlisting the young into the service of the state and as an effective sorting device, whereby manpower requirements could be assessed in the light of military necessity. When universal military service was finally defeated by those who shrank from giving the military complete control over manpower recruitment, the country adopted a system of recruitment in some ways more undemocratic still. Under the Selective Service Act of 1951, passed at the height of the Korean War, military service became a universal obligation except for those who managed to qualify for academic exemption. The system of academic deferment, when combined with educational reforms designed to recruit a scientific and technical elite, created a national system of manpower selection in which minorities and the poor provided recruits for a vast peacetime army, while the middle class, eager to escape military service, attended college in unprecedented numbers.

The National Defense Education Act of 1958, designed to speed up production of engineers and scientists, gave added impetus to the boom in higher education, which lasted until the early 1970s. Meanwhile the schools devoted increasing attention to the identification of able students and the discouragement of others. More efficient systems of tracking, together with increased emphasis on math and science, recruited growing numbers of college students but did little to improve their training. Efforts to extend techniques first perfected by teachers of the "new math" into the social sciences and humanities produced students deficient in factual knowledge and intolerant of instruction that did not address their need for "creativity" and "self-expression." "When we wrote at school," as Joyce Maynard remembers her experience in the early sixties, "we were encouraged to forget about grammar and concern ourselves with free self-expression—maybe not to write at all, but instead to nonverbally communicate."

Evidence of the spread of such methods and of their disastrous effect on the students' minds could be cited in profusion. Under cover of enlightened ideologies, teachers (like parents) have followed the line of least resistance, hoping to pacify their students and to sweeten the time they have to spend in school by making the experience as painless as possible. Hoping to avoid confrontations and quarrels, they leave the students without guidance, meanwhile treating them as if they were incapable of serious exertion. Frederick Exley, who taught briefly in the public schools of upstate New York, describes the demoralizing effects of the unwritten rule that "everybody passes":

The faculty had been rendered moral monsters. Asked to keep one eye open, cool and detached, in appraising half the students, we were to keep the other eye winking as the rest of the students were passed from grade to grade and eventually into a world that would be all too happy to teach them, as they drifted churlishly from disappointment to disaster, what the school should have been teaching them all along: that even in America *failure is a part of life.* *

Institutions of cultural transmission (school, church, family), which might have been expected to counter the narcissistic trend of our culture, have instead been shaped in its image, while a growing body of progressive theory justifies this capitulation on the ground that such institutions best serve society when they provide a mirror reflection of it. The downward drift of public education accordingly continues: the steady dilution of intellectual standards in the name of relevance and other progressive slogans; the abandonment of foreign languages; the abandonment of history in favor of "social problems"; and a general retreat from intellectual discipline of any kind, often necessitated by the need for more rudimentary forms of discipline in order to maintain minimal standards of safety.

The Civil Rights Movement and the Schools Not even the struggle over racial integration has arrested this decline, although it has challenged the status quo in other ways. In the sixties, spokesmen for the civil rights movement and later for black power attacked the gross injustice of the educational system. The disparity in the academic performance of black and white schoolchildren dramatized the failure of American education more clearly than any other issue. Precisely for this reason, educators had always attempted to explain it away either on the grounds of racial inferiority or, when racism became scientifically unaccept-

---

* When elders make no demands on the young, they make it almost impossible for the young to grow up. A former student of mine, repelled by the conditions he now faces as a teacher at Evergreen State College in Washington, writes in criticism of recent changes in the curriculum, in a statement to his colleagues: "The betrayal of youth at Evergreen starts from the assumption—shared by many teachers and administrators—that first-year students are . . . only interested in wallowing in their own subjectivity and repelled by the thought of doing academic work." Hoping to bolster flagging enrollments, he says, the faculty and administration have turned the first-year curriculum into "a playpen of self-exploration."

able, on the grounds of "cultural deprivation." Cultural anthropology, which overthrew scientific racism in the thirties, provided educators with a new excuse for their failure to educate lower-class children: they came from culturally deprived backgrounds and were therefore unteachable. As Kenneth B. Clark pointed out, "Social scientists and educators, in the use and practice of the concept of cultural deprivation, have unintentionally provided an educational establishment that was already resistant to change . . . with a justification for continued inefficiency, much more respectable and much more acceptable in the middle of the twentieth century than racism."

The struggle over desegregation brought to the surface the inherent contradiction between the American commitment to universal education on the one hand and the realities of a class society on the other. Americans in the nineteenth century had adopted a system of common schooling without giving up their belief in the inevitability of social inequality. They had endorsed the principle of equal educational opportunity while maintaining an educational system that encouraged lower-class children to settle for training commensurate with their social station and prospects. Although they had refused to institutionalize inequality in the form of a separate system of technical training, they had recreated many forms of de facto discrimination within the academically integrated school system they had devised as an alternative to the European system. In the sixties, the most glaring exception to official egalitarianism—the racially segregated system of "separate but equal" schooling—began to crumble under the combined onslaught of the courts, the attorney general's office, and the federal bureaucracy—only to give way to new patterns of discrimination in ostensibly integrated schools, together with unmistakable evidence of that discrimination in the educational impoverishment of black children.

Conflicts over educational policy in the fifties had made it clear that the country faced a choice between basic education for all and a complicated educational bureaucracy that functioned as an agency of manpower selection. The same issue, often clouded by overheated rhetoric, underlay the more bitter struggles of the sixties and seventies. For black people, especially for upwardly mobile blacks in whom the passion for education burns as brightly as it ever did in descendants of the Puritans or in Jewish immigrants, desegregation represented the promise of equal education in the basic subjects indispensable to economic survival even in an otherwise illiterate modern society: reading, writing, and arithmetic. Black parents, it would seem, clung to what seems today an old-fashioned—from the point of view of educational "innovators," a hopelessly reactionary—conception of education. According to this supposedly traditional view, the school functions best when it transmits the basic skills on which literate societies depend, upholds high standards of academic excellence, and sees to it that students make these standards their own. The struggle for desegregated schooling implied an attack not only on racial discrimination but on the proposition, long embedded in the practice of the schools, that academic standards are inherently elitist and that universal education therefore requires the dilution of standards—the downward adjustment of standards to class origins and social expectations. The demand for desegregation entailed more than a renewed commitment to equal opportunity; it also entailed a repudiation of cultural separatism and a belief that access to common cultural traditions remained the precondition of advancement for dispossessed groups.

Thoroughly middle-class in its ideological derivation, the movement for equal education nevertheless embodied demands that could not be met without a radical overhaul of the entire educational system—and of much else besides. It flew in the face of long-established educational practice. It contained implications unpalatable not merely to entrenched educational bureaucrats but to progressives, who believed that education had to be tailored to the "needs" of the young, that overemphasis on academic subjects inhibited "creativity," and that too much stress on academic competition encouraged individualism at the expense of cooperation. The attempt to revive basic education, on the part of blacks and other minorities, cut across the grain of educational experimentation—the open classroom, the school without walls, the attempt to promote spontaneity and to undermine the authoritarianism allegedly rampant in the classroom.

Cultural Pluralism and the New Paternalism   In the late
sixties, as the civil rights movement gave way to the movement
for black power, radicals in the educational world began to identify themselves with a new theory of black culture, an inverted
version of the theory of cultural deprivation, which upheld the
ghetto subculture as a functional adaptation to ghetto life, indeed
as an attractive alternative to the white middle-class culture of
competitive achievement. Radicals now criticized the school for
imposing white culture on the poor. Black-power spokesmen,
eager to exploit white liberal guilt, joined the attack, demanding
separate programs of black studies, an end to the tyranny of the
written word, instruction in English as a second language. Ostensibly a radical advance over the middle-class movement for racial
integration, black power provided a new rationale for second-
class segregated schools, just as the radical critics of "traditional"
schooling played into the hands of the educational establishment
by condemning basic education as cultural imperialism. Instead
of criticizing the expansion of the educational bureaucracy, these
critics turned their fire against the safer target of education itself,
legitimizing a new erosion of standards in the name of pedagogical creativity. Instead of urging the school to moderate its claims
and to return to basic education, they demanded a further expansion of the curriculum to include programs in black history, black
English, black cultural awareness, and black pride.

   The educational radicalism of the late sixties, for all its revolutionary militance, left the status quo intact and even reinforced it.
In default of radical criticism, it remained for moderates like Kenneth Clark to make the genuinely radical point that "black children or any other group of children can't develop pride by just
saying they have it, by singing a song about it, or by saying I'm
black and beautiful or I'm white and superior." Racial pride,
Clark insisted, comes from "demonstrable achievement." Against
the "self-righteous, positive sentimentalism" of school reformers
like Jonathan Kozol and Herbert Kohl, veterans of the civil rights
movement argued that teachers do not need to love their students
as long as they demand good work from them. In upholding standards and asking everybody to meet them, teachers convey more

respect for their students, according to these spokesmen for the much maligned Negro middle class, than they convey when they patronize the culture of the ghetto and seek, as Hylan Lewis put it, to "gild a noisome lily."

In the long run, it does not matter to the victims whether bad teaching justifies itself on the reactionary grounds that poor people cannot hope to master the intricacies of mathematics, logic, and English composition or whether, on the other hand, pseudoradicals condemn academic standards as part of the apparatus of white cultural control, which purportedly prevents blacks and other minorities from realizing their creative potential. In either case, reformers with the best intentions condemn the lower class to a second-rate education and thus help to perpetuate the inequalities they seek to abolish. In the name of egalitarianism, they preserve the most insidious form of elitism, which in one guise or another holds the masses incapable of intellectual exertion. The whole problem of American education comes down to this: in American society, almost everyone identifies intellectual excellence with elitism. This attitude not only guarantees the monopolization of educational advantages by the few; it lowers the quality of elite education itself and threatens to bring about a reign of universal ignorance.

The Rise of the Multiversity   Recent developments in higher education have progressively diluted its content and reproduced, at a higher level, the conditions that prevail in the public schools. The collapse of general education; the abolition of any serious effort to instruct students in foreign languages; the introduction of many programs in black studies, women's studies, and other forms of consciousness raising for no other purpose than to head off political discontent; the ubiquitous inflation of grades—all have lowered the value of a university education at the same time that rising tuitions place it beyond reach of all but the affluent.

The crisis of higher learning in the sixties and seventies grew out of earlier developments. The modern university took shape in the early twentieth century as the product of a series of compromises. From the 1870s down to the First World War, advocates of research, social service, and liberal culture vied for control of the university. Faculties divided into adherents of one or another of these programs, while students and administrators injected their own interests into the debate. In the end, none of these factions achieved a decisive victory, but each won substantial concessions. The introduction of electives, together with extracurricular diversions of various kinds, helped to pacify the students. The elective system also represented a compromise between the demands of the undergraduate college, still organized around an older conception of general culture, and the research-oriented graduate and professional schools that were being superimposed on it. "The hope that the lecture system would transform the teacher from a drill master into a creative scholar depended upon giving the professor enough latitude to present a subject he knew thoroughly and yet relieving him of students for whom attendance was an unwelcome task." Unfortunately the elective system also relieved the faculty from the need to think about the broader purposes of education—including the possibility that for many students attending any classes at all had become an "unwelcome task"—and about the relation of one branch of knowledge to another. At the same time, the union of college and professional schools in the same institution preserved the fiction of general education, on which university administrators heavily relied in their appeals for funds.

A greatly expanded administrative apparatus now emerged not simply as one more element in a pluralistic community but as the only body responsible for the policy of the university as a whole. The decision to combine professional training and liberal education in the same institution, and the compromises necessary in order to implement it, rendered the faculty incapable of confronting larger questions of academic policy. These now became the responsibility of administrative bureaucracies, which grew up in order to manage the sprawling complexity of institutions that included not only undergraduate and graduate colleges but professional schools, vocational schools, research and development institutes, area programs, semiprofessional athletic programs, hospitals, large-scale real estate operations, and innumerable other enterprises. The corporate policies of the university, both internal and external—addition of new departments and programs, cooperation in war research, participation in urban renewal programs—now had to be made by administrators, and the idea of the service university or multiversity whose facilities were in theory available to all (but in practice only to the highest bidders) justified their own dominance in the academic structure. The faculty accepted this new state of affairs because, as Brander Matthews once said in explaining the attraction of Columbia to humane men of letters like himself, "So long as we do our work faithfully we are left alone to do it in our own fashion."*

The best that can be said about the American university in what might be called its classic period—roughly from 1870 to 1960—is that it provided a rather undemanding environment in which the various groups that made up the university enjoyed the freedom to do much as they pleased, provided they did not intererefere with the freedom of others or expect the university as a whole to provide a coherent explanation of its existence. The

---

* Judged by this test, Matthews found that "there is no university in the United States where the position of the professor is pleasanter than it is at Columbia." Unfortunately, these observations described conditions at Columbia better than the idealistic description of what higher education ought to be, written by one of the Columbia deans, Frederick P. Keppel: "A group of young men living and working and thinking and dreaming together, free to let their thoughts and dreams determine the future for them; these young men, hourly learning much from one another, are brought into touch with the wisdom of the past, the circumstances of the present, the visions of the future, by a group of older students, striving to provide them with ideas rather than beliefs, and guiding them in observing for themselves nature's laws and human relationships." Randolph Bourne (a Columbia graduate) scathingly pointed out the gap between ideal and reality. The professors "emphatically do not look upon themselves as 'older students' "; the curriculum shows little cornern for "nature's laws and human relationships"; and there prevails an "utterly mechanical and demoralizing system of measuring intellectual progress by 'points' and 'credits,' a system which cultivates the 'taking of courses' and not the study of a subject. . . . There seems to be little halt in the process of complicating the machinery of manufacturing the degree, in getting rid of plain-speaking and idealistic teachers, and in turning more and more of the teaching over to mediocre young instructors." In short, "There is no more obvious fact about the American college than that its administrative and curricular organization has not, in these last few years of standardizing, been in any way directed by the ideal of the 'intellectual community of youth.' "

students accepted the new status quo not only because they had plenty of nonacademic diversions but because the intellectual chaos of the undergraduate curriculum was not yet fully evident; because the claim that a college degree meant a better job still bore some relation to reality; and because in its relations to society, the university seemed to have identified itself with the best rather than the worst in American life.

What precipitated the crisis of the sixties was not simply the pressure of unprecedented numbers of students (many of whom would gladly have spent their youth elsewhere) but a fatal conjuncture of historical changes: the emergence of a new social conscience among students activated by the moral rhetoric of the New Frontier and by the civil rights movement, and the simultaneous collapse of the university's claims to moral and intellectual legitimacy. Instead of offering a rounded program of humane learning, the university now frankly served as a cafeteria from which students had to select so many "credits." Instead of diffusing peace and enlightenment, it allied itself with the war machine. Eventually, even its claim to provide better jobs became suspect.

The uprising of the sixties began as an attack on the ideology of the multiversity and its most advanced expression, the University of California at Berkeley; and whatever else it subsequently became, the movement remained, in part, an attempt to reassert faculty-student control over the larger policy of the university—expansion into urban neighborhoods, war research, ROTC. The whole development of the American university—its haphazard growth by accretion, its lack of an underlying rationale, the inherent instability of the compromises that attended its expansion—rendered such an accounting almost unavoidable.

At the same time, the student movement embodied a militant anti-intellectualism of its own, which corrupted and eventually absorbed it. Demand for the abolition of grades, although defended on grounds of high pedagogical principle, turned out in practice—as revealed by experiments with ungraded courses and pass-fail options—to reflect a desire for less work and a wish to avoid judgment on its quality. The demand for more "relevant" courses often boiled down to a desire for an intellectually undemanding cirriculum, in which students could win academic credits for political activism, self-expression, transcendental meditation, encounter therapy, and the study and practice of witchcraft. Even when seriously advanced in opposition to sterile academic pedantry, the slogan of relevance embodied an underlying antagonism to education itself—an inability to take an interest in anything beyond immediate experience. Its popularity testified to the growing belief that education should be painless, free of tension and conflict. Those who interpreted "relevance" as a concerted academic assault on racism and imperialism, moreover, merely inverted the expansionism of university administrators. When they proposed to enlist the university on the side of social reform, they echoed the service ideal that justified the imperial expansion of the multiversity in the first place. Instead of trying to hold the university to a more modest set of objectives, radical critics of higher education accepted the premise that education could solve every sort of social problem.

Cultural "Elitism" and Its Critics   In the seventies, the most common criticism of higher education revolves around the charge of cultural elitism. A well-known manifesto written by two professors of English argues that "high culture propagates the values of those who rule." Two contributors to a Carnegie Commission report on education condemn the idea that "there are certain works that should be familiar to all educated men" as inherently an "elitist notion." Such criticisms often appear in company with the contention that academic life should reflect the variety and turmoil of modern society instead of attempting to criticize and thus transcend this confusion. The very concept of criticism has become almost universally suspect. According to a fashionable line of argument, criticism, instead of teaching students how to "become involved," requires them to "stand back from on-going events in order to understand and analyze them." Criticism paralyzes the capacity for action and isolates the university from the conflicts raging in the "real world." The Carnegie Commission contributors argue that since the United States is a pluralist society, "adherence exclusively to the doctrines of any one school . . . would cause higher education to be in great dissonance with society."

Given the prevalence of these attitudes among teachers and educators, it is not surprising that students at all levels of the educational system have so little knowledge of the classics of world literature. An English teacher in Deerfield, Illinois, reports, "The students are used to being entertained. They are used to the idea that if they are just the slightest bit bored, they can flip the switch and turn the channels." In Albuquerque, only four students signed up for a high school course in the English novel, whereas a course entitled "Mystery-Supernatural" attracted so many students that it had to be taught in five separate sections. At a high school "without walls" in New Orleans, students can receive English credits for working as a disc jockey at a radio station and reading *How to Become a Radio Disc Jockey* and *Radio Programming in Action*. In San Marino, California, the high school English department increased its enrollments by offering electives in "Great American Love Stories," "Myths and Folklore," "Science Fiction," and "The Human Condition."

Those who teach college students today see at first hand the effect of these practices, not merely in the students' reduced ability to read and write but in the diminished store of their knowledge about the cultural traditions they are supposed to inherit. With the collapse of religion, biblical references, which formerly penetrated deep into everyday awareness, have become incomprehensible, and the same thing is now happening to the literature and mythology of antiquity—indeed, to the entire literary tradition of the West, which has always drawn so heavily on biblical and classical sources. In the space of two or three generations, enormous stretches of the "Judaeo-Christian tradition," so often invoked by educators but so seldom taught in any form, have passed into oblivion.* The effective loss of cultural traditions

* Another source of popular wisdom, the fairly tale, has dried up, thanks again to progressive ideologues who wish to protect the child from these allegedly terrifying stories. The censorship of fairly tales, like the attack on "irrelevant" literature in general, belongs to a general assault on fantasy and imagination. A psychologistic age robs people of harmless sublimations in the name of relevance and real-

on such a scale makes talk of a new Dark Age far from frivolous. Yet this loss coincides with an information glut, with the recovery of the past by specialists, and with an unprecedented explosion of knowledge—none of which, however, impinges on everyday experience or shapes popular culture.

Education as a Commodity   The resulting split between general knowledge and the specialized knowledge of the experts, embedded in obscure journals and written in language or mathematical symbols unintelligible to the layman, has given rise to a growing body of criticism and exhortation. The ideal of general education in the university, however, has suffered the same fate as basic education in the lower schools. Even those college teachers who praise general education in theory find that its practice drains energy from their specialized research and thus interferes with academic advancement. Administrators have little use for general education, since it does not attract foundation grants and large-scale government support. Students object to the reintroduction of requirements in general education because the work demands too much of them and seldom leads to lucrative employment.

Under these conditions, the university remains a diffuse, shapeless, and permissive institution that has absorbed the major currents of cultural modernism and reduced them to a watery blend, a mind-emptying ideology of cultural revolution, personal fulfillment, and creative alienation. Donald Barthelme's parody of higher learning in *Snow White*—like all parody in an age of ab-

ism; yet the effect of this training in realism, as Bruno Bettelheim shows, is to accentuate the discontinuity between generations (since the child comes to feel that his parents inhabit a world wholly alien to his own) and to make the child distrust his own experience. Formerly religion, myth, and fairy tale retained enough childlike elements to offer a convincing view of the world to a child. Science cannot take their place. Hence the widespread regression among young people to magical thinking of the most primitive kind: the fascination with witchcraft and the occult, the belief in extrasensory perception, the proliferation of primitive Christian cults.

surdities—so closely resembles reality as to become unrecognizable as parody.

Beaver College is where she got her education. She studied *Modern Woman, Her Privileges and Responsibilities:* the nature and nurture of women and what they stand for, in evolution and in history, including householding, upbringing, peacekeeping, healing and devotion, and how these contribute to the rehumanizing of today's world. Then she studied *Classical Guitar I,* utilizing the methods and techniques of Sor, Tarrega, Segovia, etc. Then she studied *English Romantic Poets II:* Shelley, Byron, Keats. Then she studied *Theoretical Foundations of Psychology:* mind, consciousness, unconscious mind, personality, the self, interpersonal relations, psychosexual norms, social games, groups, adjustment, conflict, authority, individuation, integration and mental health. Then she studied *Oil Painting I* bringing to the first class as instructed Cadmium Yellow Light, Cadmium Yellow Medium, Cadmium Red Light, Alizarin Crimson, Ultramarine Blue, Cobalt Blue, Viridian, Ivory Black, Raw Umber, Yellow Ochre, Burnt Sienna, White. Then she studied *Personal Resources I and II:* self-evaluation, developing the courage to respond to the environment, opening and using the mind, individual experience, training, the use of time, mature redefinition of goals, action projects. Then she studied *Realism and Idealism in the Contemporary Italian Novel:* Palazzeschi, Brancati, Bilenchi, Pratolini, Moravia, Pavese, Levi, Silone, Berto, Cassola, Ginzburg, Malaparte, Calvino, Gadda, Bassani, Landolfi. Then she studied—

Here is an education eminently befitting the heroine of Barthelme's novel, a commonplace young woman who longs for experiences such as would befall a fairy-tale princess. A latter-day Madame Bovary, Snow White is a typical victim of mass culture, the culture of commodities and consumerism with its suggestive message that experiences formerly reserved for those of high birth, deep understanding, or much practical acquaintance of life can be enjoyed by all without effort, on purchase of the appropriate commodity. Snow White's education is itself a commodity, the consumption of which promises to "fulfill her creative potential," in the jargon of pseudo-emancipation. That all students are effortlessly "creative" and that the need to release this creativity takes precedence over the need, say, to train people with the vanishing capacity for silence and self-containment—these are high among the ruling dogmas of American educators. The mindless eclecticism of Snow White's education reflects the chaos of contemporary life and the unreasonable expectation that students will achieve for themselves the intellectual coherence their teachers can no longer give them. The teachers excuse their own failure under the pretense of "tailoring instruction to the needs of the individual student."

Snow White's instructors assume that higher learning ideally includes everything, assimilates all of life. And it is true that no aspect of contemporary thought has proved immune to educationalization. The university has boiled all experience down into "courses" of study—a culinary image appropriate to the underlying ideal of enlightened consumption. In its eagerness to embrace experience, the university comes to serve as a substitute for it. In doing so, however, it merely compounds its intellectual failures—notwithstanding its claim to prepare students for "life." Not only does higher education destroy the students' minds; it incapacitates them emotionally as well, rendering them incapable of confronting experience without benefit of textbooks, grades, and predigested points of view. Far from preparing students to live "authentically," the higher learning in America leaves them unable to perform the simplest task—to prepare a meal or go to a party or get into bed with a member of the opposite sex—without elaborate academic instruction. The only thing it leaves to chance is higher learning.

VII

The Socialization of Reproduction
and the Collapse of Authority

The "Socialization of Workingmen" The survival of any
form of human society depends on the production of the necessi-
ties of life and the reproduction of the labor force itself. Until
recently, the work of reproduction, which includes not merely
the propagation of the species but the care and nurture of the
young, took place largely in the family. The factory system, established in the nineteenth century, socialized production but left
other functions of the family intact. The socialization of production, however, proved to be the prelude to the socialization of
reproduction itself—the assumption of childrearing functions by
surrogate parents responsible not to the family but to the state, to
private industry, or to their own codes of professional ethics. In
the course of bringing culture to the masses, the advertising industry, the mass media, the health and welfare services, and
other agencies of mass tuition took over many of the socializing
functions of the home and brought the ones that remained under
the direction of modern science and technology.

It is in this light that we should see the school's appropriation
of many of the training functions formerly carried out by the family, including manual training, household arts, instruction in
manners and morals, and sex education. "Social, political, and industrial changes," announced a pair of leading educators in 1918,
"have forced upon the school responsibilities formerly laid upon
the home. Once the school had mainly to teach the elements of
knowledge, now it is charged with the physical, mental, and
social training of the child as well." These words reflected a consensus among the "helping professions" that the family could no

longer provide for its own needs. Doctors, psychiatrists, child development experts, spokesmen for the juvenile courts, marriage counselors, leaders of the public hygiene movement all said the same thing—usually reserving to their own professions, however, the leading role in the care of the young. Ellen Richards, founder of the modern profession of social work, argued: "In the social republic, the child as a future citizen is an asset of the state, not the property of its parents. Hence its welfare is a direct concern of the state." Experts in mental health, seeking to expand their own jurisdiction, deplored "the harm, often well-nigh irreparable, which the best intentioned parents may do their children." Many reformers despaired of instilling in parents the principles of mental health and maintained that "the only practical and effective way to increase the mental health of a nation is through its school system. Homes are too inaccessible."

Opponents of child labor argued along the same lines. Convinced that poor immigrant parents exploited their children's labor at every opportunity, they demanded not only state prohibition of child labor but the placement of the child under the custody of the school. Similarly, those who dealt with juvenile delinquency saw "broken" or otherwise flawed homes as the breeding ground of crime and tried to bring the juvenile offender under the protective custody of the courts. Parents' rights in their children, according to the new ideology of social reform, depended on the extent of their willingness to cooperate with officials of the juvenile courts. "To the competent parent all aid should be given," wrote Sophonisba P. Breckinridge and Edith Abbott, but "to the degraded parent no concessions should be made." By the same logic, as another spokesman for the helping professions explained, refusal to cooperate with the courts and other welfare agencies proved that a parent "has a warped view of authority and is thereby unable to make use of social resources," thus forfeiting his right to his children or at least raising strong doubts about his competence as a parent.

Reformers conceived of the "socialization of workingmen" as the alternative to class conflict. "If men of any country are taught from childhood to consider themselves as members of a 'class,' " wrote Edwin L. Earp, characteristically addressing himself to the "professional man" as well as to the lower orders, ". . . then it will be impossible to avoid social friction, class hatred, and class conflict." A spokesman for the social gospel, Earp went on to explain that the church could socialize the worker more effectively "than the labor unions, for they are class-conscious and . . . selfish, while the Church, on the other hand, is conscious of a world-kingdom of righteousness, peace and joy, and, in most cases at least, is hopefully altruistic."

Almost everyone agreed that the family promoted a narrow, parochial, selfish, and individualistic mentality and thus impeded the development of sociability and cooperation. This reasoning led inexorably to the conclusion that outside agencies had to replace the family, especially the working-class family, which so many reformers nevertheless wished to preserve and strengthen. If the school was reluctantly "taking the place of the home," according to Ellen Richards, this was because "the personal point of view, inculcated now by modern conditions of strife for money, just as surely as it must have been by barbarian struggle in pre-civilized days, must be supplanted by the broader view of majority welfare." The iron laws of social evolution dictated the subordination of the individual to "the destiny of the race."

The Juvenile Court The movement to bring youthful offenders under special jurisdiction illustrates in their clearest form the connections between organized altruism, the new therapeutic conception of the state, and the appropriation of familial functions by outside agencies. When penal reformers and humanitarians established a new system of juvenile justice at the end of the nineteenth century, they conceived of it as a substitute for the home. In their view, the reformatory should contain "essential elements of a good home." In Illinois, the law establishing the juvenile court (1889) announced that the act would ensure "that the care, custody, and discipline of a child shall approximate as nearly as may be that which should be given by its parents." If parents "virtually orphaned" their children "by their inadequacy, neglect, or cruel usage," the parental powers of the state—*parens patriae*—entitled it to remove children from their parents' custody without a trial and to bring them under its own care. According to Miss Breckinridge, the juvenile court "helped to rescue the child from irresponsible parents and . . . pointed the way to a new relationship between the family and the community." Because the new courts treated youthful offenders as victims of a bad environment rather than as criminals, they eliminated the adversary relationship between the child and the state and made the prevention of crime, not punishment, the chief object of the law—in reformers' eyes, a great advance toward a more humane, more scientific system of justice. "The element of conflict was absolutely eliminated," wrote Jane Addams, "and with it all notions of punishment."

An early history of the juvenile court movement noted that after the abolition of adversary proceedings, "the relations of the child to his parents and other adults and to the state or society are defined and adjusted summarily according to the scientific findings about the child and his environment." Magistrates had given way to "socially-minded judges, who hear and adjust cases according not to rigid rules of law but to what the interests of society and the interests of the child or good conscience demand." Juries, prosecutors, and lawyers had yielded to "probation officers, physicians, psychologists, and psychiatrists. . . . In this new court we tear down primitive prejudice, hatred, and hostility toward the lawbreaker in that most hidebound of all human institutions, the court of law."

As so often happens in modern history, reforms that presented themselves as the height of ethical enlightenment eroded the rights of the ordinary citizen. Conceiving of the problem of social control on the model of public health, the "helping professions" claimed to attack the causes of crime instead of merely treating its consequences. By converting the courts into agents of moral instruction and psychic "help," however, they abrogated the usual safeguards against arbitrary arrest and detention. Their reforms empowered the courts to pry into family affairs; to remove children from "unsuitable homes"; to sentence them to indeterminate periods of incarceration without proving their guilt; and to invade the delinquent's home in order to supervise the terms of probation. The probation system, according to one reformer, created "a new kind of reformatory, without walls and without much coercion"; but in fact the establishment of this reformatory without walls extended the coercive powers of the state, now disguised as a wish "to befriend and help," into every corner of society. The state could now segregate deviants for no other reason than that they or their parents had refused to cooperate with the courts, especially when refusal to cooperate appeared as *prima facie* evidence of a bad home environment. Judges who considered themselves "specialists in the art of human relations" sought to "get the whole truth about a child," in the words of Miriam Van Waters, in the same way that a "physician searches for every detail that bears on the condition of a patient." One judge prided himself on "the personal touch" with which he approached delinquent boys: "I have often observed that if I sat on a high platform behind a high desk, such as we had in our city court, with the boy on the prisoner's bench some distance away, that my words had little effect on him; but if I could get close enough to him to put my hand on his head and shoulder, or my arm around him, in nearly every case I could get his confidence." In effect, the court now certified the "patient" into what Talcott Parsons has called the sick role. Once the boy admitted his need of help—the real meaning, in this essentially therapeutic setting, of giving the judge his "confidence"—he exchanged his legal rights for the protective custody of the state, which in practice often proved to be as harsh and unrelenting as the punishment from which the new system of judicial therapy had delivered him in the first place.

Occasionally a judge with old-fashioned ideas insisted that "the true function of a court is to determine judicially the facts at issue before it"—and that "investigations of the lives, environments, or heredity of delinquents, the infliction of punishment, and the supervision of probation institutionalize the courts and are repugnant to every tenet of the science of law." Such reasoning, however, ran against the current of sociological jurisprudence, which appeared to justify a vastly enlarged role for the courts. By the mid-1920s, Van Waters argued that the state had an obligation to "protect" children not merely against broken homes, which bred crime, but "against parents whose treatment results in a crippled or warped personality." Her book, *Parents on Probation*, listed in one chapter "nineteen ways of being a bad parent," which included "perpetual chaperonage," a "warped view of authority," and failure to become "oriented in the modern world." Van Waters admitted that most children of "bad parents," given a choice between the custody of the juvenile court and the custody of their parents, preferred to return even to homes in shambles. This "incurable loyalty of children to unworthy adults," although it was "the despair of the social worker," nevertheless suggested that a child's "own home gave him something that the mere kindness and plenty of the foster home could not furnish, and that all the social workers in the world would fail to supply." But these considerations did not prevent Van Waters from arguing that not only broken homes but "normal" homes often produced broken children and that the social worker's duty to interfere in other people's domestic arrangements logically knew no limits. "As our case descriptions in clinics and conferences pile up, the wealth of evidence that the 'normal' home, as well as the broken home, fosters malnutrition, physical and spiritual, that sordid habit-settings and moral maladjustments occur in the 'best' families, the conclusion grows, not that parents need education, but that a specialized agency had better take over the whole matter of child rearing."

Parent Education   Those who resisted such a sweeping formulation of the state's powers *in loco parentis* clung to the hope that "parent education" would improve the quality of child care and make more drastic attacks on the family unnecessary. Reformers like Washington Gladden, well known as an exponent of the social gospel, accepted most of the principles associated with the new humanitarianism—with school reform and the new sociological jurisprudence in particular—yet questioned their more extreme applications. Gladden endorsed the view that "punishment must be ancillary to reformation" but wondered whether the "reaction against the retributive severities of the old penology" had not eroded "fundamental ethical principles" and "weakened, perceptibly, the sense of moral responsibility." Many "sentimental prison reformers," he noted, talked about prisoners "as if they were wholly innocent and amiable people." Although Gladden accepted the prevailing view that "the actual work of education is now largely done outside the family" and that this arrangement, moreover, represented an efficient division of labor, he accepted it only with misgivings. He agreed with Dewey that "the school must find a way to cultivate the social temper, the habit of cooperation, the spirit of service, the consciousness of fraternity"; yet while assenting to this unprecedented expansion of the school's responsibility for socialization, he nevertheless wanted education to remain "fundamentally, a parental function."

From the beginning, the movement to improve the home—the only alternative, it appeared, to bypassing or replacing it—floundered in such contradictions. Teachers of "domestic science," academic experts in "marriage and the family," marriage counselors, family therapists, and many social workers tried to strengthen the family against the forces that tended to undermine it. One social worker, Frank Dekker Watson, objected to the "deceptive philosophy that turns the back upon parents as hopeless and proposes to save the children. We cannot save the children separately," he insisted. "We must reach and save the family as a whole." Yet all these experts, in their very eagerness to "save" the family, accepted the overriding premise that the family could no longer provide for its needs without outside assistance. In particular they distrusted the immigrant family and saw the parent-education movement as part of a wider effort to civilize the masses—that is, to Americanize the immigrants and impose industrial discipline on the working class. The urban masses, wrote Gladden, "must be civilized, educated, inspired with new ideas." Florence Kelley, a noted socialist, complained that a typical Italian girl, even when exposed to years of schooling, forgot everything she learned as soon as she married and proceeded to bring up "in the most unreasonable manner the large family which continues to the second generation in the Italian colonies. She will feed her infants bananas, bologna, beer and coffee; and many of these potential native citizens will perish during their first year, poisoned by the hopeless ignorance of their school-bred mother." Such reformers, despairing of the school, hoped to make the family itself one of the chief agencies of enlightenment—but only by overhauling it according to the latest principles of marital interaction and child care.

These principles, of course, underwent continual elaboration and revision, as professional fashion dictated. If we consider the literature on childrearing alone—leaving aside the equally voluminous literature on the problems of marriage, which consisted mostly of conflicting speculations about the attraction of opposites or the importance of similar backgrounds and tastes—we find that expert opinion evolved through four stages, each claiming to represent a notable advance over the last. In the twenties and thirties, behaviorism held sway. Such authorities as John B. Watson and Arnold Gesell stressed the need for strict feeding schedules and carefully regulated child-parent contacts. In their initial revulsion against home remedies, rule-of-thumb methods, and "maternal instinct," baby doctors and psychiatrists condemned "maternal overprotection" and urged parents to respect the child's "emotional independence." Many mothers, according to Ernest and Gladys Groves, thought it "the most astonishing thing that mother love has been found by science inherently dangerous, and some of them grow panicky as they let the significance of the new teaching sink into their thoughts." In the long run, however, the new teaching would enable parents to confer on their offspring the inestimable blessing of "freedom from emotional bondage to their parents."*

* Groves and Groves were not alone in noting, even at this early date, certain disturbing effects of professional teaching on parents. Miriam Van Waters wrote: "So much alarming popular literature has been written about defective children that a diagnosis of defect, or serious handicap, like epilepsy or neurotic constitution, freezes the parents into despair." Such observations, however, seldom prompted those who made them to question the wisdom of professional teaching, which by its very nature—even when it seeks to reassure—holds up a norm of child development, deviations from which necessarily give rise to parental alarm, to further demands for professional intervention, and often to measures that intensify suffering instead of alleviating it.

Those who noted that the attack on maternal instinct undermined maternal

Permissiveness Reconsidered In the late thirties and forties, the popularization of progressive education and of debased versions of Freudian theory brought about a reaction in favor of "permissiveness." Feeding schedules gave way to feeding on demand; everything now had to be geared to the child's "needs." Love came to be regarded not as a danger but as a positive duty. Improved methods of birth control, according to the progressive creed, had freed parents from the burden of raising unwanted children, but this freedom in practice seemed to boil down to the obligation to make children feel wanted at every moment of their lives. "The common error of psychological advice," wrote Hilde Bruch in 1952, "is teaching parents techniques of conveying to the child a sense of being loved instead of relying on their innate true feelings of love."*

confidence felt no reservations about this development, because in their view the confidence destroyed by medicine rested in the first place on ignorance and complacency. According to Lorine Pruette, "The severe criticism of the average mother's way with her children coming from social workers, psychiatrists, and educators has helped to destroy a great complacency which was formerly the young mother's protection. . . . The dictum that mother knows best and the dogma of the natural instincts of motherhood have so fallen in disfavor as to be available refuges only for the ignorant or the stubborn." A writer in *Good Housekeeping* observed in 1914: "Souls full of love bring also heads full of ignorance. . . . 'Instinct tells a mother what to do.' Oh, it's an old chant, and it is as scientific as the classic statement that an upstanding fork means a caller, or that the moon is made of green cheese. Instinct forsooth!"

* In Lisa Alther's *Kinflicks*, the heroine's mother, a product of the permissive period, complains: "If anything had been drummed into her in her years of motherhood, it was that you mustn't squelch the young. It might stunt their precious development. Never mind about your own development."

The importance of "wanted" children attained the status of dogma as early as 1912, when Mary Roberts Coolidge argued that organized education for motherhood, together with improvements in contraception, would soon make motherhood "something more than a blind obedience to nature and mankind." Motherhood would soon become "a high vocation worthy of the best preparation and the profoundest devotion," according to Coolidge. Freed of the burden of raising unwanted children, women would confront childrearing not as a burdensome biological duty but as a challenging career requiring careful study and the application of rational technique. "We are rapidly passing from a purely instinctual to conscious and voluntary motherhood."

Permissiveness soon produced its own reaction, an insistence that parents should consult their own needs as well as the child's. Maternal instinct, much derided by earlier experts, made a comeback in Dr. Spock's *Baby and Child Care,* first published in 1946. "Trust yourself," Spock announced at the outset. "What good mothers and fathers instinctively feel like doing for their babies is usually best." Often blamed for the excesses of permissive child-rearing, Spock should be seen instead as one of its critics, seeking to restore the rights of the parent in the face of an exaggerated concern for the rights of the child. He and other experts of the forties and fifties had become somewhat belatedly aware of the way their own advice undermined parental confidence. They began to suggest, tentatively at first, that parents should not be held responsible for all their children's faults. "The deepest roots," wrote one pediatrician, "lie not in the mistakes of the parents but in cultural attitudes of which the parents are merely the purveyors." Another expert found that faulty approaches to parent education aroused irrational "hostility toward family experts and counsellors." Exposed to counselors who stressed "problems instead of theories," many parents "felt somehow that they had failed to do for their children what their parents had done for them, and yet, they did not know why, or wherein they had failed, or what they could do about it." Such considerations did not lead experts to withdraw, however, from the business of parent education. On the contrary, they now widened the scope of their claims, setting themselves up as doctors to all of society.

Even the more penetrating critics of permissive dogmas countered them not with a more modest statement of what medicine and psychiatry could hope to accomplish but simply with new dogmas of their own. The limits of psychiatric self-criticism emerged most clearly in Hilde Bruch's *Don't Be Afraid of Your Child,* the work of a humane and sensible psychiatrist who nevertheless left matters no better than she found them. At times, Dr. Bruch departed from her attack on permissiveness and attacked psychiatric imperialism itself, which had inhibited "spontaneity" and brought about in many parents a "state of superimposed anxiety." Afraid of repeating the mistakes of their own parents, modern parents repudiated the serviceable practices of the past and embraced the "routinized half-truths of the experts as the laws of living." Better than almost any other commentator on American psychiatry, Dr. Bruch understood its massive assault against the past and the devastation left by this demolition of older forms of authority.

It has become fashionable in the whole world of psychiatry and psychology, not only in its immediate relation to child-rearing practices, to speak in sweeping, dramatic terms of the crushing effect of authority and tradition. The failure to recognize the essentially valid and sustaining aspects of traditional ways and of differentiating them from outmoded harmful and overrestrictive measures has resulted in a demoralized confusion of modern parents and thus had a disastrous effect on children.

Dr. Bruch went even further. She grasped the social and cultural transformation that has made science the handmaiden of industry—in this case, psychiatry the handmaiden of advertising, which enlists psychiatry in the attempt to exploit "parents' desires to do right by their children." By keeping parents in a state of chronic anxiety, psychiatry thus frustrates desires that advertising can then claim to satisfy. It lays the emotional foundation for the insistence of the advertising industry that the health and safety of the young, the satisfaction of their daily nutritional requirements, their emotional and intellectual development, and their ability to compete with their peers for popularity and success all depend on consumption of vitamins, band-aids, cavity-preventing toothpaste, cereals, mouthwashes, and laxatives.

Having confronted or at least glimpsed all this, Dr. Bruch betrayed her own perceptions by attributing the troubles she identified not to the inherently expansionist ambitions of modern psychiatry but rather to the misuse of psychiatry by a few irresponsible practitioners. Too often, she wrote, parents consulted "self-appointed, unlicensed experts" when they should have gone to a "medical psychiatric expert" working in close conjunction with a physician. For all the barbs she launched against her own profession, she subscribed to most of its clichés: "parent education is here to stay"; "there is no going back"; "what was 'common sense' in a past century is apt to be useless and hopelessly out of step in our time." Her attack on permissive childrearing boiled down to a criticism of psychiatric malpractice. Although she urged parents "to recognize their own inner resources and capacity for judgment," her book, like Dr. Spock's, abounded in dire warnings of the damage ignorant parents could inflict on their offspring. Spock undermined his own plea for confidence by reminding parents that failure to give children love and security could lead to "irreparable harm." Similarly Bruch condemned permissiveness on the grounds that it could produce "deep emotional disturbance" in the child. Such pronouncements had the effect of weakening parental confidence in the very act of trying to restore it.*

---

* The same thing holds true of the critique of permissiveness that runs through a group of psychiatric essays collected in 1959 by Samuel Liebman, *Emotional Forces in the Family*. These essays contain the same mixture of sense and pseudo-sense. In "The Development of the Family in the Technical Age," Joost A. M. Meerloo analyzes, with great discernment, the "invasion" of the family by mass culture and by half-assimilated psychiatric ideas, which then become tools of sexual and generational combat. An "imposed intellectualization of the emotions," according to Meerlo, has become "a substitute for mature action." The "delusion of explanation replaces the appropriate act. Words, words, and mere words are produced rather than good will and good action. Sex itself is expressed in words instead of affection."

In the remaining essays, however, analysis of "psychologizing" and "the delusion of explanation" gives way to criticism of a single form of psychologizing, the dogma of permissiveness. Bertram Schaffner writes, in the same vein as Hilde Bruch and Dr. Spock, that "the so-called 'human relations' school of thought," both in childrearing and in industrial management, has gone too far in the direction of permissiveness and has too readily assumed that the "child could do no wrong." "In the recent confused picture of parent-child relations, some parents have taken the concept [of providing security for the child] to mean that the child should have every wish and need met, should not have the experience of being refused." Schaffner's attack on the "abdication of authority in the family and at work" recalls Bruch's plea for "a father or mother who can say 'No' without going through an elaborate song and dance."

The contributors to the Liebman volume, like other critics of permissiveness, write as if parental authority could be restored by professional exhortation, at the same time that they repeat the conventional injunction against leaving childrearing to instinct. "It is our responsibility," concludes Lawrence S. Kubie, "to re-examine critically everything which used to be left to mother's or father's uninformed impulses, under such euphemistic clichés as 'instinct' and 'love,' lest mother-love mask self-love and father-love mask unconscious impulses to destroy." Psychiatrists have the last word after all.

Gilbert J. Rose has criticized "global permissiveness in child development" along the same lines, but with more sensitivity to the evil of psychologizing as

The Cult of Authenticity   Since the critique of permissiveness seldom challenged psychiatric orthodoxy, it soon hardened into a new dogma of its own—the dogma of authenticity. Earlier experts had advised the parent to follow one or another set of prescriptions; now the experts told him to trust his own feelings. Whatever he did was right as long as he did it spontaneously. "Children are not easily fooled about true feelings," warned Dr. Bruch. "Parent effectiveness training," the latest vogue in child-rearing, has popularized the cult of authenticity that began to emerge in the fifties. Like other forms of psychic self-help, parent effectiveness training teaches the need to "get in touch with your feelings" and to base everyday intercourse on the communication of these feelings to others. If parents can understand their own needs and wishes and convey them to their children, encouraging children to reciprocate in the same fashion, they can eliminate many sources of friction and conflict. Objective statements should be excluded from discourse with the child, according to this reasoning, in the first place because no one can argue rationally about beliefs and in the second place because statements about reality convey ethical judgments and therefore arouse strong emotions. "When a child says, 'I never have good luck,' no argument or explanation will change this belief." "When a child tells of an event, it is sometimes helpful to respond, not to the event itself, but to the feelings around it." Since "all feelings are legitimate," their expression should be greeted neither with praise nor with blame. If a child does something to annoy the parent, the parent should express his annoyance instead of condemning the child or the action. If the child expresses emotions that seem

such. The "analytic tendency to look with suspicion upon action as possible acting out, . . . inappropriately transferred from analytic practice," encourages passivity in everyday life, according to Rose. "Some parents, for example, are incapable of such things as putting their child to bed in the face of protest or of curbing the children's aggression. . . . The avoidance of being judgmental in analysis is sometimes generalized into a moral detachment in everyday life. This suspension of the moral sense, often combined with a hypertrophy of the therapeutic attitude, leads to calling something 'sick' where there is no clinical evidence and not calling it 'bad' though such is obvious. The naive idea that sickness accounts for badness and that badness necessarily results from being misunderstood is the prejudice of a therapeutic morality."

incommensurate with the occasion, the parent, instead of point-
ing out this discrepancy—instead of making an objective statement about reality and the emotions appropriate to it—should indicate to the child that he understands the child's feelings and
acknowledges his right to express them. "It is more important for
a child to know what he feels than why he feels it." The child
needs to learn "that his own anger is not catastrophic, that it can
be discharged without destroying anyone."*

The cult of authenticity reflects the collapse of parental guidance and provides it with a moral justification. It confirms, and
clothes in the jargon of emotional liberation, the parent's helplessness to instruct the child in the ways of the world or to transmit
ethical precepts. By glorifying this impotence as a higher form of
awareness, it legitimizes the proletarianization of parenthood—the appropriation of childrearing techniques by the "helping professions." As John R. Seeley noted in 1959, the transfer of
parental knowledge to other agencies parallels the expropriation
of the worker's technical knowledge by modern management—"the taking over from the worker of the sad necessity of
providing himself with the means of production." By "helpfully"
relieving the worker from "such onerous responsibilities" as the
provision of his own and his children's needs, society has freed
him, as Seeley wrote, "to become a soldier in the army of production and a cipher in the process of decision."†

* The contention that parent effectiveness training and other enlightened techniques of childrearing originated in the fifties will surprise those commentators
who can remember nothing more ancient than the latest issue of the *New York
Times News of the Week in Review*, and who regard the fifties, accordingly, as the
Dark Age of "traditional" parenthood—a period, for example, in which "sex education usually didn't amount to much more than a brief embarrassed conversation." Nancy McGrath, a free-lance journalist, belatedly discovered the cult of
spontaneity in 1976 and jumped to the conclusion that it represented a complete
reversal of the "permissiveness" encouraged by Dr. Spock. In fact, Spock anticipated recent writers in his insistence that parents had rights as important as the
child's—one of the principal dogmas of parent effectiveness training. He and
Hilde Bruch condemned permissive styles of childrearing on precisely the same
grounds that Nancy McGrath now condemns Fitzhugh Dodson's *How to Parent*
and Lee Salk's *How to Raise a Human Being*—that such teaching mistakenly in-
structs parents to "adapt to a baby's needs, not expect the baby to adapt to theirs."
† As a result of the invasion of parenthood by the health industry, Seeley concluded, "One finds parents convinced of their impotence, clinging to doctrine in

The revolt against behavioral and progressive dogmas, which exaggerated the parent's power to deform the child, has encouraged society to hold the parent "only marginally accountable," as Mark Gerzon has recently observed, "for his child's growth. . . . Obstetricians take charge at birth, pediatricians are responsible for a child's ailments and cures; the teacher for his intelligence; . . . the supermarket and food industry for his food; television for his myths." Ironically, the devaluation of parenthood coincides with a belated movement to return to the family functions it has surrendered to the apparatus of organized therapy and tuition. Rising rates of crime, juvenile delinquency, suicide, and mental breakdown have finally convinced many experts, even many welfare workers, that welfare agencies furnish a poor substitute for the family. Dissatisfaction with the results of socialized welfare and the growing expense of maintaining it now prompt efforts to shift health and welfare functions back to the home.*

the face of confronting fact-at-hand, robbed of spontaneity (or, equivalently, forcing themselves as a routine to 'be spontaneous'), guilt-ridden, dubious about their own discriminatory capacity, in double tutelage—to the child himself and to his agent, the 'expert'—penetrable, defenseless, credulous, and sure only that, while it doth not yet appear, the day of salvation is at hand." In another essay in the same collection, Seeley noted that modern society presents "a social division of labor in which the burden of rationality is . . . externalized, thrust upon a body of professionals, and hence set beyond one's own capacity to mismanage. In effect, one is to become rational, not by some internal and personal struggle, but by setting in motion a public process that, once started, one cannot resist—a process in which one selects an elite to procure for oneself and others that environment that is most conducive to rational behavior."

* In 1976, the Center for Policy Research (New York) organized a conference on dependency, based on the premise that "traditional public responses have lost much, if not all, legitimacy" and that institutionalization and professional care have become widely "suspect." Both in its attack on asylums and in its suspicious attitude toward the "motive of benevolence," this conference accurately reflects the current revulsion against socialized welfare and the revisionist scholarship which supports that revulsion by disparaging the motives of reformers and depicting asylums as "total institutions." The work of Erving Goffman, Thomas Szasz, Eliot Freidson, David Rothman, and others has helped to shape a new orthodoxy, which criticizes institutionalization and "professional dominance" but fails to see the connection between these developments and the rise of modern management or the degradation of work. In practice, the critique of professionalism seldom

Psychological Repercussions of the "Transfer of Functions"

It is too late, however, to call for a revival of the patriarchal family or even of the "companionate" family that replaced it. The "transfer of functions," as it is known in the antiseptic jargon of the social sciences—in reality, the deterioration of child care—has been at work for a long time, and many of its consequences appear to be irreversible. The first step in the process, already taken in some societies in the late eighteenth century, was the segregation of children from the adult world, partly as a deliberate policy, partly as the unavoidable result of the withdrawal of many work processes from the home. As the industrial system monopolized production, work became less and less visible to the child. Fathers could no longer bring their work home or teach children the skills that went into it. At a later stage in this alienation of labor, management's monopolization of technical skills, followed at an even later stage by the socialization of childrearing techniques, left parents with little but love to transmit to their offspring; and love without discipline is not enough to assure the generational continuity on which every culture depends. Instead of guiding the child, the older generation now struggles to "keep up with the kids," to master their incomprehensible jargon, and even to imitate their dress and manners in the hope of preserving a youthful appearance and outlook.

These changes, which are inseparable from the whole development of modern industry, have made it more and more difficult for children to form strong psychological identifications with their parents. The invasion of the family by industry, the mass media, and the agencies of socialized parenthood has subtly

rises above the level of a consumers' movement, while in theory, it has already hardened into a cliché. For historians, "social control" serves the same purpose in the seventies that "status anxiety" served in the fifties. It offers a comprehensive, all-purpose explanation that fits every case and contingency and can now be manipulated with little thought. Even the best of the social-control studies tend, in the words of Richard Fox, "to exaggerate the novelty of nineteenth-century perceptions of disorder, to reify the 'controllers' to the point where they become either a homogeneous elite or, as in Rothman's case, indistinguishable from society as a whole, and to assume that institutions are imposed by that elite or that society upon passive, malleable subjects."

altered the quality of the parent-child connection. It has created an ideal of perfect parenthood while destroying parents' confidence in their ability to perform the most elementary functions of childrearing. The American mother, according to Geoffrey Gorer, depends so heavily on experts that she "can never have the easy, almost unconscious, self-assurance of the mother of more patterned societies, who is following ways she knows unquestioningly to be right." According to another observer, the "immature, narcissistic" American mother "is so barren of spontaneous manifestation of maternal feelings" that she redoubles her dependence on outside advice. "She studies vigilantly all the new methods of upbringing and reads treatises about physical and mental hygiene." She acts not on her own feelings or judgment but on the "picture of what a good mother should be."

The woman who came to a psychiatrist after reading books on child development from which she "felt that she had not been able to learn anything" dramatizes, in heightened form, the plight of the modern parent. She pursued such information, her psychiatrist reported, "as if she were interested in passing some kind of examination or in producing a child that would win some contest. . . . She had to become a perfect mother." Yet her relations with her child suffered from "a striking lack of affect." Tormented by "a feeling of inexperience and clumsiness in handling tasks with which she had no previous acquaintance," she compared herself to someone who had never seen or ridden in a car and was trying to learn to drive it from a mechanic's manual. Another mother "felt she knew nothing about mothering, literally. . . . She could go mechanically through the motions of looking after her child's needs, but she never really understood what her daughter required and she felt she was responding completely without empathy as one would automatically follow instructions from a manual."

Narcissism, Schizophrenia, and the Family Clinical evidence documents the frequently devastating effects of this kind of mothering on the child. The "shallowness and unpredictability of his mother's responses," according to Heinz Kohut, produced in one of his patients the pattern of narcissistic dependence so often found in borderline conditions, in which the subject attempts to re-create in his unconscious fantasies the omniscience of early infancy and seeks to shore up his self-esteem by attaching himself to "strong, admired figures." The mother-child connection, in the view of Kohut and many others, ideally rests on "optimal frustrations." As the child begins to perceive his mother's limitations and fallibility, he relinquishes the image of maternal perfection and begins to take over many of her functions—to provide for his own care and comfort. An idealized image of the mother lives on in the child's unconscious thoughts. Diminished, however, by the daily experience of maternal fallibility, it comes to be associated not with fantasies of infantile omnipotence but with the ego's modest, growing mastery of its environment. Disappointment with the mother, brought about not only by her unavoidable lapses of attention but by the child's perception that he does not occupy the exclusive place in her affections, makes it possible for the child to relinquish her undivided love while internalizing the image of maternal love (through a psychic process analogous to mourning) and incorporating her life-giving functions.

The narcissistic mother's incessant yet curiously perfunctory attentions to her child interfere at every point with the mechanism of optimal frustration. Because she so often sees the child as an extension of herself, she lavishes attentions on the child that are "awkwardly out of touch" with his needs, providing him with an excess of seemingly solicitous care but with little real warmth. By treating the child as an "exclusive possession," she encourages an exaggerated sense of his own importance; at the same time she makes it difficult for him to acknowledge his disappointment in her shortcomings. In schizophrenia, the disjunction between the child's perceptions of his mother's shallow, perfunctory care and her apparently undivided devotion becomes so painful that the child refuses to acknowledge it. Regressive defenses, "loss of the boundaries of the self," delusions of omniscience, and magical thinking appear, in milder form, in narcissistic disorders. Although schizophrenia can by no means be considered simply as an exaggerated form of narcissism, it shares with narcissistic disturbances a breakdown in the boundaries between the self and the world of objects. "The contemporary psychoanalytic position," according to one psychiatrist, is that "schizophrenia is above all a narcissistic disorder." It is not surprising, therefore, that studies of the family background of schizophrenic patients point to a number of features also associated with narcissistic families. In both cases, a narcissistic mother lavishes suffocating yet emotionally distant attentions on her offspring. The narcissist, like the schizophrenic, often occupies a special position in the family, either because of his real endowments or because one of the parents treats him as a substitute for an absent father, mother, or spouse. Such a parent sometimes draws the whole family into the web of his own neurosis, which the family members tacitly conspire to indulge so as to maintain the family's emotional equilibrium. In "the family caught in this way of life," according to a student of narcissism, each member tries to validate the others' expectations and projected wishes. "This family tautology, together with the work needed to maintain it, is an identifying feature of the family held together by the narcissistic way of life." According to Kohut, such families suffer more from one member's character disorder than from an overt psychosis, since the psychotic parent is confined to an asylum or at least gets less support from his immediate social environment.

Narcissism and the "Absent Father"   Families of this type arise in America not just in response to a particular member's pathology but as a normal response to prevailing social conditions. As the world of business, jobs, and politics becomes more and more menacing, the family tries to create for itself an island of security in the surrounding disorder. It deals with internal tensions by denying their existence, desperately clinging to an illusion of normality. Yet the picture of harmonious domestic life, on which the family attempts to model itself, derives not from spontaneous feeling but from external sources, and the effort to conform to it therefore implicates the family in a charade of togetherness or "pseudo-mutuality," as one student of schizophrenia calls it. The mother in particular, on whom the work of childrearing devolves by default, attempts to become an ideal parent, compensating for her lack of spontaneous feeling for the child by smothering him with solicitude. Abstractly convinced that her child deserves the best of everything, she arranges each detail of his life with a punctilious zeal that undermines his initiative and destroys the capacity for self-help. She leaves the child with the feeling, according to Kohut, that he has "no mind of his own." His idealistically inflated impressions of the mother persist unmodified by later experience, mingling in his unconscious thoughts with fantasies of infantile omnipotence.

A case reported by Annie Reich shows in exaggerated form what the absence of the father does to the relations between mother and child. The patient, a bright young woman who had embarked on a successful career as a teacher, "wavered between her feelings of grandiosity and an awareness that she was not as grandiose as she wanted to be." Secretly she believed she was a genius, who in her own words would "suddenly reveal herself and stand out as an obelisk." The girl's father had died a few months after she was born. Her mother's brother had also died young. The mother refused to remarry and showered the child with attentions, treating her as someone rare and special. She made it clear that the child was to substitute for the dead father and uncle. The daughter, putting her own construction on this communication, "imagined that the mother had devoured the father in the sexual act, which was equated with having castrated him through biting off the penis. She (the patient) was the father's penis—or the dead father or uncle come back." Like many narcissistic women, she directed her interest "to an enormous degree upon her own body," which she unconsciously equated with a phallus in the fantasy of "standing out like a tremendous obelisk," admired by everyone around her. Yet her awareness of her femininity, which contradicted this phallic fantasy, combined with "a relentless superego" (derived in part from the "megalomanic id") to produce feelings of unworthiness and violent "oscillations of self-esteem."

The most striking features of this material, as with so many cases concerning narcissistic patients, are the persistence of archaic fantasies, the regressive character of defenses against loss, and the inability to sublimate—for example, by finding pleasure in the work for which the patient had already shown considerable aptitude. We have seen how an exaggerated dependence on the mother, encouraged by the mother herself, makes it difficult for the child to reconcile himself, after a period of mourning, to her loss. In the present case, the father's death, combined with the mother's use of the child as a substitute for the father, allowed the girl's fantasy of a grandiose, phallic father to flourish without the correcting influence of everyday contact. "The normal impact of reality on this fantasy subject, which would have helped to achieve some degree of desexualization [as the child came to understand that her father had other qualities besides sexual ones] and also to reduce to normal size the figure of the father that was seen in such supernatural dimensions, was absent in this case—hence the unsublimated phallic character of the ego ideal and its megalomanic scope."

Women with "otherwise well-integrated personalities," according to Dr. Reich, unconsciously seek to please a narcissistic mother by replacing the missing father, either by elaborating grandiose fantasies of success or by attaching themselves to successful men. One patient said that "during intercourse she felt as though she were the man with the phallus-like body making love to herself, the girl." Another achieved minor success as an actress and described the euphoria of being admired by the audience as "an intense excitement experienced over the entire body surface and a sensation of standing out, erect, with her whole body. Obviously she felt like a phallus with her whole body." In such patients, the superego or ego ideal consists of archaic representations of the father unmitigated by reality. The identification of themselves with a sexual organ, their grandiose ambitions, and the feelings of worthlessness that alternate with delusions of grandeur all testify to the primitive origin of the superego and to the aggressiveness with which it punishes failure to live up to the exaggerated ideal of an all-powerful father. Behind this image of the phallic father stands an even earlier attachment to the primitive mother, equally untempered by experiences that might reduce early fantasies to human scale. Narcissistic women seek to replace the absent father, whom the mother has castrated, and thus to reunite themselves with the mother of earliest infancy.

On the assumption that pathology represents a heightened version of normality, we can now see why the absence of the American father has become such a crucial feature of the American family: not so much because it deprives the child of a role model as because it allows early fantasies of the father to dominate subsequent development of the superego. The father's absence, moreover, deforms the relations between mother and child. According to a misguided popular theory, the mother takes the father's place and confuses the child by assuming a masculine role ("Momism"). In the child's fantasies, however, it is not the mother who replaces the father but the child himself. When a narcissistic mother, already disposed to see her offspring as extensions of herself, attempts to compensate the child for the father's desertion (and also to conform to the socially defined standards of ideal motherhood), her constant but perfunctory attentions, her attempts to make the child feel wanted and special, and her wish to make it "stand out" communicate themselves to the child in a charged and highly disturbing form. The child imagines that the mother has swallowed or castrated the father and harbors the grandiose fantasy of replacing him, by achieving fame or attaching himself to someone who represents a phallic kind of success, thereby bringing about an ecstatic reunion with the mother.

The intensity of the child's dependence on the mother prevents him from acknowledging her limitations, which in any case are concealed beneath an appearance of continual solicitude. The father's emotional absence from the family makes the mother the dominant parent; yet her dominance makes itself felt chiefly in the child's fantasies (where the father too plays an active part), not in everyday life. In this sense, the American mother is an absent parent also. Outside experts have taken over many of her practical functions, and she often discharges those that remain in a mechanical manner that conforms not to the child's needs but to a preconceived ideal of motherhood. In view of the suffocating yet emotionally distant care they receive from narcissistic mothers, it is not surprising that so many young people—for example, the alienated students interviewed by Kenneth Keniston and Herbert

Hendin—describe their mothers as both seductive and aloof, devouring and indifferent. Nor is it surprising that so many narcissistic patients experience maternal seductiveness as a form of sexual assault. Their unconscious impressions of the mother are so overblown and so heavily influenced by aggressive impulses, and the quality of her care so little attuned to the child's needs, that she appears in the child's fantasies as a devouring bird, a vagina full of teeth.

The Abdication of Authority and the Transformation of the Superego   The psychological patterns associated with pathological narcissism, which in less exaggerated form manifest themselves in so many patterns of American culture—in the fascination with fame and celebrity, the fear of competition, the inability to suspend disbelief, the shallowness and transitory quality of personal relations, the horror of death—originate in the peculiar structure of the American family, which in turn originates in changing modes of production. Industrial production takes the father out of the home and diminishes the role he plays in the conscious life of the child. The mother attempts to make up to the child for the loss of its father, but she often lacks practical experience of childrearing, feels herself at a loss to understand what the child needs, and relies so heavily on outside experts that her attentions fail to provide the child with a sense of security. Both parents seek to make the family into a refuge from outside pressures, yet the very standards by which they measure their success, and the techniques through which they attempt to bring it about, derive in large part from industrial sociology, personnel management, child psychology—in short, from the organized apparatus of social control. The family's struggle to conform to an externally imposed ideal of family solidarity and parenthood creates an appearance of solidarity at the expense of spontaneous feeling, a ritualized "relatedness" empty of real substance.

Because these family patterns are so deeply rooted in the social conditions created by modern industry, they cannot be changed by prophylactic or "educational" reforms designed to improve the quality of communication, diminish tensions, and promote interpersonal skills. Such reforms, by extending the sway of the health and welfare professions, usually do more harm than good. The injunction to feel spontaneous emotion does not make it easier to feel. In any case, the psychological patterns promoted by the family are reinforced by conditions outside the family. Because those patterns seem to find their clearest expression in the pathology of narcissism, and ultimately in schizophrenia, we should not jump to the conclusion that the family produces misfits, people who cannot function efficiently in modern industrial society.* In many ways it does a good job of preparing the child for the conditions he will encounter when he leaves home. Other institutions—for example, the school and the adolescent peer group—merely strengthen earlier patterns by satisfying expectations created by the family. As Jules Henry writes, "There is a constant interplay between each family and the culture at large, one reinforcing the other; each unique family upbringing gives rise to needs in the child that are satisfied by one or another aspect of the adolescent-and-school-culture."

According to Henry and other observers of American culture, the collapse of parental authority reflects the collapse of "ancient impulse controls" and the shift "from a society in which Super Ego values (the values of self-restraint) were ascendant, to one in which more and more recognition was being given to the values of the id (the values of self-indulgence)." The reversal of the normal

---

*Kenneth Keniston, Philip Slater, and other Parsonian critics of American culture have argued that the nuclear family, in Keniston's words, "produces deep discontinuities between childhood and adulthood." The critique of "privatism," which has emerged as one of the dominant themes in recent cultural radicalism, finds an obvious target in the nuclear family, which ostensibly encourages a predatory and anachronistic individualism and thus cripples children for the demands of cooperative living in a complex, "interdependent" society. Often associated with the radical psychiatry of R. D. Laing and Wilhelm Reich and with urgent calls for a cultural revolution, this criticism of the nuclear family merely updates and clothes in the latest liberationist jargon an indictment of the family first articulated by social workers, educators, penal reformers, and other social pathologists, and used by these experts to justify their appropriation of familial functions. By associating itself with psychiatric criticism of the family, the "cultural revolution" thus reaffirms one of the strongest tendencies in the society it claims to criticize.

relations between the generations, the decline of parental discipline, the "socialization" of many parental functions, and the "self-centered, impulse-dominated, detached, confused" actions of American parents give rise to characteristics that "can have seriously pathological outcomes, when present in extreme form," but which in milder form equip the young to live in a permissive society organized around the pleasures of consumption. Arnold Rogow argues, along similar lines, that American parents, alternately "permissive and evasive" in dealing with the young, "find it easier to achieve conformity by the use of bribery than by facing the emotional turmoil of suppressing the child's demands." In this way they undermine the child's initiative and make it impossible for him to develop self-restraint or self-discipline; but since American society no longer values these qualities anyway, the abdication of parental authority itself instills in the young the character traits demanded by a corrupt, permissive, hedonistic culture. The decline of parental authority reflects the "decline of the superego" in American society as a whole.

These interpretations, which lucidly capture the prevailing styles of parental discipline, their impact on the young, and the connections between the family and society, need to be modified in one important detail. The changing conditions of family life lead not so much to a "decline of the superego" as to an alteration of its contents. The parents' failure to serve as models of disciplined self-restraint or to restrain the child does not mean that the child grows up without a superego. On the contrary, it encourages the development of a harsh and punitive superego based largely on archaic images of the parents, fused with grandiose self-images. Under these conditions, the superego consists of parental introjects instead of identifications. It holds up to the ego an exalted standard of fame and success and condemns it with savage ferocity when it falls short of that standard. Hence the oscillations of self-esteem so often associated with pathological narcissism.

The fury with which the superego punishes the ego's failures suggests that it derives most of its energy from aggressive drives in the id, unmixed with libido. The conventional oversimplification which equates superego and id with "self-restraint" and "self-indulgence," treating them as if they were radically opposed, ignores the irrational features of the superego and the alliance between aggression and a punishing conscience. The decline of parental authority and of external sanctions in general, while in many ways it weakens the superego, paradoxically reinforces the aggressive, dictatorial elements in the superego and thus makes it more difficult than ever for instinctual desires to find acceptable outlets. The "decline of the superego" in a permissive society is better understood as the creation of a new kind of superego in which archaic elements predominate. The social changes that have made it difficult for children to internalize parental authority have not abolished the superego but have merely strengthened the alliance of superego and Thanatos—that "pure culture of the death instinct," as Freud called it, which directs against the ego a torrent of fierce, unrelenting criticism.

The new permissiveness extends largely to expression of libidinal instincts, not to aggression. A bureaucratic society that stresses cooperation, interpersonal give and take, cannot allow many legitimate outlets for anger. Even in the family, which is supposed to allow expression to feelings denied expression elsewhere, anger threatens the precarious equilibrium that members of the family try so hard to preserve. At the same time, the mechanical quality of parental care, so notably lacking in affect, gives rise in the child to ravenous oral cravings and to a boundless rage against those who fail to gratify them. Much of this anger, fiercely repressed by the ego, finds its way into the superego, with the results described by Henry and Yela Lowenfeld.

The inhibiting, controlling, and guiding function of the superego, which largely merges with the ego, is weakened through the weakness of the parents, through indulgent education which fails to train the ego, and through the general social climate of permissiveness. . . . But the severe superego of early childhood still lives in the individual. The controlling function of the superego which draws its strength from the ientification with strong parental figures, and which can protect the individual from conscious and unconscious guilt feelings, functions poorly; its punishing and self-destructive power still seems to affect many. The result is restlessness, discontent, depressive moods, craving for substitute satisfactions.

In Heller's *Something Happened*, which describes with such a multitude of depressing details the psychodynamics of family life today, the father believes, with good reason, that his rebellious adolescent daughter wants him to punish her; and like so many American parents, he refuses to give her this satisfaction or even to recognize its legitimacy. Refusing to be maneuvered into administering punishment, he wins psychological victories over his daughter, on the contrary, by giving in to her wishes and thereby avoiding the quarrels she seeks to provoke. Yet both his children, notwithstanding his desire, in his son's case at least, to adopt the part of the "best friend," unconsciously regard him as a tyrant. He muses in bewilderment: "I don't know why [my son] feels so often that I am going to hit him when I never do; I never have; I don't know why both he and my daughter believe I used to beat them a great deal when they were smaller, when I don't believe I ever struck either one of them at all." The parent's abdication of authority intensifies rather than softens the child's fear of punishment, while identifying thoughts of punishment more firmly than ever with the exercise of arbitrary, overwhelming violence.*

The Family's Relation to Other Agencies of Social Control

Society reinforces these patterns not only through "indulgent education" and general permissiveness but through advertising, demand creation, and the mass culture of hedonism. At first glance, a society based on mass consumption appears to encourage self-indulgence in its most blatant forms. Strictly considered, however, modern advertising seeks to promote not so much self-indulgence as self-doubt. It seeks to create needs, not to fulfill them; to generate new anxieties instead of allaying old ones. By

---

* In the school studied by Jules Henry, an eleven-year-old boy wrote gratefully that his father "teaches me [baseball and] other sports [and] gives me as much as he can," but complained that "he never gives me a spanking when I've done wrong." Henry observes: "What this child seems to be saying is that the father . . . cannot give what the child feels he needs in order to make him a person: just punishment for his wrongdoing. It is startling for people in a permissive culture to learn that *not* to be given pain can be felt as a deprivation. Yet it is more painful for some children to bear guilt unpunished than to get a spanking."

surrounding the consumer with images of the good life, and by associating them with the glamour of celebrity and success, mass culture encourages the ordinary man to cultivate extraordinary tastes, to identify himself with the privileged minority against the rest, and to join them, in his fantasies, in a life of exquisite comfort and sensual refinement. Yet the propaganda of commodities simultaneously makes him acutely unhappy with his lot. By fostering grandiose aspirations, it also fosters self-denigration and self-contempt. The culture of consumption in its central tendency thus recapitulates the socialization earlier provided by the family.

Experiences with authority—in school, at work, in the political realm—complete the citizen's training in uneasy acquiescence to the prevailing forms of control. Here again, social control promotes neither self-indulgence nor the guilty self-criticism formerly inflicted by a moralistic superego but anxiety, uncertainty, restless dissatisfaction. In the school, the business corporation, and the courts of law, authorities conceal their power behind a façade of benevolence. Posing as friendly helpers, they discipline their subordinates as seldom as possible, seeking instead to create a friendly atmosphere in which everyone freely speaks his mind. Jules Henry found that high school teachers actually feared quiet and restraint in their classrooms, justifying their failure to enforce order on the grounds that imposition of silence interferes with spontaneous expression and creates unnecessary fears. "A quiet classroom may be an awfully fearful situation for someone," said one teacher, whose classroom grew so noisy that the students themselves clamored for quiet. According to Henry, the classroom teaches children "their first lessons in how to live in the 'friendly,' 'relaxed' climates of the contemporary bureaucracies of business and government."*

---

* When Ann Landers advised a high school student to complain to the principal about other students who carried on sexual activities in the cafeteria, she was told that the "principal is probably a gutless wonder" and that "the teachers know what goes on and who the offensive kids are, but they don't want to stir up any trouble so they keep quiet." The same column carried a letter from a sixteen-year-old girl who insisted that adolescents complaining of "being under [their] parents' thumb" should consider themselves lucky not to have "parents who take the easy way out and don't stand up to their kids because they hate the hassle."

The appearance of permissiveness conceals a stringent system of controls, all the more effective because it avoids direct confrontations between authorities and the people on whom they seek to impose their will. Because confrontations provoke arguments about principle, the authorities whenever possible delegate discipline to someone else so that they themselves can pose as advisers, "resource persons," and friends. Thus parents rely on doctors, psychiatrists, and the child's own peers to impose rules on the child and to see that he conforms to them. If the child refuses to eat what his parents think he ought to eat, the parents appeal to medical authority. If he is unruly, they call in a psychiatrist to help the child with his "problem."* In this way, parents make their own problem—insubordination—the child's. Similarly at school, the child finds himself surrounded by authorities who wish only to help. If one of the students gets "out of line," they send him to a counselor for "guidance." The students themselves, according to Edgar Friedenberg's study of the American high school, reject both authoritarian and libertarian measures and regard social control as "a technical problem, to be referred to the right expert for solution." Thus if a teacher finds an unruly student smoking in the washroom, he should neither "beat him calmly and coolly and with emotional restraint" or publicly humiliate him, on the one hand, nor ignore the offense, on the other hand, as a minor infraction that should not contribute to the student's reputation as a troublemaker. The teacher should refer him instead to the school psychiatrist. Beating him would make him more unmanageable than ever, in the students' view, whereas the psychiatric solution, in effect, enlists his own cooperation in the school's attempt to control him.

Human Relations on the Job: The Factory as a Family   Experts in personnel management have introduced similar tech-

---

* "The community has expressed its concern for childhood by creating institutions," wrote Van Waters. "It is increasingly common for births to take place in hospitals, infant feeding has become an esoteric rite few parents would attempt

niques into the modern corporation, ostensibly as a means of "humanizing" the workplace. The ideology of modern management draws on the same body of therapeutic theory and practice that informs progressive education and progressive childrearing. Recent efforts to "democratize" industrial relations bring to a full circle the development that began when experts in scientific management began to study group dynamics in the office and factory in order to remove friction and raise output. Social scientists then applied the ideas first worked out in the study of small groups to study and treatment of the family, arguing that most domestic conflicts originated in the attempt to impose outmoded authoritarian controls on an institution that was evolving from an authoritarian to a democratic form. By the 1950s, almost all psychiatrists, social workers, and social scientists condemned the values associated with the traditional or authoritarian family. "Our textbooks," wrote one team of experts, "discuss the 'democratic' family system and the sharing of authority."

In the late fifties and sixties, industrial relations experts began to extend these ideas to the problems of management. In *The Human Side of Enterprise* (1960), Douglas McGregor urged corporate executives to accept the "limits of authority." Defining authority, too crudely, as command sanctioned by force, McGregor argued that authority represented an outmoded form of social control in an age of "interdependence." Command remained effective, he reasoned, only so long as workers occupied a debased, dependent position in the industrial hierarchy and found it difficult to satisfy even their material needs. The psychiatrist Abraham Maslow had demonstrated that as soon as human beings satisfy the basic need for bread, shelter, and security, they devote their attention to satisfying the need for "self-actualization." Yet industrial managers, McGregor complained, still took a "carrot and stick" approach to the worker, unscientifically assuming that people hate work and have to be coerced into performing it or enticed with material rewards.

without expert assistance; when children are ill, they are cared for by specialists far better equipped than parents. . . . At every stage in the child's life some modern organized agency will say to the parent: 'We can do this better than you can.' "

McGregor made it clear that he did not wish to see an abdication of managerial responsibility. Like Dr. Spock and Dr. Bruch, he rejected the "permissive" approaches of his predecessors, which had allegedly contaminated early experiments in "human relations." Experience had overturned the assumption that "employee satisfaction" led to greater productivity or that "industrial health [flowed] automatically from the elimination of . . . conflict." The worker still needed direction, but he had to be approached as a partner in the enterprise, not as a child. The enlightened executive encouraged his subordinates to participate in group discussions, to "communicate" their needs and suggestions to management, and even to make "constructive" criticisms. Just as marriage counselors had learned to accept conflict as a normal part of domestic life, so McGregor tried to impress a similar point of view on corporate managers. He told them that they made a mistake in regarding the interests of the individual as opposed to those of the group. "If we look to the family, we might recognize the possibilities inherent in the opposite point of view."

Research into small groups, according to McGregor, showed that groups function best when everyone speaks his mind; when people listen as well as speak; when disagreements surface without causing "obvious tensions"; when the "chairman of the board" does not try to dominate his subordinates; and when decisions rest on consensus.* These precepts, which by this time had be-

---

* McGregor's influential book, so characteristic an expression of the culture of the fifties, not only complemented the psychiatric attack on the authoritarian family, which came to fruition in that decade, it restated many of the themes of the Parsonian sociology of the family. In 1961, Parsons criticized David Riesman's analysis of the abdication of parental authority (in *The Lonely Crowd*) on the grounds that modern parents best equip the young for life in a complex industrial society when they encourage them to become self-reliant, instead of attempting to supervise every detail of the child's upbringing. Like Parsons, McGregor argues that what looked like an abdication of authority—in this case, managerial authority—represented instead a transition to a more effective, scientific, therapeutic form of control. Just as reactionary alarmists (sometimes in common with well-meaning but misguided social theorists) prematurely deplored the collapse of parental authority, so reactionary businessmen predictably denounced the new softness imported into business by industrial relations experts, demanding a crackdown on unions, a reversal of the New Deal, and a return to the good old days of industrial

come the common coin of the social sciences, summarize the therapeutic view of authority. The growing acceptance of that view, at all levels of American society, makes it possible to preserve hierarchical forms of organization in the guise of "participation." It provides a society dominated by corporate elites with an antielitist ideology. The popularization of therapeutic modes of thought discredits authority, especially in the home and the classroom, while leaving domination uncriticized. Therapeutic forms of social control, by softening or eliminating the adversary relation between subordinates and superiors, make it more and more difficult for citizens to defend themselves against the state or for workers to resist the demands of the corporation. As the ideas of guilt and innocence lose their moral and even legal meaning, those in power no longer enforce their rules by means of the authoritative edicts of judges, magistrates, teachers, and preachers. Society no longer expects authorities to articulate a clearly reasoned, elaborately justified code of law and morality; nor does it expect the young to internalize the moral standards of the community. It demands only conformity to the conventions of everyday intercourse, sanctioned by psychiatric definitions of normal behavior.

In the hierarchies of work and power, as in the family, the decline of authority does not lead to the collapse of social constraints. It merely deprives those constraints of a rational basis. Just as the parent's failure to administer just punishment to the child undermines the child's self-esteem rather than strengthening it, so the corruptibility of public authorities—their acquiescence in minor forms of wrongdoing—reminds the subordinate of his subordination by making him dependent on the indulgence of those above him. The new-style bureaucrat, whose "ideology and character support hierarchy even though he is neither paternalistic nor authoritarian," as Michael Maccoby puts it in his study of

autocracy. McGregor had no patience with this outmoded outlook. It rested, in his view, on a misunderstanding of authority and a simplification of the alternative modes of exercising power. "Abdication is not an appropriate antithesis to authoritarianism. . . . Only if we can free ourselves from the notion that we are limited to a single dimension—that of more or less authority—will we escape from our present dilemma."

the corporate "gamesman," no longer orders his inferiors around; but he has discovered subtler means of keeping them in their place. Even though his underlings often realize that they have been "conned, pushed around, and manipulated," they find it hard to resist such easygoing oppression. The diffusion of responsibility in large organizations, moreover, enables the modern manager to delegate discipline to others, to blame unpopular decisions on the company in general, and thus to preserve his standing as a friendly adviser to those beneath him. Yet his entire demeanor conveys to them that he remains a winner in a game most of them are destined to lose.

Since everyone allegedly plays this game by the same rules, no one can begrudge him his success; but neither can the losers escape the heavy sense of their own failure. In a society without authority, the lower orders no longer experience oppression as guilt. Instead, they internalize a grandiose idea of the opportunities open to all, together with an inflated opinion of their own capacities. If the lowly man resents those more highly placed, it is only because he suspects them of grandly violating the regulations of the game, as he would like to do himself if he dared. It never occurs to him to insist on a new set of rules.

VIII

The Flight from Feeling:
Sociopsychology of the Sex War

> *Suddenly she wished she was with some other man and not with Edward. . . . Pia looked at Edward. She looked at his red beard, his immense spectacles. I don't like him, she thought. That red beard, those immense spectacles. . . .*
>
> *Pia said to Edward that he was the only person she had ever loved for this long. "How long is it?" Edward asked. It was seven months.*
>
> DONALD BARTHELME

> *I think more and more . . . that there is no such thing as rationality in relationships. I think you just have to say okay that's what you feel right now and what are we going to do about it. . . . I believe everybody should really be able to basically do what they want to do as long as it's not hurting anybody else.*
>
> LIBERATED BRIDEGROOM

The Trivialization of Personal Relations   Bertrand Russell once predicted that the socialization of reproduction—the supersession of the family by the state—would "make sex love itself more trivial," encourage "a certain triviality in all personal relations," and "make it far more difficult to take an interest in anything after one's own death." At first glance, recent developments appear to have refuted the first part of this prediction. Americans today invest personal relations, particularly the relations between men and women, with undiminished emotional importance. The

187

decline of childrearing as a major preoccupation has freed sex from its bondage to procreation and made it possible for people to value erotic life for its own sake. As the family shrinks to the marital unit, it can be argued that men and women respond more readily to each other's emotional needs, instead of living vicariously through their offspring. The marriage contract having lost its binding character, couples now find it possible, according to many observers, to ground sexual relations in something more solid than legal compulsion. In short, the growing determination to live for the moment, whatever it may have done to the relations between parents and children, appears to have established the preconditions of a new intimacy between men and women.

This appearance is an illusion. The cult of intimacy conceals a growing despair of finding it. Personal relations crumble under the emotional weight with which they are burdened. The inability "to take an interest in anything after one's own death," which gives such urgency to the pursuit of close personal encounters in the present, makes intimacy more elusive than ever. The same developments that have weakened the tie between parents and children have also undermined relations between men and women. Indeed the deterioration of marriage contributes in its own right to the deterioration of care for the young.

This last point is so obvious that only a strenuous propaganda on behalf of "open marriage" and "creative divorce" prevents us from grasping it. It is clear, for example, that the growing incidence of divorce, together with the ever-present possibility that any given marriage will end in collapse, adds to the instability of family life and deprives the child of a measure of emotional security. Enlightened opinion diverts attention from this general fact by insisting that in specific cases, parents may do more harm to their children by holding a marriage together than by dissolving it. It is true that many couples preserve their marriage, in one form or another, at the expense of the child. Sometimes they embark on a life full of distractions that shield them against daily emotional involvements with their offspring. Sometimes one parent acquiesces in the neurosis of the other (as in the family configuration that produces so many schizophrenic patients) for fear of disturbing the precarious peace of the household. More often the husband abandons his children to the wife whose company he finds unbearable, and the wife smothers the children with incessant yet perfunctory attentions. This particular solution to the problem of marital strain has become so common that the absence of the father impresses many observers as the most striking fact about the contemporary family. Under these conditions, a divorce in which the mother retains custody of her children merely ratifies the existing state of affairs—the effective emotional desertion of his family by the father. But the reflection that divorce often does no more damage to children than marriage itself hardly inspires rejoicing.

The Battle of the Sexes: Its Social History   While the escalating war between men and women has psychological roots in the disintegration of the marital relation, and more broadly in the changing patterns of socialization outlined in the preceding chapter, much of this tension can be explained without reference to psychology. The battle of the sexes also constitutes a social phenomenon with a history of its own. The reasons for the recent intensification of sexual combat lie in the transformation of capitalism from its paternalistic and familial form to a managerial, corporate, bureaucratic system of almost total control: more specifically, in the collapse of "chivalry"; the liberation of sex from many of its former constraints; the pursuit of sexual pleasure as an end in itself; the emotional overloading of personal relations; and most important of all, the irrational male response to the emergence of the liberated woman.

It has been clear for some time that "chivalry is dead." The tradition of gallantry formerly masked and to some degree mitigated the organized oppression of women. While males monopolized political and economic power, they made their domination of women more palatable by surrounding it with an elaborate ritual of deference and *politesse*. They set themselves up as protectors of the weaker sex, and this cloying but useful fiction set limits to their capacity to exploit women through sheer physical force. The counterconvention of *droit de seigneur*, which justified the predatory exploits of the privileged classes against women socially inferior to themselves, nevertheless showed that the male sex at no time ceased to regard most women as fair game. The long history of rape and seduction, moreover, served as a reminder that animal strength remained the basis of masculine ascendancy, manifested here in its most direct and brutal form. Yet polite conventions, even when they were no more than a façade, provided women with ideological leverage in their struggle to domesticate the wildness and savagery of men. They surrounded essentially exploitive relationships with a network of reciprocal obligations, which if nothing else made exploitation easier to bear.

The symbiotic interdependence of exploiters and exploited, so characteristic of paternalism in all ages, survived in male-female relations long after the collapse of patriarchal authority in other areas. Because the convention of deference to the fair sex was so closely bound up with paternalism, however, it lived on borrowed time once the democratic revolutions of the eighteenth and nineteenth centuries had destroyed the last foundations of feudalism. The decline of paternalism, and of the rich public ceremonial formerly associated with it, spelled the end of gallantry. Women themselves began to perceive the connection between their debasement and their sentimental exaltation, rejected their confining position on the pedestal of masculine adoration, and demanded the demystification of female sexuality.

Democracy and feminism have now stripped the veil of courtly convention from the subordination of women, revealing the sexual antagonisms formerly concealed by the "feminine mystique." Denied illusions of comity, men and women find it more difficult than before to confront each other as friends and lovers, let alone as equals. As male supremacy becomes ideologically untenable, incapable of justifying itself as protection, men assert their domination more directly, in fantasies and occasionally in acts of raw violence. Thus the treatment of women in movies, according to one study, has shifted "from reverence to rape."

Women who abandon the security of well-defined though restrictive social roles have always exposed themselves to sexual exploitation, having surrendered the usual claims of respectability. Mary Wollstonecraft, attempting to live as a free woman, found herself brutally deserted by Gilbert Imlay. Later feminists forfeited the privileges of sex and middle-class origin when they campaigned for women's rights. Men reviled them publicly as sexless "she-men" and approached them privately as loose women. A Cincinnati brewer, expecting to be admitted to Emma Goldman's hotel room when he found her alone, became alarmed when she threatened to wake the whole establishment. He protested, "I thought you believed in free love." Ingrid Bengis reports that when she hitchhiked across the country, men expected her to pay for rides with sexual favors. Her refusal elicited the predictable reply: "Well, girls shouldn't hitchhike in the first place."

What distinguishes the present time from the past is that defiance of sexual conventions less and less presents itself as a matter of individual choice, as it was for the pioneers of feminism. Since most of those conventions have already collapsed, even a woman who lays no claim to her rights nevertheless finds it difficult to claim the traditional privileges of her sex. All women find themselves identified with "women's lib" merely by virtue of their sex, unless by strenuous disavowals they identify themselves with its enemies. All women share in the burdens as well as the benefits of "liberation," both of which can be summarized by saying that men no longer treat women as ladies.

The Sexual "Revolution"　　The demystification of womanhood goes hand in hand with the desublimation of sexuality. The "repeal of reticence" has dispelled the aura of mystery surrounding sex and removed most of the obstacles to its public display. Institutionalized sexual segregation has given way to arrangements that promote the intermingling of the sexes at every stage of life. Efficient contraceptives, legalized abortion, and a "realistic" and "healthy" acceptance of the body have weakened the links that once tied sex to love, marriage, and procreation. Men and women now pursue sexual pleasure as an end in itself, unmediated even by the conventional trappings of romance.

Sex valued purely for its own sake loses all reference to the future and brings no hope of permanent relationships. Sexual liaisons, including marriage, can be terminated at pleasure. This means, as Willard Waller demonstrated a long time ago, that lovers forfeit the right to be jealous or to insist on fidelity as a condition of erotic union. In his sociological satire of the recently divorced, Waller pointed out that the bohemians of the 1920s attempted to avoid emotional commitments while eliciting them from others. Since the bohemian was "not ready to answer with his whole personality for the consequences of the affair, nor to give any assurance of its continuance," he lost the right to demand such an assurance from others. "To show jealousy," under these conditions, became "nothing short of a crime. . . . So if one falls in love in Bohemia, he conceals it from his friends as best he can." In similar studies of the "rating and dating complex" on college campuses, Waller found that students who fell in love invited the ridicule of their peers. Exclusive attachments gave way to an easygoing promiscuity as the normal pattern of sexual relations. Popularity replaced purity as the measure of a woman's social value; the sentimental cult of virginity gave way to "playful woman-sharing," which had "no negative effect," as Wolfenstein and Leites pointed out in their study of movies, "on the friendly relations between the men."* In the thirties and forties, the cinematic fantasy in which a beautiful girl dances with a chorus of men, favoring one no more than the others, expressed an ideal to which reality more and more closely conformed. In *Elmtown's Youth*, August Hollingshead described a freshman girl who violated conventional taboos against drinking, smoking, and "fast" behavior and still retained her standing in the school's most prominent clique, partly because of her family's wealth but largely by means of her carefully calibrated promiscuity. "To be seen with

---

* The transition in American movies from the vamp to the "good-bad girl," according to Wolfenstein and Leites, illustrates the decline of jealousy and the displacement of sexual passion by sexiness. "The dangerousness of the vamp was associated with the man's intolerance for sharing her with other men. Her seductive appearance and readiness for love carried a strong suggestion that there had been and might be other men in her life. . . . The good-bad girl is associated with a greater tolerance for sharing the woman. . . . In effect, the woman's attraction is enhanced by her association with other men. All that is needed to eliminate unpleasantness is the assurance that those these relations were not serious."

her adds to a boy's prestige in the elite peer group. . . . She pets with her dates discreetly—never goes too far, just far enough to make them come back again." In high school as in college, the peer group attempts through conventional ridicule and vitupera-tion to prevent its members from falling in love with the wrong people, indeed from falling in love at all; for as Hollingshead noted, lovers "are lost to the adolescent world with its quixotic enthusiasms and varied group activities."

These studies show that the main features of the contempo-rary sexual scene had already established themselves well before the celebrated "sexual revolution" of the sixties and seventies: cas-ual promiscuity, a wary avoidance of emotional commitments, an attack on jealousy and possessiveness. Recent developments, however, have introduced a new source of tension: the modern woman's increasingly insistent demand for sexual fulfillment. In the 1920s and 1930s, many women still approached sexual en-counters with a hesitance that combined prudery and a realistic fear of consequences. Superficially seductive, they took little pleasure in sex even when they spoke the jargon of sexual libera-tion and professed to live for pleasure and thrills. Doctors wor-ried about female frigidity, and psychiatrists had no trouble in recognizing among their female patients the classic patterns of hysteria described by Freud, in which a coquettish display of sex-uality often coexists with powerful repression and a rigid, puri-tanical morality.

Today women have dropped much of their sexual reserve. In the eyes of men, this makes them more accessible as sexual partners but also more threatening. Formerly men complained about women's lack of sexual response; now they find this re-sponse intimidating and agonize about their capacity to satisfy it. "I'm sorry they ever found out they could have orgasms too," Heller's Bob Slocum says. The famous Masters-Johnson report on female sexuality added to these anxieties by depicting women as sexually insatiable, inexhaustible in their capacity to experi-ence orgasm after orgasm. Some feminists have used the Masters report to attack the "myth of the vaginal orgasm," to assert wo-men's independence of men, or to taunt men with their sexual in-feriority. "Theoretically, a woman could go on having orgasms 'indefinitely if physical exhaustion did not intervene," writes Mary Jane Sherfey. According to Kate Millett, "While the male's sexual potential is limited, the female's appears to be biologically nearly inexhaustible." Sexual "performance" thus becomes another weapon in the war between men and women; social inhibitions no longer prevent women from exploiting the tactical advantage which the current obsession with sexual measurement has given them. Whereas the hysterical woman, even when she fell in love and longed to let herself go, seldom conquered her underlying aversion to sex, the pseudoliberated woman of *Cosmopolitan* exploits her sexuality in a more deliberate and calculating way, not only because she has fewer reservations about sex but because she manages more successfully to avoid emotional entanglements. "Women with narcissistic personalities," writes Otto Kernberg, "may appear quite 'hysterical' on the surface, with their extreme coquettishness and exhibitionism, but the cold, shrewdly calculating quality of their seductiveness is in marked contrast to the much warmer, emotionally involved quality of hysterical pseudo-hypersexuality."

Togetherness Both men and women have come to approach personal relations with a heightened appreciation of their emotional risks. Determined to manipulate the emotions of others while protecting themselves against emotional injury, both sexes cultivate a protective shallowness, a cynical detachment they do not altogether feel but which soon becomes habitual and in any case embitters personal relations merely through its repeated profession. At the same time, people demand from personal relations the richness and intensity of a religious experience. Although in some ways men and women have had to modify their demands on each other, especially in their inability to exact commitments of lifelong sexual fidelity, in other ways they demand more than ever. In the American middle class, moreover, men and women see too much of each other and find it hard to put their relations in proper perspective. The degradation of work and the impoverishment of communal life force people to turn to sexual excitement to satisfy all their emotional needs. Formerly sexual antagonism was tempered not only by chivalric, paternalistic conventions but by a more relaxed acceptance of the limitations of the other sex. Men and women acknowledged each other's shortcomings without making them the basis of a comprehensive indictment. Partly because they found more satisfaction than is currently available in casual relations with their own sex, they did not have to raise friendship itself into a political program, an ideological alternative to love. An easygoing, everyday contempt for the weaknesses of the other sex, institutionalized as folk wisdom concerning the emotional incompetence of men or the brainlessness of women, kept sexual enmity within bounds and prevented it from becoming an obsession.

Feminism and the ideology of intimacy have discredited the sexual stereotypes which kept women in their place but which also made it possible to acknowledge sexual antagonism without raising it to the level of all-out warfare. Today the folklore of sexual differences and the acceptance of sexual friction survive only in the working class. Middle-class feminists envy the ability of working-class women to acknowledge that men get in their way without becoming man-haters. "These women are less angry at their men because they don't spend that much time with them," according to one observer. "Middle-class women are the ones who were told men had to be their companions."*

* Psychiatric and sociological studies of working-class life confirm these observations. "An American middle-class wife tends to expect her husband to treat her as an equal," wrote a psychiatrist in 1957. ". . . She expects cooperation, sharing of responsibility, and individual consideration. . . . In the lower-class family of Italians, . . . the wife . . . does not expect to be treated as an equal. Rather she expects him to make the chief decisions, relieving her of the responsibility so that she can tend to the needs of the large brood of children." Rainwater, Coleman, and Handel reported in their study of working-class wives: "Middle class wives tend to see a greater interchangeability between the marriage partners in handling the work that must be done. There is much more interest in doing things together, whether it be the dishes or painting the walls; 'togetherness' is largely a middle class value."

In the twenty years since these descriptions were written, the ideology of marital companionship has made headway in working-class as well as middle-class families, while feminism, penetrating finally into the consciousness of working-

Feminism and the Intensification of Sexual Warfare   Not merely the cult of sexual companionship and "togetherness" but feminism itself has caused women to make new demands on men and to hate men when they fail to meet those demands. Feminist consciousness-raising, moreover, has had irreversible effects. Once women begin to question the inevitability of their subordination and to reject the conventions formerly associated with it, they can no longer retreat to the safety of those conventions. The woman who rejects the stereotype of feminine weakness and dependence can no longer find much comfort in the cliché that all men are beasts. She has no choice except to believe, on the contrary, that men are human beings, and she finds it hard to forgive them when they act like animals. Although her own actions, which violate the conventions of female passivity and thus appear to men as a form of aggression, help to call up animal-like actions in males, even her understanding of this dynamic does not make it any easier to make allowances for her adversary. "You want too much," an older woman says to a younger one. "You aren't willing to compromise. Men will never be as sensitive or aware as women are. It's just not in their nature. So you have to get used to that, and be satisfied with . . . either sexual satisfaction or theoretical intelligence or being loved and *not* understood or else being left alone to do the things you want to do."

A woman who takes feminism seriously, as a program that aims to put the relations between men and women on a new footing, can no longer accept such a definition of available alternatives without recognizing it as a form of surrender. The younger woman rightly replies that no one should settle for less than a combination of sex, compassion, and intelligent understanding.

class women, has made conventional sexual stereotyping suspect and has thus made it hard for people to indulge in routine depreciation of the opposite sex without self-consciousness. As working-class women begin to assert their rights or at least to listen to feminist ideas, their husbands see in this turn of events another blow to their own self-respect, the crowning indignity heaped on the workingman by a middle-class liberalism that has already destroyed his savings, bused his children to distant schools, undermined his authority over them, and now threatens to turn even his wife against him.

The attempt to implement these demands, however, exposes her to repeated disappointments, especially since men appear to find the demand for tenderness as threatening to their emotional security as the demand for sexual satisfaction. Thwarted passion in turn gives rise in women to the powerful rage against men so unforgettably expressed, for example, in the poems of Sylvia Plath.

> No day is safe from news of you,
> Walking about in Africa maybe, but thinking of me.

Women's rage against men originates not only in erotic disappointments or the consciousness of oppression but in a perception of marriage as the ultimate trap, the ultimate routine in a routinized society, the ultimate expression of the banality that pervades and suffocates modern life. For the heroine of *The Bell Jar*, marriage represents the apotheosis of the everyday: "It would mean getting up at seven and cooking him eggs and bacon and toast and coffee and dawdling about in my nightgown and curlers after he'd left for work to wash up the dirty plates and make the bed, and then when he came home after a lively, fascinating day he'd expect a big dinner, and I'd spend the evening washing up, even more dirty plates till I fell into bed, utterly exhausted." If the man protests that he is exhausted too, and that his "fascinating day" consists of drudgery and humiliation, his wife suspects that he wishes merely to give her domestic prison the appearance of a rose-covered cottage.

In theory, it should be possible for feminists to advance beyond the present stage of sexual recrimination by regarding men simply as a class enemy, involuntarily caught up in the defense of masculine privilege and therefore exempt from personal blame. The symbiotic interdependence of men and women, however, makes it hard to attain such intellectual detachment in everyday life. The "class enemy" presents himself in ordinary existence as a lover, husband, or father, on whom women proceed to make demands that men usually fail to meet. According to the feminists' own analysis of the way in which the subjection of women damages women and impoverishes the emotional life of men, men cannot possibly meet the full erotic demands of women under the existing sexual arrangements; yet feminism itself gives those demands the strongest ideological support. It therefore intensifies the problem to which it simultaneously offers the solution. On the one hand, feminism aspires to change the relations between men and women so that women will no longer be forced into the role of "victim and shrew," in the words of Simone de Beauvoir. On the other hand, it often makes women more shrewish than ever in their daily encounters with men. This contradiction remains unavoidable so long as feminism insists that men oppress women and that this oppression is intolerable, at the same time urging women to approach men not simply as oppressors but as friends and lovers.

Strategies of Accommodation   Because the contradictions exposed (and exacerbated) by feminism are so painful, the feminist movement has always found it tempting to renounce its own insights and program and to retreat into some kind of accommodation with the existing order, often disguised as embattled militancy. In the nineteenth century, American feminists edged away from their original programs, which envisioned not only economic equality but a sweeping reform of marriage and sexual relations, into a protracted campaign for woman suffrage. Today many feminists argue, once again in the name of political realism, that women need to establish their influence within the two-party system, as a kind of loyal opposition, before they can raise broader issues. Such tactics merely serve to postpone the discussion of broader issues indefinitely. Just as the women's rights movement of the nineteenth century drew back from discussions of love and marriage when they met with public hostility, so strong forces in the National Organization for Women today propose to improve woman's image, to show that feminism in no way threatens men, and to blame "social conditions" or bad attitudes, not male supremacy, for the subordination of the female sex.

More subtle forms of accommodation pose as radical challenges to mainstream feminism and the status quo. Some militants have revived discredited theories of matriarchal origins or myths of the moral superiority of women, thereby consoling themselves for their lack of power. They appeal to the illusory solidarity of sisterhood in order to avoid arguments about the proper goals of the feminist movement. By institutionalizing women's activities as "alternatives to the male death-culture," they avoid challenging that culture and protect women from the need to compete with men for jobs, political power, and public attention. What began as a tactical realization that women have to win their rights without waiting for men to grant them has degenerated into the fantasy of a world without men. As one critic has noted, the movement's "apparent vigor turns out to be mere busyness with self-perpetuating make-work: much of it serving in the short run to provide its more worldly experts with prestige, book contracts, and grants, its dreamers with an illusory matriarchal utopia."

"Radical lesbians" carry the logic of separation to its ultimate futility, withdrawing at every level from the struggle against male domination while directing a steady stream of abuse against men and against women who refuse to acknowledge their homosexual proclivities. Proclaiming their independence from men, militant lesbians in fact envision a protected enclave for themselves within a male-dominated society. Yet this form of surrender—the dream of an island secure against male intrusion—remains attractive to women who repeatedly fail to find a union of sexuality and tenderness in their relations with men. As such disappointments become more and more common, sexual separatism commends itself as the most plausible substitute for liberation.

All these strategies of accommodation derive their emotional energy from an impulse much more prevalent than feminism: the flight from feeling. For many reasons, personal relations have become increasingly risky—most obviously, because they no longer carry any assurance of permanence. Men and women make extravagant demands on each other and experience irrational rage and hatred when their demands are not met. Under these conditions, it is not surprising that more and more people long for emotional detachment or "enjoy sex," as Hendin writes, "only in situations where they can define and limit the intensity of the relationship." A lesbian confesses: "The only men I've ever been able to enjoy sex with were men I didn't give a shit about. Then I could let go, because I didn't feel vulnerable."

Sexual separatism is only one of many strategies for controlling or escaping from strong feeling. Many prefer the escape of drugs, which dissolve anger and desire in a glow of good feeling and create the illusion of intense experience without emotion. Others simply undertake to live alone, repudiating connections with either sex. The reported increase in single-member households undoubtedly reflects a new taste for personal independence, but it also expresses a revulsion against close emotional attachments of any kind. The rising rate of suicide among young people can be attributed, in part, to the same flight from emotional entanglements. Suicide, in Hendin's words, represents the "ultimate numbness."

The most prevalent form of escape from emotional complexity is promiscuity: the attempt to achieve a strict separation between sex and feeling. Here again, escape masquerades as liberation, regression as progress. The progressive ideology of "nonbinding commitments" and "cool sex" makes a virtue of emotional disengagement, while purporting to criticize the depersonalization of sex. Enlightened authorities like Alex Comfort, Nena and George O'Neill, Robert and Anna Francoeur insist on the need to humanize sex by making it into a "total experience" instead of a mechanical performance; yet in the same breath they condemn the human emotions of jealousy and possessiveness and decry "romantic illusions." "Radical" therapeutic wisdom urges men and women to express their needs and wishes without reserve—since all needs and wishes have equal legitimacy—but warns them not to expect a single mate to satisfy them. This program seeks to allay emotional tensions, in effect, by reducing the demands men and women make on each other, instead of making men and women better able to meet them. The promotion of sex as a "healthy," "normal" part of life masks a desire to divest it of the emotional intensity that unavoidably clings to it: the reminders of earlier entanglements with parents, the "unhealthy" inclination to re-create those relations in relation with lovers. The enlightened insistence that sex is not "dirty" expresses a wish to sanitize it by washing away its unconscious associations.

The humanistic critique of sexual "depersonalization" thus sticks to the surface of the problem. Even while preaching the need to combine sex with feeling, it gives ideological legitimacy to the protective withdrawal from stong emotions. It condemns the overemphasis on technique while extolling sexual relations that are hermetically free of affect. It exhorts men and women to "get in touch with their feelings" but encourages them to make "resolutions about freedom and 'non-possessiveness,'" as Ingrid Bengis writes, which "tear the very heart out of intimacy." It satirizes the crude pornographic fantasies sold by the mass media, which idealize hairless women with inflated mammaries, but it does so out of an aversion to fantasy itself, which so rarely conforms to social definitions of what is healthy minded. The critics of dehumanized sex, like the critics of sport, hope to abolish spectatorship and to turn everyone into a participant, hoping that vigorous exercise will drive away unwholesome thoughts. They attack pornography, not because they wish to promote more complicated and satisfying fantasies about sex, but because, on the contrary, they wish to win acceptance for a realistic view of womanhood and of the reduced demands that men and women have a right to make of each other.

The Castrating Woman of Male Fantasy The flight from feeling, whether or not it tries to justify itself under an ideology of nonbinding commitments, takes the form above all of a flight from fantasy. This shows that it represents more than a defensive reaction to external disappointments. Today men and women seek escape from emotion not only because they have suffered too many wounds in the wars of love but because they experience their own inner impulses as intolerably urgent and menacing. The flight from feeling originates not only in the sociology of the sex war but in the psychology that accompanies it. If "many of us," as Ingrid Bengis observes of women and as others have observed of men as well, "have had to anesthetize ourselves to [our] needs," it is the very character of those needs (and of the defenses erected against them) which gives rise to the belief that they cannot be satisfied in heterosexual relations—perhaps should not be satisfied in any form—and which therefore prompts people to withdraw from intense emotional encounters.

Instinctual desires always threaten psychic equilibrium and for this reason can never be given direct expression. In our society, however, they present themselves as intolerably menacing, in part because the collapse of authority has removed so many of the external prohibitions against the expression of dangerous impulses. The superego can no longer ally itself, in its battle against impulse, with outside authorities. It has to rely almost entirely on its own resources, and these too have diminished in their effectiveness. Not only have the social agents of repression lost much of their force, but their internal representations in the superego have suffered a similar decline. The ego ideal, which cooperates in the work of repression by making socially acceptable behavior itself an object of libidinal cathexis, has become increasingly pallid and ineffective in the absence of compelling moral models outside the self. This means, as we have seen, that the superego has to rely more and more on harsh, punitive dictation, drawing on the aggressive impulses in the id and directing them against the ego.

The narcissist feels consumed by his own appetites. The intensity of his oral hunger leads him to make inordinate demands on his friends and sexual partners; yet in the same breath he repudiates those demands and asks only a casual connection without promise of permanence on either side. He longs to free himself from his own hunger and rage, to achieve a calm detachment beyond emotion, and to outgrow his dependence on others. He longs for the indifference to human relationships and to life itself that would enable him to acknowledge its passing in Kurt Vonnegut's laconic phrase, "So it goes," which so aptly expresses the ultimate aspiration of the psychiatric seeker.

But although the psychological man of our times frightens himself with the intensity of his inner needs, the needs of others appall him no less than his own. One reason the demands he inadvertently imposes on others make him uneasy is that they may justify others in making demands on himself. Men especially fear the demands of women, not only because women no longer hesitate to press them but because men find it so difficult to imagine an emotional need that does not wish to consume whatever it seizes on.

Women today ask for two things in their relations with men: sexual satisfaction and tenderness. Whether separately or in combination, both demands seem to convey to many males the same message—that women are voracious, insatiable. Why should men respond in this fashion to demands that reason tells them have obvious legitimacy? Rational arguments notoriously falter in the face of unconscious anxieties; women's sexual demands terrify men because they reverberate at such deep layers of the masculine mind, calling up early fantasies of a possessive, suffocating, devouring, and castrating mother. The persistence of such fantasies in later life intensifies and brings into the open the secret terror that has always been an important part of the male image of womanhood. The strength of these pre-Oedipal fantasies, in the narcissistic type of personality, makes it likely that men will approach women with hopelessly divided feelings, dependent and demanding in their fixation on the breast but terrified of the vagina which threatens to eat them alive; of the legs with which popular imagination endows the American heroine, legs which can presumably strangle or scissor victims to death; of the dangerous, phallic breast itself, encased in unyielding armor, which in unconscious terror more nearly resembles an implement of destruction than a source of nourishment. The sexually voracious female, long a stock figure of masculine pornography, in the twentieth century has emerged into the daylight of literary respectability. Similarly the cruel, destructive, domineering woman, *la belle dame sans merci*, has moved from the periphery of literature and the other arts to a position close to the center. Formerly a source of delicious titillation, of sadomasochistic gratification tinged with horrified fascination, she now inspires unambiguous loathing and dread. Heartless, domineering, burning (as Leslie Fiedler has said) with "a lust of the nerves rather than of the flesh," she unmans every man who falls under her spell. In

American fiction, she assumes a variety of guises, all of them variations on the same theme: the bitchy heroine of Hemingway, Faulkner, and Fitzgerald; Nathanael West's Faye Greener, whose "invitation wasn't to pleasure but to struggle, hard and sharp, closer to murder than to love"; Tennessee Williams's Maggie Tolliver, edgy as a cat on a hot tin roof; the domineering wife whose mastery of her husband, as in the joyless humor of James Thurber, recalls the mastery of the castrating mother over her son; the man-eating Mom denounced in the shrill falsetto of Philip Wylie's *Generation of Vipers*, Wright Morris's *Man and Boy*, Edward Albee's *The American Dream*; the suffocating Jewish mother, Mrs. Portnoy; the Hollywood vampire (Theda Bara), scheming seductress (Marlene Dietrich), or bad blonde (Marilyn Monroe, Jayne Mansfield); the precocious female rapist of Nabokov's *Lolita* or the precocious female killer of William March's *The Bad Seed.*

Child or woman, wife or mother, this female cuts men to ribbons or swallows them whole. She travels accompanied by eunuchs, by damaged men suffering from nameless wounds, or by a few strong men brought low by their misguided attempts to turn her into a real woman. Whether or not the actual incidence of impotence has increased in American males—and there is no reason to doubt reports that it has—the specter of impotence haunts the contemporary imagination, not least because it focuses the fear that a played-out Anglo-Saxon culture is about to fall before the advance of hardier races. The nature of impotence, moreover, has undergone an important historical shift. In the nineteenth century, respectable men sometimes experienced embarrassing sexual failures with women of their own class, or else suffered from what Freud called "psychic impotence"—the characteristic Victorian split between sensuality and affection. Although most of these men dutifully had intercourse with their wives, they derived sexual satisfaction only from intercourse with prostitutes or with women otherwise degraded. As Freud explained, this psychic syndrome—"the most prevalent form of degradation" in the erotic life of his time—originated in the Oedipus complex. After the painful renunciation of the mother, sensuality seeks only those objects that evoke no reminder of her, while the mother herself, together with other "pure" (socially respectable) women, is idealized beyond reach of the sensual.

Today, impotence typically seems to originate not in renunciation of the mother but in earlier experiences, often reactivated by the apparently aggressive overtures of sexually liberated women. Fear of the devouring mother of pre-Oedipal fantasy gives rise to a generalized fear of women that has little resemblance to the sentimental adoration men once granted to women who made them sexually uncomfortable. The fear of women, closely associated with a fear of the consuming desires within, reveals itself not only as impotence but as a boundless rage against the female sex. This blind and impotent rage, which seems so prevalent at the present time, only superficially represents a defensive male reaction against feminism. It is only because the recent revival of feminism stirs up such deeply rooted memories that it gives rise to such primitive emotions. Men's fear of women, moreover, exceeds the actual threat to their sexual privileges. Whereas the resentment of women against men for the most part has solid roots in the discrimination and sexual danger to which women are constantly exposed, the resentment of men against women, when men still control most of the power and wealth in society yet feel themselves threatened on every hand—intimidated, emasculated—appears deeply irrational, and for that reason not likely to be appeased by changes in feminist tactics designed to reassure men that liberated women threaten no one. When even Mom is a menace, there is not much that feminists can say to soften the sex war or to assure their adversaries that men and women will live happily together when it is over.

The Soul of Man and Woman under Socialism

Would men and women live more happily together under some other form of social organization? Would they live more happily under socialism? The answer to this question no longer strikes many people as self-evident, as it struck earlier generations of socialists. The feminist movement has unceremoniously exposed the shallowness of the old socialist analysis, according to which a revolution in property relations would automatically revolutionize the relations between men and women. All but the most rigid and dogmatic of socialists have now admitted the justice of this feminist criticism and incorporated it into their own work, notably in the recent studies by Juliet Mitchell, Eli Zaretsky, and Bruce Dancis. For the first time, large numbers of socialists have begun to grasp the historic challenge of feminism to socialism. As Mary White Ovington put it as early as 1914, socialism "does not mean simply a full stomach—that was often attained under chattel slavery—but a full life." Discussion of personal issues can no longer be dismissed as a form of "bourgeois subjectivity." On the contrary, it appears that the exploitation of women by men, far from constituting a secondary formation dependent in one way or another on the organization of production, antedates the establishment of production based on private property and may well survive its demise.

The justice of the feminist critique of socialism, however, does not justify the conclusions some feminists draw from it— that the oppression of women represents the basic and primal form of exploitation and that it underlies and determines all other social relations. The exploitation of women has evolved through many historical forms, and the importance of these changes must not be obscured by treating sexism as an unchanging fact of life, which can be abolished only by abolishing sexuality itself and instituting the reign of androgyny. The form of sexual oppression specific to late capitalist society has raised sexual tensions to a new intensity, at the same time encouraging a new independence among women that leads them to reject subordination. It does not seem unreasonable to believe, even in the political passivity and quietism of the 1970s, that a thoroughgoing transformation of our social arrangements remains a possibility, and that a socialist revolution would abolish the new paternalism—the dependence of the ordinary citizen on experts, the degradation of both work and domestic life—from which so much of the antagonism between men and women now derives. The establishment of equality between the sexes, the transformation of the family, and the development of new structures of personality would by no means usher in the androgynous utopia, but neither would it leave the battle of the sexes essentially unchanged. The abolition of sexual tensions is an unworthy goal in any case; the point is to live with them more gracefully than we have lived with them in the past.

IX

The Shattered Faith
in the Regeneration of Life

The Dread of Old Age   In some ways the most characteristic expression of the times is the campaign against old age, which holds a special terror for people today. As the proportion of old people in the population increases, the problem of old age attracts the anxious attention of doctors, demographers, psychiatrists, medical researchers, sociologists, social reformers, policy makers, and futurologists. A growing number of sciences and pseudo-sciences concern themselves specifically with aging and death: geriatrics, gerontology, thanatology, cryonics, "immortalism." Many others, notably genetics, genetic engineering, and community medicine, have enlisted in the struggle to alleviate or abolish the ravages of time—a struggle dear to the heart of a dying culture.

Two approaches to the problem of age have emerged. The first seeks not to prolong life but to improve its quality, especially the quality of what used to be known as the declining years. Resisting the equation of old age with loss of powers, proponents of this approach demand a more active social role for those who, though past middle age, have by no means outlived their usefulness. Humanitarians insist that old age is a social category, not a biological one. The modern problem of old age, from this point of view, originates less in physical decline than in society's intolerance of old people, its refusal to make use of their accumulated wisdom, and its attempt to relegate them to the margins of social existence.

The second approach proposes to deal with old age as a "medical problem," in Albert Rosenfeld's words—"something your doctor may some day hope to do something about." Falsely attributing to modern medicine an increase in life expectancy that actually derives from a higher standard of living, it assumes that medicine has the power to lengthen life still further and to abolish the horrors of old age.* By the year 2025, Rosenfeld believes, "most of the major mysteries of the aging process will have been solved."

In spite of their differences, the medical and social solutions to old age have more in common than first appears. Both rest more on hope—and on a powerful aversion to the prospect of bodily decay—than on critical examination of evidence. Both regard old age and death as "an imposition on the human race," in the words of the novelist Alan Harrington—as something "no longer acceptable." †

What lies behind this loathing of the aging process, which ap-

---

* Most historians and demographers now believe that improvements in diet, sanitation, and general standards of living, not improvements in medical technology, account for the increase in life expectancy since the eighteenth century. The superficially plausible explanation of the decline in mortality accepted by Rosenfeld and other technological determinists—that it derived from improvements in medicine—was "so completely demolished by Thomas McKeown and R. G. Brown in 1955," in the words of William L. Langer, "that it has since been generally abandoned by other students of the problem." Whatever those students think about the real cause of the population explosion, they agree in discounting the influence of medicine. Recently McKeown has estimated that between 1848 and 1971, vaccination against smallpox accounted for only 1.6 percent of the decline in the English death rate. Even antibiotics, which have undeniably influenced the mortality rate, were not introduced until the 1930s and therefore could not have contributed to a demographic revolution that had been in progress since the eighteenth century.

† Advocates of the social theory of aging could easily agree with Harrington's description of its symptoms and the fear they evoke—"the fear of losing our powers and being left alone, or in the hands of indifferent nurses, and knowing that the moment must come when we will not see the people we love any more, and everything will go black." But whereas Harrington turns for "salvation" to "medical engineering and nothing else," insisting that "our messiahs will be wearing white coats," those who regard aging as a social problem argue that "losing our powers," "being left alone," and being handed over to "indifferent nurses" are experiences needlessly inflicted on the aged by a callous society, and made still more painful by old people's unthinking acceptance of the social devaluation of themselves.

pears to be growing more and more common in advanced industrial society?

Narcissism and Old Age   Obviously men have always feared death and longed to live forever. Yet the fear of death takes on new intensity in a society that has deprived itself of religion and shows little interest in posterity. Old age inspires apprehension, moreover, not merely because it represents the beginning of death but because the condition of old people has objectively deteriorated in modern times. Our society notoriously finds little use for the elderly. It defines them as useless, forces them to retire before they have exhausted their capacity for work, and reinforces their sense of superfluity at every opportunity. By insisting, ostensibly in a spirit of respect and friendship, that they have not lost the right to enjoy life, society reminds old people that they have nothing better to do with their time. By devaluing experience and setting great store by physical strength, dexterity, adaptability, and the ability to come up with new ideas, society defines productivity in ways that automatically exclude "senior citizens." The well-known cult of youth further weakens the social position of those no longer young.

Thus "our attitudes toward aging," as a recent critic observes, "are not accidental." They derive from long-term social changes that have redefined work, created a scarcity of jobs, devalued the wisdom of the ages, and brought all forms of authority (including the authority of experience) into disrepute. Because the declining power and status of the aged has deeply rooted social causes, merely propagandizing on their behalf or formulating more humane policies will not be enough to alleviate their lot. Those who argue that old age is a social rather than a medical issue have yet to grasp how deeply social it is and how resistant, therefore, to palliative solutions. Nothing short of a complete reordering of work, education, the family—of every important institution—will make old age more bearable. Even then, biology sets limits to the degree to which old age can be made genuinely pleasant, as opposed to less painful—another stubborn fact which the social theorists of aging and death (as optimistic in their reformist meliorism as are the "prolongevity" theorists in their faith in medical miracles) steadfastly refuse to confront.

The problem of old age remains intractable for another reason. It has a psychological as well as a social and a biological dimension. Social change manifests itself inwardly as well as outwardly, in changing perceptions, habits of mind, unconscious associations. If our era has a special dread of old age and death, this dread must arise out of some inner predisposition. It must reflect not only objective changes in the social position of the elderly but subjective experiences that make the prospect of old age intolerable. The fear of old age may stem from a rational, realistic assessment of what happens to old people in advanced industrial society; but it has its roots in irrational panic. The most obvious sign of this panic is that it appears in people's lives so prematurely. Men and women begin to fear growing old before they even arrive at middle age. The so-called midlife crisis presents itself as a realization that old age looms just around the corner. Americans experience the fortieth birthday as the beginning of the end. Even the prime of life thus comes to be overshadowed by the fear of what lies ahead.

This irrational terror of old age and death is closely associated with the emergence of the narcissistic personality as the dominant type of personality structure in contemporary society. Because the narcissist has so few inner resources, he looks to others to validate his sense of self. He needs to be admired for his beauty, charm, celebrity, or power—attributes that usually fade with time. Unable to achieve satisfying sublimations in the form of love and work, he finds that he has little to sustain him when youth passes him by. He takes no interest in the future and does nothing to provide himself with the traditional consolations of old age, the most important of which is the belief that future generations will in some sense carry on his life's work. Love and work unite in a concern for posterity, and specifically in an attempt to equip the younger generation to carry on the tasks of the older. The thought that we live on vicariously in our children (more broadly, in future generations) reconciles us to our own supersession—the central sorrow of old age, more harrowing even than frailty and loneliness. When the generational link begins to fray, such consolations no longer obtain.

The emergence of the narcissistic personality reflects among other things a drastic shift in our sense of historical time. Narcissism emerges as the typical form of character structure in a society that has lost interest in the future. Psychiatrists who tell parents not to live through their offspring; married couples who postpone or reject parenthood, often for good practical reasons; social reformers who urge zero population growth, all testify to a pervasive uneasiness about reproduction—to widespread doubts, indeed, about whether our society should reproduce itself at all. Under these conditions, the thought of our eventual supersession and death becomes utterly insupportable and gives rise to attempts to abolish old age and to extend life indefinitely. When men find themselves incapable of taking an interest in earthly life after their own death, they wish for eternal youth, for the same reason they no longer care to reproduce themselves. When the prospect of being superseded becomes intolerable, parenthood itself, which guarantees that it will happen, appears almost as a form of self-destruction. In Lisa Alther's *Kinflicks*, a young man explains that he doesn't want to have children. "I always saw the world as a stage. . . . And any child of mine would be a ballsy young actor wanting to run me off stage altogether, watching and waiting to bury me, so that *he* could assume center stage."

The Social Theory of Aging: "Growth" as Planned Obsolescence The social interpretation of old age, under a veneer of realism, easily degenerates into a kind of positive thinking that aims merely to upgrade the "image" of the elderly and to encourage old people to acknowledge their infirmities without losing the zest for life. Alex Comfort, well known as a proponent of a more relaxed style of sexuality, has advocated a similar approach to the problems of aging. "Tragic intensities," in Comfort's view, "tend to produce bad trips." Just as he seeks "to transfer sex and its anxieties from the 'hot' category prescribed by an irradiated culture to the 'cool' category based on nonanxiety, noncompulsion and recognition of personhood," so Comfort pleads for "a change in our vision of age." Modern science, he argues, "indicates that a high proportion of the mental and attitudinal changes seen in 'old' people are not biological effects" but "the result of role playing."*

In the same vein, Gail Sheehy tries to convince people that old age is not necessarily a disaster—without, however, challenging the social conditions that cause so many people to experience it as such. Reassurance of this kind easily defeats its own object. As reviewers have pointed out, Sheehy does for adulthood what Dr. Spock did for childhood. Both assure the anxious reader that conduct he finds puzzling or disturbing, whether in his children, his spouse, or himself, can be seen as merely a normal phase of emotional development. But although it may be comforting to know that a two-year-old child likes to contradict his parents and often refuses to obey them, if the child's development fails to conform to the proper schedule, the parent will be alarmed and seek medical or psychiatric advice, which may stir up further fears. The application of the psychology of the "life cycle" to adult life will have the same effect. Measuring experience against a normative model set up by doctors, people will find themselves as troubled by departures from the norm as they are currently troubled by the "predictable crises of adult life" themselves, against which medical norms are intended to provide reassurance. The spirit of Sheehy's book, like that of Comfort's, is generous and humane, but it rests on medical definitions of reality that remain highly suspect, not least because they make it so difficult to get through life without the constant attention of doctors, psychiatrists, and faith healers. Sheehy brings to the subject of aging, which needs to be approached from a moral and philosophical perspective, a therapeutic sensibility incapable of transcending its own limitations.

---

* Comfort's emergence as an advocate of more "humanistic" approaches to old age invites the same suspicion as the emergence of Masters and Johnson as advocates of a less mechanistic approach to sex. Benjamin DeMott writes of their belated recognition of "loyalty and faithfulness, honor and trust": "It seems to me at least questionable whether a decision by Masters and Johnson to rehabilitate this lost language, unaccompanied by any acknowledgment of their own role in discrediting and soiling it, can stand as a significant act of mind."

Sheehy recognizes that wisdom is one of the few comforts of age, but she does not see that to think of wisdom purely as a consolation divests it of any larger meaning or value. The real value of the accumulated wisdom of a lifetime is that it can be handed on to future generations. Our society, however, has lost this conception of wisdom and knowledge. It holds an instrumental view of knowledge, according to which technological change constantly renders knowledge obsolete and therefore nontransferable. The older generation has nothing to teach the younger, according to this kind of reasoning, except to equip it with the emotional and intellectual resources to make its own choices and to deal with "unstructured" situations for which there are no reliable precedents or precepts. It is taken for granted that children will quickly learn to find their parents' ideas old-fashioned and out-of-date, and parents themselves tend to accept the social definition of their own superfluity. Having raised their children to the age at which they enter college or the work force, people in their forties and fifties find that they have nothing left to do as parents. This discovery coincides with another, that business and industry no longer need them either. The superfluity of the middle-aged and elderly originates in the severance of the sense of historical continuity. Because the older generation no longer thinks of itself as living on in the next, of achieving a vicarious immortality in posterity, it does not give way gracefully to the young. People cling to the illusion of youth until it can no longer be maintained, at which point they must either accept their superfluous status or sink into dull despair. Neither solution makes it easy to sustain much interest in life.

Sheehy appears to acquiesce in the devaluation of parenthood, for she has almost nothing to say about it. Nor does she criticize the social pressures that push people out of their jobs into increasingly early retirement. Indeed she accepts this trend as desirable. "A surprisingly large number of workers are choosing to accept early retirement," she says brightly, "provided it will not mean a drastic drop in income." Her solution to the crisis of aging is to find new interests, new ways of keeping busy. She equates growth with keeping on the move. She urges her readers to discover "the thrill of learning something new *after* forty-five." Take up skiing, golf, or hiking. Learn to play the piano. You won't make much progress, "but so what! . . . The point is to defeat the entropy that says slow down, give it up, watch TV, and to open up another pathway that can enliven all the senses, including the sense that one is not just an old dog."

According to Sheehy, "it is our own view of ourselves that determines the richness or paucity of the middle years." In effect, she urges people to prepare for middle age and old age in such a way that they can be phased out without making a fuss. The psychology of growth, development, and "self-actualization" presents survival as spiritual progress, resignation as renewal. In a society in which most people find it difficult to store up experience and knowledge (let alone money) against old age, or to pass on accumulated experience to their descendants, the growth experts compound the problem by urging people past forty to cut their ties to the past, embark on new careers and new marriages ("creative divorce"), take up new hobbies, travel light, and keep moving. This is a recipe not for growth but for planned obsolescence. It is no wonder that American industry has embraced "sensitivity training" as an essential part of personnel management. The new therapy provides for personnel what the annual model change provides for its products; rapid retirement from active use. Corporate planners have much to learn from the study of the life cycle carried out by humanistic psychology, which provides techniques by means of which people can prematurely phase themselves out of active life, painlessly and without "panic."

Prolongevity: The Biological Theory of Aging   Alex Comfort and other advocates of the cultural approach to aging have cautioned their followers against hoping for a medical extension of the life span, even though Comfort himself, in an unguarded moment, once predicted that "if the scientific and medical resources of the United States alone were mobilized, aging could be conquered within a decade." After his discovery of humanism, Comfort became more cautious. Medical research could hope merely "to make it take, say, seventy years to reach today's sixty." Those who subscribe to a biological theory of aging, on the other hand, put their faith in a great medical breakthrough. August Kinzel, former president of the Salk Institute, declared in 1967 that "we will lick the problem of aging completely, so that accidents will be essentially the only cause of death." Ten years later Robert Sinsheimer of the California Institute of Technology said flatly, "We know of no intrinsic limits to the life span. How long would you like to live?"

Such statements always contain the qualification, implicit or explicit, that progress depends on the commitment of enormous resources to the battle against old age. Their purpose is not to describe what science actually knows but to raise money for more research, or in the case of Sinsheimer's sweeping prediction, to scare scientists into self-restraint. "Curiosity," says Sinsheimer, "is not necessarily the highest virtue—and science . . . may not merit *total* commitment." We can agree wholeheartedly with this sentiment while remaining unconvinced that medical science stands on the verge of "eradicating" old age, as Albert Rosenfeld puts it. Biologists still do not agree about the causes of aging and have postulated a great variety of conflicting theories to explain it. The superabundance of theories suggests that gerontologists work in a field still in the early stages of development. Yet Rosenfeld and other publicists of the medical profession, confident that all these ideas will somehow prove to contain part of the truth—as if the sheer proliferation of hypotheses added up to scientific progress—take the medical conquest of old age for granted and devote most of their attention to the attempt to allay doubts and "misgivings" that we shortsightedly feel, Rosenfeld says, about tampering with the human life span.

By associating this "disquiet" with sentimental humanitarianism and superstitious resistance to scientific progress, these publicists pose as hardheaded realists willing to "think the unthinkable," as another futurologist, Herman Kahn, once put it when he tried to reconcile mankind to the prospect of nuclear war. The prophets of prolongevity take pride in their ability to confront forbidding questions. Would society stagnate if death lost its sting? Would people avoid risk, devoting all their energies merely to staying alive? Would old people, still young in mind and body, refuse to make room for new arrivals? Would society become indifferent to the future? Needless to say, Rosenfeld reassures himself in each case that things would not turn out so badly. Thus people would pay more, not less attention to the future, he contends, if they became their "own posterity" and had to live with the consequences of their heedless folly.

But the remarkable thing about this reasoning is not that Rosenfeld has loaded the dice by arguing that medical progress is inevitable, in spite of the "qualms" it arouses in the tender-minded, but that his fixation on the hypothetical consequences of prolongevity prevents him from seeing that possibilities he projects into an imaginary, science-fiction future have already rooted themselves in the prosaic, everyday reality of the present. Futurology, in its infatuation with a technological utopia in the offing (so different from a genuine concern for posterity), cannot see what is under its nose. Devoid of historical perspective, it has no way of recognizing the future when the future has become the here and now. Those who pride themselves on facing "future shock" without fear retreat from the scariest thought of all: that social stagnation is not just a hypothetical possibility but a reality, which already has us in its grip. Indeed the prolongevity movement (together with futurology in general) itself reflects the stagnant character of late capitalist culture. It arises not as a natural response to medical improvements that have prolonged life expectancy but from changing social relations and social attitudes, which cause people to lose interest in the young and in posterity, to cling desperately to their own youth, to seek by every possible means to prolong their own lives, and to make way only with the greatest reluctance for new generations.

"In the end, the discovery that one is old is inescapable," writes David Hackett Fischer. "But most Americans are not prepared to make it." He describes with sympathetic irony the desperation with which adults now ape the styles of youth.

This historian observed a Boston matron on the far side of fifty, who might have worn a graceful palla in ancient Rome, dressed in a miniskirt and leather boots. He saw a man in his sixties, who might have draped himself in the dignity of a toga, wearing 'hiphugger' jeans and a tie-dyed T-shirt. He witnessed a conservative businessman, who in an earlier generation might have hesitated each morning, wondering whether to wear black or charcoal gray, going to the office in white plastic shoes, chartreuse trousers and cerise shirt, purple aviator glasses, and a Prince Valiant haircut. Most astonishing were college professors who put aside their Harris tweeds and adopted every passing adolescent fad with an enthusiasm out of all proportion to their years. One season it was the Nehru jacket; another, dashikis; the next, railroad overalls. In the early 1970's it was love beads and leather jackets. Every twist and turn of teenage fashion revolutionized their costumes. But always, old was out and young was in.

The denial of age in America culminates in the prolongevity movement, which hopes to abolish old age altogether. But the dread of age originates not in a "cult of youth" but in a cult of the self. Not only in its narcissistic indifference to future generations but in its grandiose vision of a technological utopia without old age, the prolongevity movement exemplifies the fantasy of "absolute, sadistic power" which, according to Kohut, so deeply colors the narcissistic outlook. Pathological in its psychological origins and inspiration, superstitious in its faith in medical deliverance, the prolongevity movement expresses in characteristic form the anxieties of a culture that believes it has no future.

X

Paternalism Without Father

The New Rich and the Old   Most of the evils discussed in this book originate in a new kind of paternalism, which has risen from the ruins of the old paternalism of kings, priests, authoritarian fathers, slavemasters, and landed overlords. Capitalism has severed the ties of personal dependence only to revive dependence under cover of bureaucratic rationality. Having overthrown feudalism and slavery and then outgrown its own personal and familial form, capitalism has evolved a new political ideology, welfare liberalism, which absolves individuals of moral responsibility and treats them as victims of social circumstance. It has evolved new modes of social control, which deal with the deviant as a patient and substitute medical rehabilitation for punishment. It has given rise to a new culture, the narcissistic culture of our time, which has translated the predatory individualism of the American Adam into a therapeutic jargon that celebrates not so much individualism as solipsism, justifying self-absorption as "authenticity" and "awareness."

Ostensibly egalitarian and antiauthoritarian, American capitalism has rejected priestly and monarchical hegemony only to replace it with the hegemony of the business corporation, the managerial and professional classes who operate the corporate system, and the corporate state. A new ruling class of administrators, bureaucrats, technicians, and experts has appeared, which retains so few of the attributes formerly associated with a ruling class—pride of place, the "habit of command," disdain for the lower orders—that its existence as a class often goes unnoticed. The difference between the new managerial elite and the old propertied elite defines the difference between a bourgeois culture that now survives only on the margins of industrial society and the new therapeutic culture of narcissism.

The difference emerges most clearly in contrasting styles of childrearing. Whereas the new rich share the prevailing confusion about the values parents should transmit to the young, the old rich have firm ideas about childrearing and do not hesitate to put them into practice. They try to impress the child with the responsibilities that go along with the privileges he will inherit. They do what they can to inculcate a certain toughness, which includes not only a readiness to overcome obstacles but an unsentimental acceptance of social differences. In order for the children of privilege to become the administrators and custodians of great wealth—chairmen of the board, mineowners, collectors, connoisseurs, mothers and fathers of new dynasties—they have to accept the inevitability of inequality, the inescapability of social class. These children have to stop wondering whether life is fair to its victims. They have to stop "daydreaming" (as their parents see it) and get on with the serious business of life: studies, preparations for a career, music lessons, riding lessons, ballet lessons, tennis lessons, parties, dancing, socializing—the busy round of activities, seemingly pointless to a casual observer (or even to a close observer like Veblen) through which the propertied rich acquire discipline, courage, persistence, and self-possession.

In the families of the old propertied elite, parents seem to make more demands on their children than more "modern" parents make, and wealth gives them the power to back up these demands. They control the schools and churches their children attend. When they have to seek professional advice, they deal with experts from a position of strength. They have the self-confidence that comes with success—with a pattern of success repeated, in many cases, over several generations. In dealing with their children, they insist not only on their own authority but on the authority of the past. Rich families invent historical legends about themselves, which the young internalize. In many ways the most important thing they give their children is the sense of generational continuity so rarely encountered elsewhere in American society. James, the son of a New Orleans cotton broker, "assumes," according to Robert Coles, that he himself "will have a son" and that "the family will persist" as it "has for centuries—through wars, revolutions, natural and man-made disasters."

The sense of continuity notably weakens as the managerial

elite displaces the old propertied upper class. The old bourgeoisie, which derives its income from the ownership of property
rather than from salaries, still represents the summit of wealth,
but although it owns department stores and urban real estate and
big plantations in the South and West, it no longer controls national and multinational corporations or plays a dominant role in
national politics. It is a dying class, obsessed, indeed, with its
own decline. Even in decline, however, it implants in the young a
powerful sense of local pride, often tinged with the apprehension
that outside influences (Yankees, immigrants to the Sun Belt,
government) are tearing the place apart. The class loyalty propertied families instill in their children is forged in the midst of striking scenes of class struggle, in sections of the country—the Mis-
sissippi delta, the Florida orange groves, Appalachia—where the
struggle remains vivid and intense. The generalization that children today seldom see their fathers at work hardly applies to
children who experience all too vividly what their parents do for a
living: boss the poor. Fathers in the old entrepreneurial class are
neither absent nor impotent. Indeed their capacity to command
not just respect but fear makes their children uneasy. Yet most of
these children eventually learn to suppress their sense of fair play,
to accept the responsibilities of wealth, and to identify themselves
with the family fortunes in every sense.

When we move from the propertied rich to the much more
numerous corporate rich (which is to move from families where
the average annual income ranges as high as $400,000 to the more
modest but still select level exceeding $50,000), the pattern
changes. Here we find executives always on the move, whose
children learn no sense of place. Work becomes abstract, class
conflict institutionalized, the fact of it evaded or denied. In the
big cities of the North, the poor tend to become invisible, and the
problem of injustice no longer presents itself as starkly as it does
elsewhere. In old entrepreneurial families, children worry that
their families' houses will be broken into and their possessions
stolen. Children of managerial families do not have the sense of
permanence that gives rise to such a fear. Life for them amounts
to a series of moves, and their parents reproach themselves for not
providing a real home—not being "better parents."

In one of the families studied by Coles, which exemplifies to perfection this emerging managerial pattern of rootlessness and anomie, the father, an executive in a New England electronics company, drinks too much and wonders at times "if it's all worth it—the struggle he's had to get to the top." The mother drinks in secret and apologizes to her children for "not being a better mother." Their daughter, raised by a succession of maids, is growing up with ill-defined anxieties and resentments, with little guilt but much anxiety. She has become a problem child. Twice she has run away from home. Now she sees a psychiatrist and no longer feels "peculiar" about it, since most of her friends go to psychiatrists too. The family is about to move again.

The Managerial and Professional Elite as a Ruling Class

As even the rich lose the sense of place and historical continuity, the subjective feeling of "entitlement," which takes inherited advantages for granted, gives way to what clinicians call "narcissistic entitlement"—grandiose illusions, inner emptiness. The advantages the rich confer on their children dwindle down to money alone. As the new elite discards the outlook of the old bourgeoisie, it identifies itself not with the work ethic and the responsibilities of wealth but with an ethic of leisure, hedonism, and self-fulfillment. Although it continues to administer American institutions in the interests of private property (corporate property as opposed to entrepreneurial property), it has replaced character building with permissiveness, the cure of souls with the cure of the psyche, blind justice with therapeutic justice, philosophy with social science, personal authority with an equally irrational authority of professional experts. It has tempered competition with antagonistic cooperation, while abolishing many of the rituals in which aggressive impulses formerly found civilized expression. It has surrounded people with "symbolically mediated information" and has substituted images of reality for reality itself. Without intending to, it has created new forms of illiteracy even in the act of setting up a system of universal education. It has undermined the family while attempting to rescue the family.

It has torn away the veil of chivalry that once tempered the exploitation of women and has brought men and women face to face as antagonists. It has expropriated the worker's knowledge of his craft and the mother's "instinct" for childrearing, and has reorganized this knowledge as a body of esoteric lore accessible only to the initiated. The new ruling class has elaborated new patterns of dependence as effectively as its forebears eradicated the dependence of the peasant on his lord, the apprentice on his master, and the woman on her man.

I do not wish to imply a vast conspiracy against our liberties. These things have been done in broad daylight and have been done, on the whole, with good intentions. Nor have they arisen as a unified policy of social control. Social policy in the United States has unfolded in response to a series of immediate emergencies, and those who make policy seldom see beyond the problems at hand. The cult of pragmatism, moreover, justifies their unwillingness or inability to make far-reaching plans for the future. What unifies their actions is the need to promote and defend the system of corporate capitalism from which they—the managers and professionals who operate the system—derive most of the benefits. The needs of the system shape policy and set the permissible limits of public debate. Most of us can see the system but not the class that administers it and monopolizes the wealth it creates. We resist a class analysis of modern society as a "conspiracy theory." Thus we prevent ourselves from understanding how our current difficulties arose, why they persist, or how they might be solved.

Progressivism and the Rise of the New Paternalism   The new paternalism emerged in the second half of the nineteenth century, found political expression in the progressive movement and later in the New Deal, and gradually worked its way into every corner of American society. The democratic revolution of the eighteenth and early nineteenth centuries, culminating in the Civil War, not only did away with monarchy but undermined established religion, landed elites, and finally overthrew the slaveholding oligarchy in the South. The revolution gave rise to a society based on individualism, competition, and the pursuit of the main chance. It also generated demands for further change, which came to a head in the period immediately following the Civil War. Having destroyed slavery in the name of free labor, the leaders of the democratic movement inadvertently encouraged northern workers to ask for the freedom to control the terms of their work, not merely to sell their labor at ruinous prices. The logic of democracy demanded the confiscation of Confederate estates and their distribution among the freedmen; it demanded woman suffrage; it demanded, in short, a more sweeping reorganization of society than its leaders had contemplated. Seeking merely to free property from its feudal and mercantile restrictions, bourgeois radicals in the 1860s and early 1870s found themselves confronted with an incipient attack on property itself, from which most of them recoiled in horror.

After the collapse of reconstruction and the radical agitation associated with it, American liberalism no longer spoke for the artisan, the small farmer, and the independent entrepreneur—the "producing classes" that had been the backbone of the democratic movement. Faced with unrest at home and with the spectacle of the Paris commune abroad, liberalism now identified itself, in the words of E. L. Godkin, with "the more well-to-do and observing classes." It undertook to reform society from the top down—to professionalize the civil service, break the power of the urban machine, and put "the best men" into office. When such measures failed to stem the rising tide of labor militancy and agrarian radicalism, reformers brought forward their own version of the "cooperative commonwealth" in the name of progressivism: universal education, welfare capitalism, scientific management of industry and government. The New Deal completed what progressivism had begun, solidifying the foundations of the welfare state and adding much of the superstructure as well. In industry, scientific management gave way to the school of human relations, which tried to substitute cooperation for authoritarian control. But this cooperation rested on management's monopoly of technology and the reduction of work to routines imperfectly understood by the worker and controlled by the capitalist. Similarly the expansion of welfare services presupposed the reduction of the citizen to a consumer of expertise.

American progressivism, which has successfully countered agrarian radicalism, the labor movement, and the feminist movement by enacting selective parts of their program, has now lost almost all trace of its origin in nineteenth-century liberalism. It has rejected the liberal conception of man, which assumed the primacy of rational self-interest, and has installed in its place a therapeutic conception which acknowledges irrational drives and seeks to divert them into socially constructive channels. It has rejected the stereotype of economic man and has attempted to bring the "whole man" under social control. Instead of regulating the conditions of work alone, it now regulates private life as well, organizing leisure time on scientific principles of social and personal hygiene. It has exposed the innermost secrets of the psyche to medical scrutiny and has thus encouraged habits of anxious self-scrutiny, superficially reminiscent of religious introspection but rooted in anxiety rather than a guilty conscience—in a narcissistic rather than a compulsive or hysterical type of personality.

Liberal Criticism of the Welfare State   The new modes of social control associated with the rise of progressivism have stabilized capitalism without solving any of its underlying problems— the gap between wealth and poverty, the failure of purchasing power to keep pace with productivity, economic stagnation. The new paternalism has kept social tensions from assuming political form, but it has not removed their source. As those tensions increasingly find expression in crime and random violence, critics have begun to ask whether the welfare system delivers all it promised. The system, moreover, has become more and more expensive to operate. Even those who remain loyal to the underlying premises of American capitalism have begun to express alarm about the mounting cost of maintaining it. Proposals to replace the welfare system with a guaranteed income or a negative income tax have gained a sympathetic hearing. In his book on old age, David Hackett Fischer argues that a national inheritance system, whereby a gift of capital at birth would accumulate interest and provide for the citizen in his old age, would prove "cheaper than present arrangements." The modification or abandonment of the welfare system now presents itself not as a utopian dream but as a matter of sound business practice.

The health and welfare industries, which have done so much to promote the new paternalism by professionalizing activities formerly carried on in the workshop, the neighborhood, or the home, have themselves begun to harbor second thoughts about the results of their own labors. Members of the "helping professions" have begun to question the efficiency of the public institutions and welfare agencies that monopolize the knowledge formerly administered by ordinary citizens—the hospital, the mental asylum, the juvenile court. The medical profession, after upholding the hospital as an indispensable alternative to the family, now begins to think that patients might be better off if they were allowed to die at home. Psychiatrists have been speculating along similar lines, not only because existing facilities are overcrowded but because they have failed to achieve the high rates of cure once predicted with such confidence. Lawyers have begun to criticize the courts for removing "neglected" children from their homes without evidence that such children suffer serious harm and without proof that institutionalization or transfer to foster parents provides any solution. Even the school's claim on the child has begun to give way to parental claims. In *Wisconsin* v. *Yoder* (1972), the Supreme Court ruled that Amish parents have a right to keep their children out of the public schools. "The child is not the mere creature of the State," the court said; "those who nurture him and direct his destiny have the right, coupled with the high duty, to recognize and prepare him for additional obligations."*

* Justice William O. Douglas, dissenting in *Yoder*, presented the argument for state intervention in its most attractive form. Suppose an Amish child wished to follow an occupation that required him to break from the cultural tradition of his parents. Suppose he wished to become "a pianist or an astronaut or an oceanographer." The court's decision made this impossible, Douglas argued. Without consulting the preferences of the children themselves, the court had delivered them into a narrow, backward, and parochial environment, barring them "forever"

Even with the best intentions, however, those who criticize the welfare state within the assumptions underlying a capitalist economy cannot bring themselves to confront the revolution in social relations that abandonment of the welfare system would require. Liberal criticism of the new paternalism resembles the "humanization" of the workplace, which tries to give the worker the illusion of participation while leaving management in undiminished control. The attempt to mitigate the monotony of the assembly line by allowing the worker to perform more than a single operation does not alter the condition that degrades work— the monopoly of technical knowledge by means of which management designs all phases of production, while the worker merely carries out the bidding of the planning department. Recent proposals to modify the welfare system suffer from the same kind of limitation. Thus a study of the family commissioned by the Carnegie Corporation takes issue with the conventional assumption of parental incompetence while leaving unchallenged the definition of parents as consumers of professional services. Kenneth Keniston and the other authors of the Carnegie report, conscious of belonging to "an emerging consensus," hold that parents "are still the world's greatest experts about the needs of their own children." They recognize that many of the agencies ostensibly ministering to the family have undermined the family instead. The parental "malaise," according to Keniston, lies in "the sense of having no guidelines or supports for raising children, the feeling of not being in control as parents, and the widespread sense of personal guilt for what seems to be going awry."

from the "new and amazing world of diversity." Persuasive as it appears at first sight, this argument on examination proves to be a classic example of the sentimentality of liberal humanitarianism, which invokes "diversity" to support a system of uniform compulsory schooling and proposes to rescue the child from the backward culture of his parents by delivering him into the tender care of the state. The argument is sentimental above all in its assumption that the state can spare the child who does decide to break from his parents' traditions the pain, suffering, and guilt that such a break necessarily exacts—the confrontation with which, however, constitutes the psychological and educative value of such an experience. In true paternalist fashion, Douglas would smooth away the painful obstacles to the child's progress, forgetting that progress consists precisely in overcoming those obstacles.

The rehabilitation of parenthood, it appears, implies an attack on professionalism and the welfare state. Yet Keniston stops well short of such an attack. He takes for granted the family's dependence on experts and seeks merely to regularize and regulate this relationship. "Few people would dispute that we live in a society where parents must increasingly rely on others for help and support in raising their children." The family economy has disappeared; children represent a financial liability rather than an asset; the school has taken over the family's educational functions; and the medical profession has assumed most of the responsibility for health care. These changes, according to Keniston, leave parents in the position of "executives in a large firm—responsible for the smooth coordination of the many people and processes that must work together to produce the final product."

This line of analysis leads to the conclusion not that parents should collectively assert their control over childrearing but that federal policy should seek to equalize the relationship between experts and parents. Yet Keniston's own reasoning shows that parents occupy a position closer to proletarians than to executives. As things now stand, according to Keniston, "parents have little authority over those with whom they share the task of raising their children"; they "deal with those others from a position of inferiority or helplessness." The obvious reason for this is that the state, not the parents, pays the bill for professional services, or at least signs the paychecks. (The citizens, as taxpayers, pay in the end.) If parents organized and hired their own experts, things might be different.

It goes without saying that such solutions do not commend themselves to members of the policy-making establishment. Measures of this kind are too closely associated with populism, localism, and residual resistance to centralized progress. They have become doubly objectionable, and for reasons the force of which even enemies of the establishment must acknowledge, in the wake of the Ocean Hill-Brownsville battle of the late sixties, when "community control" degenerated into reverse racism and education into racial propaganda. Yet the alternative to community control is more bureaucracy. Instead of confronting the choice, liberal reformers try to have things both ways. While advocating an expansion of government services to the family, a federal guarantee of full employment, improved protection of children's legal rights, and a vastly expanded program of health care, they propose to strengthen "parent participation" in all these programs. They treat the ascendancy of experts as an unavoidable condition of industrial society, even when they seek to qualify this ascendancy by improving the position of consumers. They assume that the requirements of a complex society dictate the triumph of factory production over handicraft production and the ascendancy of the "helping professions" over the family.

Bureaucratic Dependence and Narcissism   Recent studies of professionalization show that professionalism did not emerge, in the nineteenth and early twentieth centuries, in response to clearly defined social needs. Instead, the new professions themselves invented many of the needs they claimed to satisfy. They played on public fears of disorder and disease, adopted a deliberately mystifying jargon, ridiculed popular traditions of self-help as backward and unscientific, and in this way created or intensified (not without opposition) a demand for their own services. The evidence of professional self-promotion can no longer be dismissed by reasserting the sociological truism that "modern society involves the individual in relations . . . that are vastly more complex than [those] his ancestors . . . had to contend with."*

* Since the author of these words, Thomas L. Haskell, has tried to equate criticism of the professions with a blind and willful opposition to the pursuit of truth, I should make it clear that my argument must not be misunderstood as an unqualified condemnation of professionalism. Obviously professions uphold important values. In particular, they uphold standards of accuracy, honesty, verification, and service that might otherwise disappear altogether. But it is not true, as Paul Goodman argued in his otherwise compelling defense of professionalism ("The New Reformation," cited by Haskell and others as the last word on the subject), that "professionals are autonomous individuals beholden to the nature of things and the judgment of their peers, and bound by an explicit or implicit oath to benefit their clients and the community." The way in which professionals construe and discharge these responsibilities naturally reflects the social surroundings in which they operate. American professionalism has been corrupted by the man-

The family's dependence on professional services over which it has little control represents one form of a more general phenomenon: the erosion of self-reliance and ordinary competence by the growth of giant corporations and of the bureaucratic state that serves them. The corporations and the state now control so much of the necessary know-how that Durkheim's image of society as the "nourishing mother," from whom all blessings flow, more and more coincides with the citizen's everyday experience. The new paternalism has replaced personal dependence not with bureaucratic rationality, as theorists of modernization (beginning with Max Weber) have almost unanimously assumed, but with a new form of bureaucratic dependence. What appears to social scientists as a seamless web of "interdependence" represents in fact the dependence of the individual on the organization, the citizen on the state, the worker on the manager, and the parent on the "helping professions." The "consensus of the competent," as Thomas L. Haskell refers to the professions in his study of the professionalization of social science, came into being by reducing the layman to incompetence.

As retributive justice gives way to therapeutic justice, what began as a protest against moral oversimplification ends by destroying the very sense of moral responsibility. Therapeutic justice perpetuates childlike dependence into adulthood and deprives the citizen of legal resources against the state. Formerly law rested on an adversary relation between the state and the offender and acknowledged the superior power of the state by giving important procedural advantages to the defendant. Medical jurisprudence, on the other hand, implicates the offender in his own control. Relieved of moral responsibility when certified into

agerial capitalism with which it is so closely allied, just as professionalism in the Soviet Union has been much more completely corrupted by the dictatorship of the party.

Haskell writes: "Membership in a truly professional community [cannot] be based on charm, social standing, personal connection, good character, or perhaps even decency, but on demonstrated intellectual merit alone." Haskell does not appreciate how easily "intellectual merit" can be confused with the mere acquisition of professional credentials or, worse, with loyalty to an unspoken ideological consensus—how easily the indispensable ideal of professional disinterestedness can be warped and distorted by the social and political context in which it has grown up.

the sick role, he cooperates with the doctors in his own "cure."

The psychiatric critique of the law, like the therapeutic attack on authority in general, makes a virtue of substituting personal treatment for the impersonal, arbitrary authority of the courts. Thus a specialist in the sociology of law, acknowledging his intention to "substitute scientific therapies for legal sanctions—for 'justice' "—once deplored the irrationality of legal procedures: "There is in the concept of justice an element of 'fate,' which is absent in the concept of scientific treatment. The offender simply gets what he himself initiated. . . . Society as a whole is blameless. The criminal himself was the one who chose." Whereas "the lawyer's way of handling a human problem is typically nonscientific," therapy treats the criminal or patient as a victim and thus puts matters in their proper light. The shift from "sin" to "sickness," according to this writer, represents the first step toward "the introduction of science and personal reactions [into] human conflicts" and to the recognition of social problems as medical problems, in which "cooperation with the therapist" becomes "probably the most critical problem for the deviant."

Medical justice shares with enlightened childrearing and pedagogy a tendency to promote dependence as a way of life. Therapeutic modes of thought and practice exempt their object, the patient, from critical judgment and relieve him of moral responsibility. Sickness by definition represents an invasion of the patient by forces outside his conscious control, and the patient's realistic recognition of the limits of his own responsibility—his acceptance of his diseased and helpless condition—constitutes the first step toward recovery (or permanent invalidism, as the case may be). Therapy labels as sickness what might otherwise be judged as weak or willful actions; it thus equips the patient to fight (or resign himself to) the disease, instead of irrationally finding fault with himself. Inappropriately extended beyond the consulting room, however, therapeutic morality encourages a permanent suspension of the moral sense. There is a close connection, in turn, between the erosion of moral responsibility and the waning of the capacity for self-help—in the categories used by John R. Seeley, between the elimination of culpability and the elimination of competence. "What says 'you are

not guilty' says also 'you cannot help yourself.' " Therapy legiti-
mates deviance as sickness, but it simultaneously pronounces the
patient unfit to manage his own life and delivers him into the
hands of a specialist. As therapeutic points of view and practice
gain general acceptance, more and more people find themselves
disqualified, in effect, from the performance of adult responsibilities and become dependent on some form of medical authority.

The psychological expression of this dependence is narcissism. In its pathological form, narcissism originates as a defense
against feelings of helpless dependency in early life, which it tries
to counter with "blind optimism" and grandiose illusions of personal self-sufficiency. Since modern society prolongs the experience of dependence into adult life, it encourages milder forms of
narcissism in people who might otherwise come to terms with the
inescapable limits on their personal freedom and power—limits
inherent in the human condition—by developing competence as
workers and parents. But at the same time that our society makes
it more and more difficult to find satisfaction in love and work,
it surrounds the individual with manufactured fantasies of total
gratification. The new paternalism preaches not self-denial but
self-fulfillment. It sides with narcissistic impulses and discourages their modification by the pleasure of becoming self-reliant,
even in a limited domain, which under favorable conditions accompanies maturity. While it encourages grandiose dreams of
omnipotence, moreover, the new paternalism undermines more
modest fantasies, erodes the capacity to suspend disbelief, and
thus makes less and less accessible the harmless substitute-
gratifications, notably art and play, that help to mitigate the sense
of powerlessness and the fear of dependence that otherwise express themselves in narcissistic traits.

Our society is narcissistic, then, in a double sense. People
with narcissistic personalities, although not necessarily more numerous than before, play a conspicuous part in contemporary
life, often rising to positions of eminence. Thriving on the adula-
tion of the masses, these celebrities set the tone of public life and
of private life as well, since the machinery of celebrity recognizes
no boundaries between the public and the private realm. The

beautiful people—to use this revealing expression to include not merely wealthy globetrotters but all those who bask, however briefly, in the full glare of the cameras—live out the fantasy of narcissistic success, which consists of nothing more substantial than a wish to be vastly admired, not for one's accomplishments but simply for oneself, uncritically and without reservation.

Modern capitalist society not only elevates narcissists to prominence, it elicits and reinforces narcissistic traits in everyone. It does this in many ways: by displaying narcissism so prominently and in such attractive forms; by undermining parental authority and thus making it hard for children to grow up; but above all by creating so many varieties of bureaucratic dependence. This dependence, increasingly widespread in a society that is not merely paternalistic but maternalistic as well, makes it increasingly difficult for people to lay to rest the terrors of infancy or to enjoy the consolations of adulthood.

The Conservative Critique of Bureaucracy   Criticism of the new paternalism, insofar as it remains imprisoned in the assumptions of political liberalism, objects to the cost of maintaining a welfare state—the "human cost" as well as the cost to the taxpayers—without criticizing the ascendancy of the managerial and professional class. Another line of attack, which singles out bureaucracy as the overriding evil, arises out of a conservative idealization of old-fashioned individualism. Less equivocal in its opposition to bureaucratic centralization—except when it comes from right-wingers who denounce government regulation of industry and still plead for a gigantic military establishment—the conservative critique of bureaucracy superficially resembles the radical critique outlined in the present study. It deplores the erosion of authority, the corruption of standards in the schools, and the spread of permissiveness. But it refuses to acknowledge the connection between these developments and the rise of monopoly capitalism—between bureaucracy in government and bureaucracy in industry.

"The great historical conflict between individualism and collectivism is dividing mankind into two hostile camps," wrote Ludwig von Mises in his study of bureaucracy. Capitalist free enterprise, he argued, rests on the rational calculation of profit and loss, whereas bureaucratic management "cannot be checked by economic calculation." Extended beyond its legitimate domain of law enforcement and national defense, bureaucracy undermines individual initiative and substitutes "government control for free enterprise." It substitutes the dictatorship of the state for the rule of law. Free-market capitalism, by turning labor into a commodity, "makes the wage earner free from any personal dependence" and detaches "appraisal of each individual's effort . . . from any personal considerations." Bureaucratic collectivism, on the other hand, undermines the "cool rationality and objectivity of capitalist relations" and renders the "plain citizen" dependent on the "professional propagandist of bureaucratization," who confuses the citizen with his "empty catchwords" and esoteric obfuscation. "Under capitalism everybody is the architect of his own fortune." But under socialism—and "there is no compromise possible between these two systems," according to Mises, "no third system"—the "way toward promotion is not achievement but the favor of the superiors."

This argument suffers from the conservative's idealization of the personal autonomy made possible by the free market and his willingness to concede enormous warmaking powers to the state, so long as they do not interfere with "private" enterprise. It cannot explain the spread of bureaucracy into industry itself. "The trend toward bureaucratic rigidity is not inherent in the evolution of business," according to Mises. "It is an outcome of government meddling with business." Such is his reply to the liberal argument that the inexorable trend toward economic concentration gives rise to a growing gap between ownership and control of the corporation, creates a new managerial elite, and calls into being a centralized state as the only agency capable of controlling it. The liberal analysis itself, however, needs modification. It is not the "divorce between ownership and control" that has created the managerial oligarchy but the divorce between production and planning. Having achieved a complete separation of handwork and brain work, management monopolizes technical knowledge and reduces the worker to a human machine; but the administration and continual elaboration of this knowledge require an ever-growing managerial apparatus, itself organized on the principles of the factory with its intricate subdivision of tasks. Studies of progressivism and the New Deal have shown that government regulation of business often arose in response to the demands of businessmen themselves. Regulatory agencies draw most of their personnel from business. Neither the regulatory nor the welfare policies of the state rest on "an implicable hatred of private business and free enterprise," as Mises claims. On the contrary, regulation controls competition and stabilizes the market, while the welfare system socializes the "human costs" of capitalist production—rising unemployment, inadequate wage scales, inadequate insurance against sickness and old age—and helps to forestall more radical solutions.

It is true that a professional elite of doctors, psychiatrists, social scientists, technicians, welfare workers, and civil servants now plays a leading part in the administration of the state and of the "knowledge industry." But the state and the knowledge industry overlap at so many points with the business corporation (which has increasingly concerned itself with every phase of culture), and the new professionals share so many characteristics with the managers of industry, that the professional elite must be regarded not as an independent class but as a branch of modern management. The therapeutic ethic, which has replaced the nineteenth-century utilitarian ethic, does not serve the "class interest" of professionals alone, as Daniel P. Moynihan and others have argued; it serves the interests of monopoly capitalism as a whole. Moynihan points out that by emphasizing impulse rather than calculation as the determinant of human conduct, and by holding society responsible for the problems confronting individuals, a "government-oriented" professional class has attempted to create a demand for its own services. Professionals, he observes, have a vested interest in discontent, because discontented people turn to professional services for relief. But the same principle underlies all of modern capitalism, which continually tries to create new demands and new discontents that can be assuaged only by the consumption of commodities. Moynihan, aware of this connection, tries to present the professional as the successor to the capitalist. The ideology of "compassion," he says, serves the class interest of the "post-industrial surplus of functionaries who, in the manner of industrialists who earlier turned to advertising, induce demand for their own products."

Professional self-aggrandizement, however, grew up side by side with the advertising industry and must be seen as another phase of the same process, the transition from competitive capitalism to monopoly capitalism. The same historical development that turned the citizen into a client transformed the worker from a producer into a consumer. Thus the medical and psychiatric assault on the family as a technologically backward sector went hand in hand with the advertising industry's drive to convince people that store-bought goods are superior to homemade goods. Both the growth of management and the proliferation of professions represent new forms of capitalist control, which first established themselves in the factory and then spread throughout society. The struggle against bureaucracy therefore requires a struggle against capitalism itself. Ordinary citizens cannot resist professional dominance without also asserting control over production and over the technical knowledge on which modern production rests. A reassertion of "common sense," according to Mises, will "prevent man from falling prey" to the "illusory fantasies" of professional bureaucrats. But common sense is not enough. In order to break the existing pattern of dependence and put an end to the erosion of competence, citizens will have to take the solution of their problems into their own hands. They will have to create their own "communities of competence." Only then will the productive capacities of modern capitalism, together with the scientific knowledge that now serves it, come to serve the interests of humanity instead.

In a dying culture, narcissism appears to embody—in the guise of personal "growth" and "awareness"—the highest attainment of spiritual enlightenment. The custodians of culture hope, at bottom, merely to survive its collapse. The will to build a better society, however, survives, along with traditions of localism, self help, and community action that only need the vision of a new society, a decent society, to give them new vigor. The moral discipline formerly associated with the work ethic still retains a value independent of the role it once played in the defense of property rights. That discipline—indispensable to the task of building a new order—endures most of all in those who knew the old order only as a broken promise, yet who took the promise more seriously than those who merely took it for granted.

Notes

Preface

page

xiv   David Donald on the irrelevance of history
New York *Times*, 8 September 1977.

xvii "rules out entirely . . . precincts of nostalgia."
A. E. Parr, "Problems of Reason, Feeling and Habitat," *Architectural Association Quarterly* 1 (1969): 9.

xviii "As people become apt pupils . . . seriously undersupplied."
Ivan Illich, *Toward a History of Needs* (New York: Pantheon, 1978), p. 31.

I. The Awareness Movement and the Social Invasion of the Self

page

3   "The Marivaudian being . . . surrounds him."
Donald Barthelme, "Robert Kennedy Saved from Drowning," in *Unspeakable Practices, Unnatural Acts* (New York: Farrar, Straus and Giroux, 1968), p. 46.

3   "It is only irritating . . . are now."
John Cage, *Silences*, quoted in Susan Sontag, *Styles of Radical Will* (New York: Farrar, Straus and Giroux, 1969), p. 94.

4   "The sense of an ending . . . too deep."
Frank Kermode, *The Sense of an Ending: Studies in the Theory of Fiction* (New York: Oxford University Press, 1967), pp. 98–100.

4   "people take . . . without great agitation."
Susan Sontag, "The Imagination of Disaster" (1965) in *Against Interpretation* (New York: Dell, 1969), pp. 212–28.

4   "everyone seems to share . . . fastest moving items."
Sara Davidson, "Open Land: Getting Back to the Communal Garden" (1970) reprinted in Gwen B. Carr, ed., *Marriage and Family in a Decade of Change* (Reading, Mass.: Addison-Wesley, 1972), p. 197.

5   Leslie A. Fiedler, "The Birth of God and the Death of Man," *Salmagundi*, no. 21 (1973), pp. 3–26; Tom Wolfe, "The 'Me' Decade and the Third Great Awakening," *New York*, 23 August 1976, pp. 26–40; Jim Hougan, *Decadence: Radical Nostalgia, Narcissism, and Decline in the Seventies* (New York: Morrow, 1975), pp. 32–37, 137, 144, 151, 186–88, 234.

6   Revolutionary of the Upper Rhine
     Norman Cohn, *The Pursuit of the Millennium*, 2d ed. (New York: Harper Torchbooks, 1961), pp. 114–23.

6   Peter Marin, "The New Narcissism," *Harper's*, October 1975, p. 46; Wolfe, "The 'Me' Decade," p. 40.

7   Susan Stern, *With the Weathermen: The Personal Journal of a Revolutionary Woman* (New York: Doubleday, 1975), pp. 23, 27, 87.

8   R. W. B. Lewis, *The American Adam: Innocence, Tragedy, and Tradition in the Nineteenth Century* (Chicago: University of Chicago Press, 1955); Quentin Anderson, *The Imperial Self* (New York: Knopf, 1971); Michael Paul Rogin, *Fathers and Children: Andrew Jackson and the Subjugation of the American Indian* (New York: Knopf, 1975) and "Nature as Politics and Nature as Romance in America," *Political Theory* 5 (1977):5–30.

9   "their whole destiny . . . propinquity to himself."
     Alexis de Tocqueville, *Democracy in America* (New York: Knopf, 1951), 2: 99.

9   "the individual will . . . isolation of the self '; "immense middle ground of human community"
     Marin, "New Narcissism," p. 48.

9   "genial middle ground of human tradition."
     Van Wyck Brooks, *America's Coming-of-Age* (New York: Doubleday, 1958 [1915]), p. 38.

9   "The work of destruction . . . hostility to the past."
     Orestes Brownson, 1857, quoted in Perry Miller, ed., *The American Transcendentalists: Their Prose and Poetry* (New York: Doubleday, 1957), pp. 40–41.

12   "the self shrinks back . . . dissolving into this cavity."
     Morris Dickstein, *Gates of Eden: American Culture in the Sixties* (New York: Basic Books, 1977), pp. 227–28.

14   Jerry Rubin, *Growing (Up) at Thirty-seven* (New York: M. Evans, 1976), pp. 19 ("journey into myself"); 20 ("make peace"; "massive self-examination"; "smorgasbord course in New Consciousness"); 34 ("permission to be healthy"; "like twenty-five"); 45 ("female in me"); 56 ("addiction"); 93 ("media freak"); 100 ("liked what I saw"; "entered rooms"); 103 ("puritan conditioning"; "it's O.K."); 116 ("fear of pleasure"); 120 ("propagandized as a child"); 122 ("in its proper place"); 124 ("negative programming"); 139 ("judge"); 154 ("forgive").

15 "released him . . . private life."
    Paul Zweig, *Three Journeys: An Automythology* (New York: Basic Books, 1976), p. 96.

17 "the deep sources of grandiosity . . . find access to"
    Heinz Kohut, *The Analysis of the Self: A Systematic Approach to the Psychoanalytic Treatment of Narcissistic Personality Disorders* (New York: International Universities Press, 1971), pp. 178, 315.

18 "After the concert . . . on their backs."
    Donald Barthelme, "Critique de la Vie Quotidienne" and "Perpetua," both in *Sadness* (New York: Farrar, Straus and Giroux, 1972), pp. 3, 40.

19 "Good Lord . . . five years in the future."
    Woody Allen, *Without Feathers* (New York: Warner, 1976), pp. 8–10, 205.

19 Dan Greenberg, *Scoring: A Sexual Memoir* (New York: Doubleday, 1972), pp. 13, 81–82.

21 Allen, *Without Feathers*, pp. 199–204.

21 "conviction, amounting to a faith . . . come close to."
    Zweig, *Three Journeys*, pp. 46, 67.

21 Frederick Exley, *A Fan's Notes: A Fictional Memoir* (New York: Random House, 1968), pp. 99 ("microscopic space"); 131 ("illusion that fame was possible)"; 231 ("awful dream"; "bleak anonymity"); 328 ("everything!"); 361 ("aversion for the herd").

22 Frederick Exley, *Pages from a Cold Island* (New York: Random House, 1974), pp. 37, 41, 170, 206.

23 Stern, *With the Weathermen*, pp. 89 ("niche in life"); 143–44 (Bernadine Dohrn); 231 ("flashy and vulgar"; "frozen inside"); 243 ("nude and armed"); 255 ("people hanging around me"); 262 ("people loved me").

24 Zweig, *Three Journeys*, pp. 49 ("inner dryness"); 73 ("*je ne veux pas*"); 79 ("impersonate his existence"); 80 ("a few bracing weeks"); 82 ("vacant spin"); 106 ("impassibility"); 108–9 ("terror and vulnerability"; schizophrenia); 149–50 ("experience of inner emptiness"); 150 ("delirium of release"); 150, 158 ("cure"), 156 ("futility of mental processes"); 164 ("healed and buoyant"); 167 ("labor of self-defense"); 172 ("double"; "mental busyness").

25 "eases their troubled conscience."
    Marin, "New Narcissism," pp. 47–48.

26 Edwin Schur, *The Awareness Trap: Self-Absorption instead of Social Change* (New York: Quadrangle-New York Times, 1976), pp. 89–91 ("middle-class values and experience"); 99 ("social discontent to personal inadequacy"); 122 ("ethic of self-preservation"); 182 ("criminal"); 193 ("real" problems).

27 "narcissism . . . self-love"
    Richard Sennett, *The Fall of Public Man* (New York: Knopf, 1977), p. 324.

28 "civility"
    ibid., pp. 264–65.

28 "Strangers . . . speak to each other."
   ibid., p. 86.
   "signs"/ibid., pp. 73 *ff.*

28 "what's in it . . . is him"; "suspends ego interests"
   ibid., pp. 220, 223.

29 "to take rather than to desire"; "ideology of intimacy"; "culture of personality"
   ibid., pp. 220, 259 and *passim;* p. 264.

30 "assertiveness"; "fighting fair"; "open marriage"
   For examples of this ideology, see Nena O'Neill and George O'Neill, *Open
   Marriage: A New Life Style for Couples* (New York: New American Library,
   1972); Robert Francoeur and Anna Francoeur, *Hot and Cool Sex: Cultures in
   Conflict* (New York: Harcourt Brace Jovanovich, 1975); Mel Krantzler, *Cre-
   ative Divorce: A New Opportunity for Personal Growth* (New York: New Ameri-
   can Library, 1973); George R. Bach and Peter Weyden, *The Intimate Enemy:
   How to Fight Fair in Love and Marriage* (New York: Avon, 1968); Manuel J.
   Smith, *When I Say No, I Feel Guilty: How to Cope, Using the Skills of Systematic
   Assertive Therapy* (New York: Bantam, 1975).

II. The Narcissistic Personality of Our Time

page
31 Erich Fromm, *The Heart of Man: Its Genius for Good and Evil* (New York:
   Harper and Row, 1964), ch. 4.

32 "we must recognize the id . . . libido."
   Sigmund Freud, *Group Psychology and the Analysis of the Ego* (1921), in James
   Strachey, ed., *The Standard Edition of the Complete Psychological Works of Sig-
   mund Freud* (London, Hogarth Press, 1955–64), 18:130.

33 Shirley Sugerman, *Sin and Madness: Studies in Narcissism* (Philadelphia: West-
   minster Press, 1976), p. 12.

34 "Psychosis . . . culture."
   Jules Henry, *Culture against Man* (New York: Knopf, 1963), p. 322.

35 T. W. Adorno, "Sociology and Psychology," *New Left Review*, no. 47 (1968),
   pp. 80, 96.

35 Otto F. Kernberg, *Borderline Conditions and Pathological Narcissism* (New
   York: Jason Aronson, 1975), p. 223.

35 "we do see certain symptom constellations . . . understanding of personality structure."
   James H. Gilfoil to the author, 12 October 1976.

37 Recent theories of narcissism
   Warren R. Brodey, "Image, Object, and Narcissistic Relationships," *Ameri-*

can Journal of Orthopsychiatry 31 (1961): 505 ("love rejected"); Therese Bene-dek, "Parenthood as a Developmental Phase," *Journal of the American Psycho-analytic Association* 7 (1959): 389–90 ("several weeks of postnatal development"); Thomas Freeman, "The Concept of Narcissism in Schizo-phrenic States," *International Journal of Psychoanalysis* 44 (1963): 295 ("annul the pain"; "recreate a wished-for love relationship"); Kernberg, *Borderline Conditions and Pathological Narcissism,* p. 283 ("cannot be considered"). On the distinction between primary and secondary narcissism and the character-istics of the latter, see also H. G. Van der Waals, "Problems of Narcissism," *Bulletin of the Menninger Clinic* 29 (1965): 293–310; Warren M. Brodey, "On the Dynamics of Narcissism," *Psychoanalytic Study of the Child* 20 (1965):165–93; James F. Bing and Rudolph O. Marburg, "Narcissism," *Journal of the American Psychoanalytic Association* 10 (1962): 593–605; Lester Schwartz, "Techniques and Prognosis in Treatment of the Narcissistic Per-sonality," *Journal of the American Psychoanalytic Association* 21 (1973): 617–32; Edith Jacobson, *The Self and the Object World* (New York: International Uni-versities Press, 1964), ch. 1, especially pp. 17–19; James F. Bing, Francis McLaughlin, and Rudolph Marburg, "The Metapsychology of Narcis-sism," *Psychoanalytic Study of the Child* 14 (1959): 9–28. Freud's "On Narcis-sism: An Introduction" (1914) appears in *Standard Edition,* 3:30–59.

37–38   characteristics of character disorders; Peter L. Giovachinni, *Psychoanalysis of Character Disorders* (New York: Jason Aronson, 1975), pp. xv ("very seldom resembled the classical neuroses"), 1 ("vague, diffuse dissatisfactions"), 31 ("general inability to get along"); Heinz Kohut, *The Analysis of the Self* (New York: International Universities Press, 1971), p. 16 ("feelings of emptiness and depression"), 62 ("sense of heightened self-esteem"), 172 ("elaborate the sexual impulse"); Annie Reich, "Pathologic Forms of Self-Esteem Regula-tion," *Psychoanalytic Study of the Child* 15 (1960): 224 ("violent oscillations"). See also, for an early description of borderline conditions, Robert P. Knight, "Borderline States" (1953) in Robert P. Knight and Cyrus R. Fried-man, eds. *Psychoanalytic Psychiatry and Psychology: Clinical and Theoretical Papers* (New York: International Universities Press, 1954), pp. 97–109; and for the importance of magical thinking in these conditions, Thomas Free-man, "The Concept of Narcissism in Schizophrenic States," *International Journal of Psychoanalysis* 44 (1963): 293–303; Géza Róheim, *Magic and Schizo-phrenia* (New York: International Universities Press, 1955).

38–41   psychodynamics of pathological narcissism
          Melanie Klein, "The Oedipus Complex in the Light of Early Anxieties" (1945), in her *Contributions to Psychoanalysis* (New York: McGraw-Hill, 1964), pp. 339–67; Melanie Klein, "Notes on Some Schizoid Mechanisms" (1946) and Paula Heimann, "Certain Functions of Introjection and Projec-tion in Early Infancy," in Melanie Klein et al., *Developments in Psychoanalysis* (London: Hogarth Press, 1952), pp. 122–68, 292–320; Paula Heimann, "A Contribution to the Reevaluation of the Oedipus Complex: The Early Stages," in Melanie Klein et al., *New Directions in Psychoanalysis* (New York:

Basic Books, 1957), pp. 23–38; Kernberg, *Borderline Conditions and Patholog-ical Narcissism*, especially pp. 36 ("constant projection"), 38 ("blind op-timism"), 161 ("pseudo-insight"), 213 ("emptiness"), 282 ("grandiose self "), 310–11 (aging and death); Roy R. Grinker et al., *The Borderline Syndrome* (New York: Basic Books, 1968), pp. 102 ("parasitic" attachments), 105 ("two month relationship"); Otto Kernberg, "A Contribution to the Ego-Psychological Critique of the Kleinian School," *International Journal of Psy-choanalysis* 50 (1969); 317–33 (quoting Herbert A. Rosenfeld on the narcissis-tic patient's use of words to defeat interpretation).

On the psychogenesis of secondary narcissism, see also Kohut, *Analysis of the Self;* Giovacchini, *Psychoanalysis of Character Disorders;* Brodey, "Dy-namics of Narcissism"; Thomas Freeman, "Narcissism and Defensive Pro-cesses in Schizophrenic States,' *International Journal of Psychoanalysis* 43 (1962); 415–25; Nathaniel Ross, "The 'As If' Concept," *Journal of the Ameri-can Psychoanalytic Association* 15 (1967): 59–83.

On mourning, see Freud's "Mourning and Melancholia" (1917), *Standard Edition*, 8:152–70; Martha Wolfenstein, "How Is Mourning Possible?" *Psy-choanalytic Study of the Child* 21 (1966): 93–126; and on psychoanalysis as a way of life, Gilbert J. Rose, "Some Misuses of Analysis as a Way of Life: Analysis Interminable and Interminable 'Analysts'," *International Review of Psychoanalysis* 1 (1974): 509–15.

42   changing patterns of pathology
Giovacchini, *Psychoanalysis of Character Disorders*, pp. 316–17; Allen Whee-lis, *The Quest for Identity* (New York: Norton, 1958), pp. 40–41; Heinz Lich-tenstein, "The Dilemma of Human Identity," *Journal of the American Psycho-analytic Association* 11 (1963): 186–87; Herbert Hendin, *The Age of Sensation* (New York: Norton, 1975), p. 13; Michael Beldoch, "The Therapeutic as Narcissist," *Salmagundi*, no. 20 (1972), pp. 136, 138; Burness E. Moore, "Toward a Clarification of the Concept of Narcissism," *Psychoanalytic Study of the Child*, 30 (1975): 265; Sheldon Bach, quoted in *Time*, 20 September 1976, p. 63; Rose, "Some Misuses of Analysis," p. 513; Joel Kovel, *A Com-plete Guide to Therapy* (New York: Pantheon, 1976), p. 252; Ilza Veith, *Hyste-ria: The History of a Disease* (Chicago: University of Chicago Press, 1965), p. 273.

44   "visibility," "momentum"
Rosabeth Moss Kanter, *Men and Women of the Corporation* (New York: Basic Books, 1977), *passim;* Eugene Emerson Jennings, *Routes to the Executive Suite* (New York: McGraw-Hill, 1971), *passim*, especially ch. 5 ('The Essence of Visiposure").

44   Michael Maccoby, *The Gamesman: The New Corporate Leaders* (New York: Simon and Schuster, 1976), pp. 100 ("the exhilaration . . . labeled a loser"); 104 ("need to be in control"); 106 ("open to new ideas"; "renounce adolescent rebelliousness"); 107 ("illusion of limitless options"); 108 ("pushed around by the company"; "very big customer"); 110 ("Once his youth . . . starkly alone"); 115 ("totally emasculated"); 122 ("seductive"), 162 ("adoring, mini-skirted secretaries").

44   "not simply getting ahead . . . of others."
      Jennings, *Routes to the Executive Suite*, p. 3.

45   "Overidentification . . . widest set of options possible."
      ibid., pp. 307–8.

45   Seymour B. Sarason, *Work, Aging, and Social Change* (New York: Free Press, 1977), ch. 12.

46   Wilfrid Sheed, *Office Politics* (New York: Farrar, Straus and Giroux, 1966), p. 172.

47   Jennings, *Routes to the Executive Suite*, pp. 61, 64, 66, 69, 72, 181.

48   Sontag on the camera
      Susan Sontag, "Photography Unlimited," *New York Review*, 23 June 1977, pp. 26, 28, 31.

49   "the struggle . . . identity or ego."
      Jennings, *Routes to the Executive Suite*, p. 4.

49   Gail Sheehy, *Passages: Predictable Crises of Adult Life* (New York: Dutton, 1976), pp. 59, 199, 201, 345.

51   Kernberg, *Borderline Conditions and Pathological Narcissism*, p. 238.

III. Changing Modes of Making it

page
52   "American society . . . became president."
      Robin Williams, *American Society* (New York, Knopf, 1970), pp. 454–55.

52   "The man of ambition . . . underlying mechanisms."
      Philip Rieff, *Freud: The Mind of the Moralist* (New York: Doubleday, 1961), p. 372.

54   Cotton Mather, *A Christian at His Calling* (1701), reprinted in Moses Rischin, ed., *The American Gospel of Success* (Chicago: Quadrangle Books, 1965), pp. 23, 25, 28. John Cotton, "Christian Calling" (164), reprinted in Perry Miller and Thomas H. Johnson, eds., *The Puritans* (New York: American Book Company, 1938), p. 324.

55   "All Franklin's moral attitudes . . . purpose of his life."
      Max Weber, *The Protestant Ethic and the Spirit of Capitalism*, trans. Talcott Parsons (New York: Scribner's, 1958 [1904–5]), pp. 52–53. For another interpretation of the eighteenth-century meaning of self-improvement, more attentive to its nuances, see John G. Cawelti, *Apostles of the Self-Made Man* (Chicago: University of Chicago Press, 1965), ch. 1.

56   P. T. Barnum, "The Art of Money-Getting," in Rischin, *Gospel of Success*, pp. 47–66.

57   Beecher on the *"beau ideal* of happiness"
      quoted in Cawelti, *Apostles of the Self-Made Man*, p. 53.

57   "work has been the chief . . . pleasure in my life."
      quoted in Irvin G. Wyllie, *The Self-Made Man in America: The Myth of Rags to Riches* (New York: Free Press, 1966), p. 43.

57   "accumulated capital means progress"
      James Freeman Clarke, *Self-Culture: Physical, Intellectual, Moral and Spiritual* (Boston: Osgood, 1880), p. 266; "discipline of daily life": unidentified industrialist quoted in Wyllie, *Self-Made Man*, p. 96. On self-culture, see also Cawelti, *Apostles of the Self-Made Man*, ch. 3.

58   Cawelti, *Apostles of the Self-Made Man*, pp. 171; 176–77; 182–83 ("willpower"; "salesmanship and boosterism").

58   "the old adage . . . our desires."
      Dale Carnegie, quoted in ibid., p. 210.

58   Napoleon Hill
      quoted in ibid., p. 211.

59   "Although I'm not being original . . . portray to others."
      Robert L. Shook, *Winning Images* (New York: Macmillan, 1977), p. 22.

60   "relevant audiences"; "our reputation as a guarantor"; "our allies . . . 'underwriters')"
      John McNaughton, quoted in Neil Sheehan et al., *The Pentagon Papers* (New York: New York Times-Quadrangle, 1971), pp. 366, 442.

61   "talk constantly . . . of their images."
      Daniel Boorstin, *The Image: A Guide to Pseudo-Events in America* (New York: Atheneum, 1972 [1961]), p. 204.

61   "Hard work . . . cause of upward mobility."
      Emerson Jennings, *Routes to the Executive Suite* (New York: McGraw-Hill, 1971), pp. 29–30.

61   "in neither, I realized . . . important things."
      Pat Watters, *The Angry Middle-Aged Man* (New York: Grossman, 1976), p. 24.

61   "self-sacrificing company man . . . anachronism"; "does not view . . . organization man"; "antiorganizational posture . . . characteristic"
      Jennings, *Routes to the Executive Suite*, pp. 12, 240.

61   should executives marry?
      O. William Battalia and John J. Tarraut, *The Corporate Eunuch* (New York: Crowell, 1973), pp. 65, 71.

62   Thomas S. Szasz, *The Myth of Mental Illness* (New York: Harper and Row, 1961), pp. 275–76.

62   Joseph Heller, *Something Happened* (New York: Knopf, 1974), p. 414.

62   "be too easily simulated . . . winning."
      Jennings, *Routes to the Executive Suite*, p. 7.

63   "subdue the refractory tempers of work people."
      quoted in Stephen Marglin, "What Do Bosses Do?" *Review of Radical Political Economics* 6 (1974): 60–112; 7 (1975): 20–37.

63   "homeopathic doses of humiliation"
      Michael Maccoby, *The Gamesman: The New Corporate Leaders* (New York:
      Simon and Schuster, 1976), p. 102.

63–64 changing American character
      see David Riesman, *The Lonely Crowd: A Study of the Changing American Char-
      acter* (New Haven: Yale University Press, 1950); William H. Whyte, Jr.,
      The Organization Man (New York: Simon and Schuster, 1956); Erich
      Fromm, *Escape from Freedom* (New York: Rinehart, 1941) and *Man for Himself*
      (New York: Holt, Rinehart, and Winston, 1947); Karen Horney, *The Neu-
      rotic Personality of Our Time* (New York: Norton, 1937); Margaret Mead, *And
      Keep Your Powder Dry* (New York: Morrow, 1943); Geoffrey Gorer, *The
      American People: A Study in National Character* (New York: Norton, 1948);
      Allen Wheelis, *The Quest for Identity* (New York: Norton, 1958).

64   "essential aims . . . commercialized friendliness"; "If you do not smile . . .
      physician."
      Fromm, *Escape from Freedom*, pp. 242–43.

65   fun morality
      Martha Wolfenstein, "Fun Morality" (1951), reprinted in Margaret Mead
      and Martha Wolfenstein, eds., *Childhood in Contemporary Cultures* (Chicago:
      University of Chicago Press, 1955), pp. 168–76.

65   assertiveness therapy; game-free intimacy
      Manuel J. Smith, *When I Say No, I Feel Guilty* New York: Bantam, 1975), p.
      22; Eric Berne, *Games People Play: The Psychology of Human Relationships* (New
      York, Ballantine, 1974), *passim*.

66   David Riesman, Robert J. Potter, and Jeanne Watson, "Sociability, Permis-
      siveness, and Equality," *Psychiatry* 23 (1960): 334–36.

67   Lee Rainwater, *Behind Ghetto Walls: Black Families in a Federal Slum* (Chicago:
      Aldine, 1970), pp. 388–89.

69–70 Sade, "On the Republican Utopia," *La Philosophia dams le Boudoir*, in *Oeuvres
      complèts du Marquis de Sade* (Paris: Cercle du Livre Précieux, 1966), 3: 504–6.

IV. *The Banality of Pseudo-self awareness*

page
71   "The death of conscience is not the death of self-consciousness."
      quoted in Malcolm Cowley, *Exile's Return: A Literary Odyssey of the 1920s*
      (New York: Penguin, 1976 [1934]), p. 261.

71–72 the efficiency movement and scientific management
      Raymond E. Callahan, *Education and the Cult of Efficiency* (Chicago: Univer-
      sity of Chicago Press, 1962); Samuel Haber, *Efficiency and Uplift: Scientific
      Management in the Progressive Era* (Chicago: University of Chicago Press,
      1964); David F. Noble, *America by Design: Science, Technology, and the Rise of*

Corporate Capitalism (New York: Knopf, 1977); Harry Braverman, *Labor and Monopoly Capital* (New York: Monthly Review Press, 1974), part 1. The quotation from Taylor comes from Callahan, *Education and the Cult of Efficiency*, p. 40. For the statements by Filene, see Stuart Ewen, *Captains of Consciousness: Advertising and the Social Roots of the Consumer Culture* (New York: McGraw-Hill, 1976), pp. 54–55. On Ford's experiments in "sociology," see Roger Burlingame, *Henry Ford* (New York: New American Library, 1956), pp. 64–65.

72   Coolidge
quoted in Ewen, *Captains of Consciousness*, p. 37.

72   Guy Debord, *La Société du spectacle* (Paris: Buchet-Chastel, 1967), p. 36.

73   Paul H. Nystrom, *Economics of Fashion* (New York: Ronald Press, 1928), pp. 67–68.

74   ibid., pp. 73, 134–37.

75   Boorstin, *The Image*, p. 34.

76   Jacques Ellul, *Propaganda: The Formation of Men's Attitudes*, trans. Konrad Kellen and Jean Lerner (New York: Knopf, 1965), pp. 53n (Allied handbook) and 57n (Rommel); for the OWI's position on the holocaust, see memorandum, Arthur Sweetser to Leo Rosten, 1 February 1942, quoted in Eric Hanin, "War on Our Minds: The American Mass Media in World War II" (Ph.D. dissertation, University of Rochester, 1976), ch. 4, n. 6.

77   "Most of us are conditioned . . . comprehension of most men."
quoted in David Eakins, "Policy-Planning for the Establishment," in Ronald Radosh and Murray Rothbard, eds., *A New History of Leviathan* (New York: Dutton, 1972), p. 198.

78   "with the growth of the complexity of society . . . about these events."
quoted in Andrew Kopkind, "The Future Planners," *New Republic*, 25 February 1967, p. 19.

79   Theodore C. Sorensen, *Kennedy* (New York: Harper and Row, 1965), pp. 245–48, 592.

80   Nixon-Kennedy debate
Richard M. Nixon, *Six Crises* (New York: Doubleday, 1962), pp. 251, 277, 353–58; Bruce Mazlish, *In Search of Nixon* (New York: Basic Books, 1972), pp. 72–73.

81   Watergate
J. Anthony Lukas, *Nightmare: The Underside of the Nixon Years* (New York: Viking, 1976), especially p. 297, for Nixon's talk with Haldeman, 20 March 1973.

82   new left street theater
Dotson Rader, "Princeton Weekend with the SDS," *New Republic*, 9 December 1967, pp. 15–16 ("blood"); Greg Calvert quoted in New York *Times*, 7 May 1967 ("guerrilla force"). On the rise and fall of SDS, see Kirkpatrick Sale, *SDS* (New York: Random House, 1973).

82–83 "to live by your wits . . . low-class socialist."
       R. G. Davis, quoted in San Francisco *Express-Times*, 21 March 1968.

83   "Yippie . . . ending repressions."
       Jerry Rubin, *Growing (Up) at Thirty-seven* (New York: M. Evans, 1976), p. 49.

84   "are afraid of not belonging . . . sense of the term."
       Otto F. Kernberg, *Borderline Conditions and Pathological Narcissism* (New York: Jason Aronson, 1975), p. 234.

84   "Unconsciously fixated . . . derive strength."
       Heinz Kohut, *The Analysis of the Self* (New York: International Universities Press, 1971), p. 84.

84   humanization of the Olympians
       Edgar Morin, *L'Esprit du temps* (Paris: Bernard Grasset, 1962), ch. 10.

85   Kernberg, *Borderline Conditions and Pathological Narcissism*, pp. 234–36; Jules Henry, *Culture against Man* (New York: Knopf, 1963), pp. 223, 226, 228–29.

86   Joseph Heller, *Something Happened* (New York: Knopf, 1974), p. 72.

86   Joyce Maynard, *Looking Back: A Chronicle of Growing Up Old in the Sixties* (New York: Doubleday, 1973), pp. 3–4.

88   realism and antirealism in the theater
       Elizabeth Burns, *Theatricality: A Study of Convention in the Theatre and in Social Life* (New York: Harper and Row, 1972), pp. 47, 76–77; Richard Sennett, *The Fall of Public Man* (New York: Knopf, 1977), p. 208.

89   Eric Bentley, "I Reject the Living Theater," New York *Times*, 20 October 1968.

89   theater of the absurd
       Norman S. Litowitz and Kenneth M. Newman, "The Borderline Personality and the Theatre of the Absurd," *Archives of General Psychiatry* 16 (1967): 268–70.

90   Erving Goffman, *The Presentation of Self in Everyday Life* (New York: Doubleday, 1959), p. 56. On the "performing self," see also Richard Poirier, *The Performing Self* (New York: Oxford University Press, 1971), especially the title essay, pp. 86–111.

91   Kurt Vonnegut, Jr., *Slaughterhouse-Five* (New York: Delacorte Press, 1969), pp. 19–76; Marshall McLuhan, *The Mechanical Bride* (New York: Vanguard Press, 1951), p. 3; William Phillips and Philip Rahv, "Some Aspects of Literary Criticism," *Science and Society* 1 (1937): 213; Litowitz and Newman, "Borderline Personality and the Theatre of the Absurd," p. 275.

91   "the first art work . . . his own personality."
       Norman Mailer, *The Presidential Papers* (London: André Deutsch, 1964), p. 284.

92   "the women in ads . . . Your Masterpiece—Yourself."
       Ewen, *Captains of Consciousness*, pp. 177, 179–80.

93   "Every painter . . . aware of them."
Edgar Wind, *Art and Anarchy* (New York: Knopf, 1963), p. 40.

93   obliteration of the idea of detail in modern art
Richard Wollheim, "What Is Art?" (review of Wind's *Art and Anarchy*), *New York Review*, 30 April 1964, p. 8.

93   "decoding isolated details . . . whole man."
Sennett, *Fall of Public Man*, p. 169.

93   "Day after day . . . seeing no one, nothing."
Andy Warhol, *The Philosophy of Andy Warhol* (New York: Harcourt Brace Jovanovich, 1975), pp. 7–10.

95   ironic distance from daily routine
For an account of these mechanisms, see Stanley Cohen and Laurie Taylor, *Escape Attempts: The Theory and Practice of Resistance to Everyday Life* (London: Allen Lane, 1976).

97   writing about writing
Morris Dickstein, *Gates of Eden* (New York: Basic Books, 1977), pp. 219–20, 226–27, 233, 238, 240.

98   Kohut, *Analysis of the Self*, pp. 172–73, 211, 255; Heller, *Something Happened*, p. 170.

98   "The best love . . . get lost in."
Warhol, *Philosophy*, pp. 48–49.

99   "I established in my mind . . . I will perform."
Luke Rhinehart, *The Dice Man* (1971), quoted in Cohen and Taylor, *Escape Attempts*, p. 184.

V. *The Degradation of Sport*

page
100   Roger Caillois, "The Structure and Classification of Games," in John W. Loy, Jr., and Gerald S. Kenyon, *Sport, Culture, and Society* (New York: Macmillan, 1969), p. 49.

101   capitalist and socialist versions of the ideology of national fitness
John F. Kennedy, "The Soft American" (1960), reprinted in John T. Talamini and Charles H. Page, *Sport and Society: An Anthology* (Boston: Little, Brown, 1973), p. 369; Philip Goodhart and Christopher Chataway, *War without Weapons* (London: W. H. Allen, 1968), pp. 80, 84.

102   Johan Huizinga, *Homo Ludens: A Study of the Play Element in Culture* (Boston: Beacon Press, 1955 [1944]), pp. 197–98, 205; Huizinga, *In the Shadow of Tomorrow* (New York: Norton, 1936), p. 177.

104   recent criticism of sports
      Harry Edwards, *The Sociology of Sport* (Homewood, Ill.: Dorsey Press, 1973)
      and *The Revolt of the Black Athlete* (New York, Free Press, 1969); Dorcas
      Susan Butt, *Psychology of Sport* (New York: Van Nostrand Reinhold, 1976);
      Dave Meggyesy, *Out of Their League* (Berkeley: Ramparts Press, 1970); Chip
      Oliver, *High for the Game* (New York: Morrow, 1971); Paul Hoch, *Rip Off the
      Big Game: The Exploitation of Sports by the Power Elite* (New York: Doubleday,
      1972); Jack Scott, *The Athletic Revolution* (New York: Free Press, 1971).

105   Podhoretz on excellence
      quoted in Michael Novak, *The Joy of Sports* (New York: Basic Books, 1976),
      p. 176.

106   track and surfing/Scott, *Athletic Revolution*, pp. 97–98.

106   "new sports for the noncompetitive"
      "Games Big People Play," *Mother Jones*, September-October 1976, p. 43; see
      also Terry Orlick, *The Cooperative Sports and Games Book: Challenge without
      Competition* (New York: Pantheon, 1978).

109   Huizinga, *Homo Ludens*, p. 48.

110   Vilas–Connors match
      I am indebted for these suggestions to Herbert Benham.

111   nineteenth-century campaign against popular amusements
      Robert W. Malcolmson, *Popular Recreations in English Society, 1750–1850*
      (Cambridge: Cambridge University Press, 1973), p. 70.

111   Lee Benson, *The Concept of Jacksonian Democracy* (New York: Atheneum,
      1964), p. 201.

112   Thorstein Veblen, *The Theory of the Leisure Class* (New York: Modern Li-
      brary, 1934 [1899]), p. 256.

112   Goodhart and Chataway, *War without Weapons*, pp. 4–5, 28–29.

113   "In most countries, the 'Bourgeoisie' . . . major portion of your energies."
      Elting E. Morison, ed., *The Letters of Theodore Roosevelt* (Cambridge, Mass.:
      Harvard University Press, 1951), 2: 1444; 3: 615.

113   "grand do-or-die spirit . . . Chateau-Thierry."
      Donald Meyer, "Early Football," unpublished paper.

113   "Upon the fields of friendly strife . . . seeds of victory."
      quoted in Scott, *Athletic Revolution*, p. 21.

114   reactionary rhetoric
      ibid., pp. 17–21; Hoch, *Rip Off the Big Game*, pp. 2–4.

114–115 Although the clichés alluded to here can be found throughout the radical cri-
      tique of sports, Hoch's book provides them in richest profusion and ex-
      presses them in the purest revolutionary jargon. See *Rip Off the Big Game*,
      pp. 7, 18, 20, 122, 154, 158, 162–6, 117

117   "dominant sports creed"
      Edwards, *Sociology of Sport*, p. 334. Cf. Jerry Rubin, *Growing (Up) at Thirty-*

seven (New York: M. Evans, 1976), p. 180: "The ethic of competition, achievement, and domination is the core of the American system."

117 Heinz Kohut, *The Analysis of the Self* (New York: International Universities Press, 1971), p. 196; Herbert Hendin, *The Age of Sensation* (New York: Norton, 1975), p. 167.

118–119 Butt, *Psychology of Sport*, pp. 18, 32, 41, 55–58, and *passim;* Hoch, *Rip Off the Big Game*, p. 158; Jack Scott, "Sport" (1972), quoted in Edwards, *Sociology of Sport*, p. 338.

119 Cosell/quoted in Novak, *Joy of Sports*, p. 273.

120 alumni culture/Meyer, "Early Fooball"; Frederick Rudolph, *The American College and University* (New York: Vintage, 1962), p. 385.

120 Walter Camp
Meyer, "Early Football."

122 Novak, *Joy of Sports*, ch. 14.

124 Edgar Wind, *Art and Anarchy* (New York: Knopf, 1963), p. 18.

124 "sports are not separate . . . above criticism"
quoted in Novak, *Joy of Sports*, p. 276.

VI. Schooling and the New Illiteracy

page
126 decline of standards at elite colleges
Newsweek, 6 February 1978, pp. 69–70.

127 R. P. Blackmur, "Toward a Modus Vivendi," in *The Lion and the Honeycomb* (New York: Harcourt, Brace and World, 1955), pp. 3–31.

128 evidence of and commentary on declining skills and literacy
see the survey by Jack McCurdy and Don Speich, originally published in the Los Angeles *Times* and reprinted in the Rochester *Democrat and Chronicle*, 29 August 1976; an Associated Press report on test scores, Rochester *Democrat and Chronicle*, 19 September, 1976; and an item in the New York *Times*, 7 November 1974, on the simplification of textbooks.

129 citizens' ignorance of their rights
New York *Times*, 2 January 1977.

131 Thomas Jefferson, *Notes on the State of Virginia* (New York: Harper Torchbooks, 1964 [1785]), pp. 139–40, 142.

131 Michael Chevalier, *Society, Manners, and Politics in the United States: Letters on North America* (New York: Doubleday, 1961 [1838]), ch. 34.

133 Veblen on industrial discipline
Thorstein Veblen, *The Theory of Business Enterprise* (New York: Scribner's, 1904), ch. 9, "The Cultural Incidence of the Machine Process."

134 Eastman, NAM on industrial education

Carl W. Ackerman, *George Eastman* (Boston: Houghton Mifflin, 1930), p. 467; Raymond E. Callahan, *Education and the Cult of Efficiency* (Chicago: University of Chicago Press, 1962), p. 10.

134 The attack on "gentleman's education" and the statement that the mob should not aspire to culture appeared in a series of articles in the *Saturday Evening Post* (1912); the attack on "cultured ease," in an article in *Educational Review* (1913); both are quoted by Callahan, *Education and the Cult of Efficiency*, pp. 50, 102. On the efficiency movement in education, see also Joel H. Spring, *Education and the Rise of the Corporate State* (Boston: Beacon Press, 1972). For an account of the progressive movement in education, unfortunately almost completely uncritical, see Lawrence A. Cremin, *The Transformation of the School: Progressivism in American Education* (New York: Vintage, 1964).

135 Randolph Bourne, "Trans-National America" (1916), reprinted in Carl Resek, ed., *War and the Intellectuals* (New York: Harper Torchbooks, 1964), pp. 107–23; Mary Antin, *The Promised Land* (Boston: Houghton Mifflin, 1912), pp. 224–25; Norman Podhoretz, *Making It* (New York: Random House, 1967), ch. 1.

136 Robert S. Lynd and Helen Merrell Lynd, *Middletown: A Study in American Culture* (New York: Harcourt, Brace, 1956 [1929]), ch. 14.

137 "By bringing into the school . . . earlier day." Katherine Glover and Evelyn Dewey, *Children of the New Day* (New York: Appleton-Century, 1934), pp. 318–19.

137 life adjustment Joel Spring, *The Sorting Machine: National Educational Policy since 1945* (New York: David McKay, 1976), pp. 18–21.

138 "The school reinforces a regular schedule . . . encourages ambition." quoted in ibid., p. 87.

138 student sociability Willard Waller, "The Rating and Dating Complex," *American Sociological Review* 2 (1937): 727–34; August B. Hollingshead, *Elmtown's Youth* (New York: Wiley, 1949), ch. 9; James S. Coleman, *The Adolescent Society: The Social Life of the Teenager and Its Impact on Education* (Glencoe, Ill.: Free Press, 1962); Ernest A. Smith, *American Youth Culture: Group Life in Teenage Society* (Glencoe: Free Press, 1962); Henry, *Culture against Man*, chs. 6, 7.

139 debates on educational policy in the 1950s Spring, *Sorting Machine*, chs. 1–3.

140 "When we wrote at school . . . nonverbally communicate." Joyce Maynard, *Looking Back* (New York: Doubleday, 1973), p. 154.

141 Frederick Exley, *A Fan's Notes* (New York: Random House, 1968), pp. 6–7.

142 Kenneth B. Clark et al., *The Educationally Deprived* (New York: Metropolitan Applied Research Center, 1972), p. 79.

144 "black children or any other group . . . white and superior"; "demonstrable achievement"; "self-righteous, positive sentimentalism"

Kenneth B. Clark, interview, 18 October 1969, mimeographed, distributed by the Council for Basic Education, Washington, D.C.

144 "gild a noisome lily."
Clark et al., *The Educationally Deprived*, p. 36.

145 emergence of the university
Laurence R. Veysey, *The Emergence of the American University* (Chicago: University of Chicago Press, 1965), part 1; Oscar Handlin and Mary F. Handlin, *Facing Life: Youth and the Family in American History* (Boston: Little, Brown, 1971), pp. 203–4; Burton Bledstein, *The Culture of Professionalism: The Middle Class and the Development of Higher Education in America* (New York: Norton, 1976), ch. 8.

147 "So long as we do our work . . . in our own fashion."
quoted in Randolph Bourne, "A Vanishing World of Gentility," *Dial* 64 (1918): 234–35.

147 Randolph Bourne, review of Frederick P. Keppel, *The Undergraduate and His College, Dial* 64 (1918): 151–52.

149 "high culture propagates the values of those who rule."
Louis Kampf and Paul Lauter in the introduction to their anthology, *The Politics of Literature* (New York: Pantheon, 1972), p. 8. For similar views, see Richard Ohmann, *English in America: A Radical View of the Profession* (New York: Oxford University Press, 1975); and for a criticism of them, Gerald Graff, "Radicalizing English," *Salmagundi*, no. 36 (1977), pp. 110–16.

149 "there are certain works . . . elitist notion . . . adherence exclusively . . . dissonance with society." Quoted in an unpublished manuscript by Gerald Graffe.

149 "become involved"; "stand back . . . analyze them." These words appear in an article, the reference to which I have mislaid, criticizing the training of Peace Corps volunteers.

150 disappearance of the classics
New York *Times,* 29 May 1977.

151 fairy tales
Bruno Bettelheim, *The Uses of Enchantment: The Meaning and Importance of Fairy Tales* (New York: Vintage, 1977), especially pp. 49, 65.

152 Donald Barthelme, *Snow White* (New York: Atheneum, 1967), pp. 25–26.

VII. *The Socialization of Reproduction and The Collapse of Authority*

page
154 "have forced upon the school . . . home."
Abraham Flexner and Frank P. Bachman, *The Gary Schools: A General Account* (New York: General Education Board, 1918), p. 17.

155 "In the social republic . . . concern of the state."
Ellen H. Richards, *Euthenics: The Science of Controllable Environment* (Boston: Whitcomb and Barrows, 1910), p. 133.

155 "the harm, often well-nigh irreparable . . . their children."
James H. S. Bossard, *Problems of Social Well-Being* (New York: Harper and Brothers, 1927), pp. 577–78.

155 "the only practical and effective way . . . too inaccessible."
Jessie Taft, "The Relation of the School to the Mental Health of the Average Child," *Mental Hygiene* 7 (1923): 687.

155 Sophonisba P. Breckinridge and Edith Abbott, *The Delinquent Child and the Home* (New York: Charities Publication Committee, 1912), pp. 173–74.

155 "warped view of authority"/Miriam Van Waters, *Parents on Probation* (New York: New Republic, 1927), p. 80.

156 Edwin L. Earp, *The Social Engineer* (New York: Eaton and Mains, 1911), pp. 40–41, 246.

156 Richards, *Euthenics*, pp. 78–79.

156–57 rise of the juvenile court
Anthony Platt, *The Child Savers: The Invention of Delinquency* (Chicago: University of Chicago Press, 1969), p. 63 (R. R. Reeder, 1905, on the reformatory as a "good home"; G. E. Howe, 1880, on "virtual orphans"); Robert M. Mennel, *Thorns and Thistles: Delinquents in the United States, 1825–1940* (Hanover, N.H.: University of New Hampshire Press, 1973), p. 149 (quotations from Herbert Lou's *Juvenile Courts in the United States*), p. 156 (Breckinridge on rescue); Jane Addams, *My Friend, Julia Lathrop* (New York: Macmillan, 1935), p. 137.

158 impact of the juvenile court on the family
Platt, *The Child Savers*, p. 143 (Van Waters on "the art of human relations"; Judge Stubbs, Indianapolis juvenile court, on the "personal touch"); Van Waters, *Parents on Probation*, p. 35 ("warped or crippled personality"), p. 61 ("oriented in the modern world"), p. 95 ("perpetual chaperonage"), p. 169 ("incurable loyalty"), p. 170 ("mere kindness and plenty"), p. 253 ("take over the whole matter"); Mennel, *Thistles and Thorns*, pp. 142–43 (Homer Folks on "a new kind of reformatory"); Joseph M. Hawes, *Children in Urban Society: Juvenile Delinquency in Nineteenth-Century America* (New York: Oxford University Press, 1971), p. 188 (unidentified Colorado county judge on "the true function of a court"). On the sick role, see Talcott Parsons, *The Social System* (Glencoe, Ill.: Free Press, 1951), ch. 10; Talcott Parsons, "Illness and the Role of the Physician: A Sociological Perspective," in Clyde Kluckhohn and Henry A. Murray, eds., *Personality in Nature, Society, and Culture*, 2d ed. (New York, Knopf, 1954), pp. 609–17.

159 Washington Gladden, *Social Salvation* (Boston: Houghton Mifflin, 1902), pp. 105–6 ("retributive severities," "sentimental prison reformers"), p. 136 ("weakened the sense of moral responsibility"), p. 179 ("actual work of education"), p. 181 ("fundamentally, a parental function"), p. 192 ("cultivate the social temper"), p. 228 ("civilized, educated, inspired").

160   parent education
      Frank Dekker Watson, *The Charity Organization Movement in the United States*
      (New York: Macmillan, 1922), p. 115 ("cannot save the children sepa-
      rately"); Florence Kelley, *Some Ethical Gains through Legislation* (New York:
      Macmillan, 1905), pp. 180–84 (on Italian mothers).

161   revulsion against "maternal overprotection"
      John B. Watson, *Psychological Care of Infant and Child* (New York: Norton,
      1928); Arnold Gesell and Frances L. Ilg, *The Child from Five to Ten* (New
      York: Harper, 1946); Ernest R. Groves and Gladys H. Groves, *Parents and
      Children* (Philadelphia: Lippincott, 1928), pp. 5, 116. On changing fashions
      in childrearing technique, see Daniel R. Miller and Guy E. Swanson, *The
      Changing American Parent: A Study in the Detroit Area* (New York: Wiley,
      1958), *passim;* Hilde Bruch, *Don't Be Afraid of Your Child* (New York: Farrar,
      Straus, and Young, 1952), pp. 38–39.

161   Van Waters, *Parents on Probation*, p. 42; Lorine Pruette, "Why Women
      Fail," in Samuel Schmalhausen, ed., *Woman's Coming of Age* (New York:
      Liveright, 1931), p. 247; Sarah Comstock, "Mothercraft: A New Profession
      for Women," *Good Housekeeping* 59 (1914): 677.

162   Bruch, *Don't Be Afraid of Your Child*, p. 57.

162   Lisa Alther, *Kinflicks* (New York: Knopf, 1976), p. 152; Mary Roberts Coo-
      lidge, *Why Women Are So* (New York: Holt, 1912), p. 334.

163   Benjamin Spock, *Baby and Child Care* (New York: Pocket Books, 1957), pp.
      3–4.

163   "The deepest roots . . . merely the purveyors."
      Judd Marmor, "Psychological Trends in American Family Relationships,"
      Marriage and Family Living 13 (1951); 147.

163   "hostility toward family experts . . . what they could do about it."
      Jerome D. Folkman, "A New Approach to Family Life Education," *Mar-
      riage and Family Living* 17 (1955): 20, 24.

163–165 Bruch, *Don't Be Afraid of Your Child*, pp. 7–8 ("superimposed anxiety"), p. 12
      ("inner resources and capacity for judgment"), p. 13 ("here to stay"), pp.
      16–17 ("no going back"; "hopelessly out of step"), p. 33 ("routinized half-
      truths"), p. 45 ("desires to do right"), p. 54 ("crushing effect of authority and
      tradition"), p. 85 ("deep emotional disturbance"), pp. 164–65 ("self-ap-
      pointed, unlicensed experts"); Spock, *Baby and Child Care*, pp. 575, 597.

165   Samuel Liebman, ed., *Emotional Forces in the Family* (Philadelphia: Lippin-
      cott, 1959), pp. 9 (Meerloo), 127–29 (Schaffner), 136 (Kubie); Bruch, *Don't
      Be Afraid of Your Child*, p. 75 ("a father or mother who can say 'No' "); Gil-
      bert J. Rose, "Some Misuses of Analysis as a Way of Life," *International
      Review of Psychoanalysis* 1 (1974): 513–14.

166   parent effectiveness training
      Bruch, *Don't Be Afraid of Your Child*, p. 59 ("not easily fooled"); Haim G.
      Ginott, *Between Parent and Child: New Solutions to Old Problems* (New York:
      Avon Books, 1965), p. 31 ("not to the event itself"), p. 36 ("I never have

good luck"), p. 38 ("all feelings are legitimate"), p. 39 ("more important for a child"), p. 59 ("discharged without destroying anyone"). See also Thomas Gordon, *P.E.T. in Action* New York: Wyden, 1976).

167   Nancy McGrath, "By the Book," *New York Times Magazine*, 27 June 1976, pp. 26–27; Fitzhugh Dodson, *How to Parent* (Los Angeles: Nash, 1970); Lee Salk, *How to Raise a Human Being* (New York: Random House, 1969).

168   John R. Seeley, "Parents–The Last Proletariat?" (1959), in *The Americanization of the Unconscious* (New York: International Science Press, 1967), pp. 134, 323, 326.

168   Mark Gerzon, *A Childhood for Every Child: The Politics of Parenthood* (New York: Outerbridge and Lazard, 1973), p. 222.

168–169   Erving Goffman, *Asylums: Essays on the Social Situation of Mental Patients and Other Inmates* (New York: Doubleday, 1961); Thomas S. Szasz, *The Myth of Mental Illness* (New York: Harper and Row, 1961); Eliot Freidson, *Professional Dominance: The Social Structure of Medical Care* (New York, Atherton, 1970); David Rothman, *The Discovery of the Asylum* (Boston: Houghton Mifflin, 1971); Richard Fox, "Beyond 'Social Control': Institutions and Disorder in Bourgeois Society," *History of Education Quarterly* 16 (1976): 203–7.

170   Geoffrey Gorer, *The American People: A Study in National Character* (New York: Norton, 1948), p. 74.

170   "immature, narcissistic . . . good mother should be."
Beata Rank, "Adaptation of the Psychoanalytical Technique for the Treatment of Young Children with Atypical Development," *American Journal of Orthopsychiatry*, 19 (1949): 131–32.

170   examples of "perfect motherhood"
Peter L. Giovachinni, *Psychoanalysis of Character Disorders* (New York: Jason Aronson, 1975), pp. 32, 108–9.

171   psychodynamics of "optimal frustration"
Heinz Kohut, *The Analysis of the Self* (New York: International Universities Press, 1971), pp. 61–64.

171   narcissistic mothering
Warren M. Brodey, "On the Dynamics of Narcissism," *Psychoanalytic Study of the Child* 20 (1965): 184; Giovacchini, *Psychoanalysis of Character Disorders*, p. 27.

171   schizophrenia
Gregory Bateson et al., "Toward a Theory of Schizophrenia," *Behavioral Science* 1 (1956): 251–64; Theodore Lidz, "Schizophrenia and the Family," *Psychiatry* 21 (1958): 21–27; William McCord et al., "The Familial Genesis of Psychoses," *Psychiatry* 25 (1962): 60–71.

172   schizophrenia and narcissism
Warren R. Brodey, "Image, Object, and Narcissistic Relationships," *American Journal of Orthopsychiatry* 31 (1961): 69–73; L. R. Ephron, "Narcissism and the Sense of Self," *Psychoanalytic Review* 54 (1967): 507–8; Thomas Free-

258 : *Notes*

man, "The Concept of Narcissism in Schizophrenic States," *International Journal of Psychoanalysis* 44 (1963): 293–303.

172   "family tautology" of narcissism
        Brodey, "Dynamics of Narcissism," p. 188; Kohut, *Analysis of the Self*, p. 255.

172   pseudo-mutuality
        Lyman C. Wynne et al., "Pseudo-Mutuality in the Family Relations of Schizophrenics," *Psychiatry* 21 (1958): 207, 210–11; Kohut, *Analysis of the Self*, pp. 40–41, 81.

173   Annie Reich, "Early Identifications as Archaic Elements in the Superego," *Journal of the American Psychoanalytic Association* 2 (1954): 218–38; Annie Reich, "Narcissistic Object Choice in Women," *American Journal of Psychoanalysis* 1 (1953): 22–44. See also B. D. Lewin, "The Body as Phallus," *Psychoanalytic Quarterly* 2 (1933): 24–27.

175   alienated students and their mothers
        Kenneth Keniston, *The Uncommitted: Alienated Youth in American Society* (New York: Harcourt, Brace, 1965); Herbert Hendin, *The Age of Sensation* (New York: Norton, 1975), pp. 72, 75, 98, 108, 129, 130, 133, 215, 297; Giovacchini, *Psychoanalysis of Character Disorders*, pp. 60–62.

177   Keniston, *The Uncommitted*, pp. 309–10; Philip Slater, *The Pursuit of Loneliness* (Boston: Beacon Press, 1970), ch. 3.

178   "decline of the superego"
        Jules Henry, *Culture against Man* (New York: Knopf, 1963), p. 127 (collapse of "ancient impulse controls"), p. 238 (interplay of family and culture), p. 337 ("pathological outcomes"); Arnold A. Rogow, *The Dying of the Light* (New York: Putnam's, 1975), ch. 2, "The Decline of the Superego," especially p. 67.

179   changing structure of the superego
        Sigmund Freud, *The Ego and the Id* (New York: Norton, 1962 [1923]), pp. 42–43; Henry Lowenfeld and Yela Lowenfeld, "Our Permissive Society and the Superego," *Psychoanalytic Quarterly* 39 (1970): 590–607.

180   Joseph Heller, *Something Happened* (New York: Knopf, 1974), pp. 141, 160, 549.

181   Henry, *Culture against Man*, p. 139.

181   "friendly" classrooms
        ibid., pp. 314–17.

181   Ann Landers, Rochester *Democrat and Chronicle*, 18 February 1978.

182   Van Waters, *Parents on Probation*, p. 36.

182   social control as a "technical problem"
        Edgar Z. Friedenberg, *Coming of Age in America: Growth and Acquiescence* (New York: Random House, 1965), pp. 73–92.

183   "Our textbooks discuss . . . sharing of authority."

Simon Dinitz et al., "Preferences for Male or Female Children: Traditional or Affectional?" *Marriage and Family Living* 16 (1954): 127.

183 Douglas McGregor, *The Human Side of Enterprise* (New York: McGraw-Hill, 1960), p. 21 ("limitations of authority"), p. 23 ("interdependence"), pp. 35–42 (Maslow's hierarchy of needs), p. 46 (criticism of permissiveness), ch. 9 (participation), p. 234 ("constructive" criticism), pp. 232–35 (characteristics of a smoothly functioning group), p. 240 (analogy between industry and the family). For a popularization of some of these ideas, see O. William Battalia and John J. Tarrant, *The Corporate Eunuch* (New York: Crowell, 1973).

184 Talcott Parsons, "The Link between Character and Society," in *Social Structure and Personality* (New York: Free Press, 1964), pp. 183–235; McGregor, *Human Side of Enterprise*, p. 31.

185 Michael Maccoby, *The Gamesman* (New York: Simon and Schuster, 1976), pp. 102, 122, 129, 137.

VIII. *The Flight from Feeling*

page
187 Donald Barthelme, "Edward and Pia," in *Unspeakable Practices, Unnatural Acts* (New York: Farrar, Straus and Giroux, 1968), p. 87; Riane Tennenhaus Eisler, *Dissolution: Divorce, Marriage, and the Future of American Women* (New York: McGraw-Hill, 1977), pp. 170–71.

187 Bertrand Russell, *Marriage and Morals* (New York: Bantam, 1959 [1929]), pp. 127, 137.

188 celebrations of the new marital intimacy
Alvin Toffler, *Future Shock* (New York: Random House, 1970), chs. 11, 14; Margaret Mead, "Marriage in Two Steps" (1966), in Robert S. Winch and Graham B. Spanier, eds., *Selected Studies in Marriage and the Family* (New York: Holt, Rinehart, and Winston, 1974), pp. 507–10.

190 Molly Haskell, *From Reverence to Rape: The Treatment of Women in the Movies* (Baltimore: Penguin, 1974).

191 free women
Wollstonecraft: Ralph M. Wardle, *Mary Wollstonecraft: A Critical Biography* (Lawrence, Kan.: University of Kansas Press, 1951), chs. 7–8; Margaret George, *One Woman's "Situation": A Study of Mary Wollstonecraft* (Urbana, Ill.: University of Illinois Press, 1970), ch. 8; Goldman: Richard Drinnon, *Rebel in Paradise* (Chicago: University of Chicago Press, 1961), p. 151; Bengis: Ingrid Bengis, *Combat in the Erogenous Zone* (New York: Knopf, 1972), p. 16.

192   decline of jealousy
      Willard Waller, *The Old Love and the New: Divorce and Readjustment* (New York, Liveright, 1930), pp. 6–7, 84, 88; "The Rating and Dating Complex," *American Sociological Review* 2 (1937): 727–34; Martha Wolfenstein and Nathan Leites, *Movies: A Psychological Study* (New York: Atheneum, 1970 [1950]), p. 33; August B. Hollingshead, *Elmtown's Youth: The Impact of Social Classes on Adolescents* (New York: Wiley, 1949), pp. 237, 317–18.

192   movies Wolfenstein and Leites, *Movies*, pp. 31–33.

193   the female orgasm
      Heller, *Something Happened*, p. 424; William H. Masters and Virginia Johnson, *Human Sexual Response* (Boston: Little, Brown, 1966); Anne Koedt, "The Myth of the Vaginal Orgasm," *Notes from the Second Year: Women's Liberation* (1970), pp. 37–41; Mary Jane Sherfey, "The Evolution and Nature of Female Sexuality in Relation to Psychoanalytic Theory," *Journal of the American Psychoanalytic Association* 14 (1966): 117; Kate Millett, *Sexual Politics* (New York: Doubleday, 1970), pp. 117–18.

194   "Women with narcissistic personalities . . . hysterical pseudo-hypersexuality."
      Kernberg, *Borderline Conditions and Pathological Narcissism*, p. 238.

195   "These women are less angry . . . had to be their companions."
      quoted in Veronica Geng, "Requiem for the Women's Movement," *Harper's*, November 1976, p. 68.

196   (Note) John P. Spiegel, "The Resolution of Role Conflict within the Family," *Psychiatry* 20 (1957): 1–16; Lee Rainwater, Richard P. Coleman, and Gerald Handel, *Workingman's Wife* (New York: MacFadden, 1962 [1959]), p. 89.

196   "You want too much . . . things you want to do."
      Bengis, *Combat in the Erogenous Zone*, pp. 210–11.

197   "No day is safe . . . thinking of me."
      Sylvia Plath, "The Rival," in *Ariel* (New York: Harper and Row, 1966), p. 48.

197   Sylvia Plath, *The Bell Jar* (New York: Harper and Row, 1971 [1963]), p. 93.

199   "apparent vigor . . . illusory matriarchal utopia."
      Geng, "Requiem for the Women's Movement," p. 53. For the retreat of nineteenth-century feminists, see Aileen S. Kraditor, *The Ideas of the Woman Suffrage Movement* (New York: Columbia University Press, 1965) and Ann Douglas, *The Feminization of American Culture* (New York: Knopf, 1977).

199   "enjoy sex . . . limit the intensity of the relationship."
      Hendin, *Age of Sensation*, p. 49.

200   "The only men . . . didn't feel vulnerable."
      Bengis, *Combat in the Erogenous Zone*, p. 185.

201   "resolutions about freedom . . . heart out of intimacy."
      ibid., p. 199

201–202   "many of us have had to anesthetize ourselves to [our] needs" ibid., p. 219.

203   "lust of the nerves rather than of the flesh"
        Leslie A. Fiedler, *Love and Death in the American Novel* (New York: Criterion
        Books, 1960), p. 313.

204   Freud on "psychic impotence"
        Sigmund Freud, "The Most Prevalent Form of Degradation in Erotic Life"
        (1912), *Standard Edition*, 12: 203–16.

206   Juliet Mitchell, *Psychoanalysis and Feminism* (New York: Pantheon, 1974); Eli
        Zaretsky, *Capitalism, the Family, and Personal Life* (New York: Harper and
        Row, 1976); Bruce Dancis, "Socialism and Women in the United States,
        1900–1917," *Socialist Revolution*, no. 27 (January–March 1976), pp. 81–144.

206   "does not mean simply a full stomach . . . but a full life."
        quoted in ibid., p. 132.

IX. *The Shattered Faith in the Regeneration of Life*

page

207   The title of this chapter comes from Mark Gerzon, *A Childhood for Every
        Child: The Politics of Parenthood* (New York: Outerbridge and Lazard, 1973),
        p. 221.

207   Albert Rosenfeld, *Prolongevity* (New York: Knopf, 1976), pp. 8, 166. For an
        even more blatant example of the medical approach to aging, see Joel Kurtz-
        man and Phillip Gordon, *No More Dying: The Conquest of Aging and the Exten-
        sion of Human Life* (Los Angeles: D. P. Tarcher, 1976).

208   See Thomas McKeown and R. G. Brown, "Medical Evidence related to En-
        glish Population Changes in the Eighteenth Century," *Population Studies*
        (1955); Thomas McKeown, *The Modern Rise of Population* (New York: Aca-
        demic Press, 1976), ch. 5; William L. Langer, "What Caused the Explo-
        sion?" *New York Review*, 28 April 1977, pp. 3–4.

208   Alan Harrington, *The Immortalist*, quoted in Rosenfeld, *Prolongevity*, p. 184.

209   "our attitudes toward aging are not accidental."
        H. Jack Geiger, review of Rosenfeld and Comfort on aging, *New York Times
        Book Review*, 28 November 1976, p. 5.

211   "I always saw the world . . . assume center stage."
        Lisa Alther, *Kinflicks* (New York: Knopf, 1976), p. 424.

212   On Comfort, Masters, and Johnson, see Benjamin DeMott, "Sex in the
        Seventies: Notes on Two Cultures," *Atlantic*, April 1975, pp. 88–91.

213   Gail Sheehy, *Passages: Predictable Crises of Adult Life* (New York: Dutton,
        1976).

214   For the statements by Comfort, Kinzel, and Sinsheimer, see Kurtzman

215   and Gordon, *No More Dying,* pp. 3, 36, 153; Geiger, review of Rosenfeld and Comfort, p. 5.

216   David Hackett Fischer, *Growing Old in America* (New York: Oxford University Press, 1977), pp. 132–34.

X. *Paternalism without Father*

page

219   On styles of socialization among the rich, see Robert Coles, *Privileged Ones: The Well-Off and the Rich in America* (Boston: Little, Brown, 1978).

223   E. L. Godkin on "the more well-to-do and observing classes." quoted in David Montgomery, *Beyond Equality: Labor and the Radical Republicans, 1862–1872* (New York: Knopf, 1967), p. 371.

224   David Hackett Fischer, *Growing Old in America* (New York: Oxford University Press, 1977), p. 206.

226   Kenneth Keniston et al., *All Our Children: The American Family under Pressure* (New York: Harcourt Brace Jovanovich, 1977).

229   Thomas L. Haskell, "Power to the Experts," *New York Review,* 13 October 1977, p. 33; Thomas L. Haskell, *The Emergence of Professional Social Science* (Urbana, Ill.: University of Illinois Press, 1977), p. 236; Paul Goodman, "The New Reformation" (1969), reprinted in Irving Howe, ed., *Beyond the New Left* (New York: McCall, 1970), p. 86.

229   psychiatric critique of law
      Vilhelm Aubert, "Legal Justice and Mental Health," *Psychiatry* 21 (1958): 111–12.

230   Seeley, *Americanization of the Unconscious,* p. 90.

233   Ludwig von Mises, *Bureaucracy* (New Haven: Yale University Press, 1962 [1944]), pp. vi ("two hostile camps"); 4 ("government control for free enterprise"); 9 ("implacable hatred"), 10, ("no compromise possible"), 11–12 ("trend toward bureaucratic rigidity"), 38 ("makes the wager earner free"), 39 ("cool rationality"), 48 ("cannot be checked by economic calculation"), 100 ("architect of his own fortune"; "not achievement but the favor of the superiors"); 125 ("empty catchwords"). For a similar critique of bureaucracy, see Frederick Hayek, *The Road to Serfdom* (Chicago: University of Chicago Press, 1944).

234   Daniel Patrick Moynihan, "Social Policy: From the Utilitarian Ethic to the Therapeutic Ethic," in Commission on Critical Choices, *Qualities of Life* (Lexington, Mass.: D. C. Heath, 1976), 7:44, p. 44.

235   Mises on common sense
      Bureaucracy, p. 125.

Index